Between Voice and Silence

Between Voice and Silence

—

Women and Girls,
Race and Relationship

Jill McLean Taylor
Carol Gilligan
Amy M. Sullivan

———

HARVARD UNIVERSITY PRESS
Cambridge, Massachusetts
London, England
1995

Library of Congress Cataloging-in-Publication Data

Taylor, Jill McLean, 1944–
    Between voice and silence : women and girls, race and relationship
Jill McLean Taylor, Carol Gilligan, Amy M. Sullivan.
        p.   cm.
    Includes bibliographical references and index.
    ISBN 0-674-06879-3 (alk. paper)
    1. Teenage girls—United States—Psychology—Longitudinal studies.
2. Socially handicapped teenagers—United States—Psychology—
Longitudinal studies.   3. Minority teenagers—United States—
Psychology—Longitudinal studies.   4. Oral communication—United
States—Psychological aspects—Longitudinal studies.
5. Intergenerational relations—United States—Longitudinal studies.
I. Gilligan, Carol, 1936–   .   II. Sullivan, Amy M. 1958–   .
III. Title.
HQ798.T39   1995   95–36209
305.23'5—dc20   CIP

Acknowledgments

We want to thank all the girls whose voices are at the heart of this book. Their generosity of spirit, their openness in speaking their minds and their hearts, and their willingness to join us in this inquiry into girls' and women's lives have made this work possible. From them we have learned more fully what is at risk in girls' development and what is at stake. To protect their privacy and preserve confidentiality, we have changed their names and altered some details of their lives. We wish that we could thank each girl individually and in public for her contribution to this research. Our thanks to their teachers and to the school staff and administrators for their flexibility and help in finding space and time for research in crowded schools and schedules.

We also want to thank the women whose participation in the Women and Race retreats has made it possible for us to join women's and girls' voices in our discussion of race and relationship. Teresa Bernardez, Lyn Mikel Brown, Katie Cannon, Judy Dorney, Joyce Grant, Kristin Linklater, Wendy Puriefoy, Christine Robinson, and Janie Ward gave of their psychic energy, their experience, and their knowledge. Their commitment to girls' development and education as well as their efforts on behalf of women have been a continuing inspiration.

We are grateful to the many people who went out of their way to make this project possible. Elsa Wasserman's interest in the research and her many years of experience in public education were critical in guiding our study of at-risk adolescents through an urban school system, making it possible for us to interview a culturally diverse group of girls. Wendy Puriefoy's vision brought our research to women working within the racially and ethnically diverse Boston Public Schools, and Joyce Grant's enthusiastic leadership made the Women Teaching Girls, Girls Teaching Women retreats happen.

We want to thank Valeria Lowe-Barehmi and Brenda Jones, the principals of the Mary Curley and the Lewis middle schools, the teachers Mary Ahern, Janet Ferone, Maria-Amy Moreno, Georgina Perry, Suzanne Ricco, Audrey Sturgis, and Patricia Woodruff, and the counselors Emily Carrington, Maria Gonzales-Baugh, and Ceil Parteleno-Barehmi, who took part in the Women Teaching Girls, Girls Teaching Women retreats. Their active involvement in girls' development and education and the diversity of their cultural, racial, and class backgrounds led the retreat discussions into some of the most challenging areas of relationship between women and girls in public education. To Judy Dorney of the Harvard Project, who developed the curriculum for the retreats, and Katie Cannon, who joined in organizing the retreat process and brought race to the center of consideration, our special thanks.

We are grateful to Betty Bardige and the Mailman Foundation for supporting this research in its initial stages and to Wendy Puriefoy and the Boston Foundation for encouraging its expansion and for two years of substantial funding. The retreats were supported by royalties from previous work of the Harvard Project.

The collaborative Harvard Project on Women's Psychology and Girls' Development provided the overarching framework for this study, and we are indebted to our colleagues for their encouragement, their ideas, and their good company. Most centrally, we thank Deborah Tolman, who was a crucial member of the research group. Her commitment to studying culturally diverse girls from poor and working-class families, her insights into girls' development, her interest in research methods, and her research on girls' sexuality have greatly contributed to this book. We also thank other project members who made vital contributions, including Judy Dorney for her work on the retreats and Janie Ward for her consultation to the research, her active involvement in the retreats, her analysis of the retreat transcripts, and her deep and generous commitment to this inquiry into race and relationship. Janie's astute and thoughtful responses to earlier drafts of this book have had a profound effect on our thinking. Elizabeth Debold was also most generous in bringing to this work her insights into mind/body relationships in girls' development and her keen eye for the effects of social class. We are enormously grateful to her for her willingness to read the manuscript on short notice and for her immensely valuable analysis.

We were fortunate to have the assistance of thoughtful and enthusiastic graduate students, Sarah Ingersoll and Mark Schernwetter, who worked with us at the beginning stages of the research, and Pamela Pleasants, who brought her experience in working with girls in public schools, her questions, and her courage into our interpretive community and stayed to work through some of the difficult interpretive problems surrounding racial differences. Our research assistants Kate Adler, Annie Blais, Elizabeth Brewer, Taryn Shea LaRaja, Lisa Machoian, and Ruth Slocum contributed their energy and ideas to the project. Jamelle Gardine and Beverly Smith added to our analysis with their close readings of the interviews with the black girls in the study. Nancy Jacobs transcribed tapes that were often difficult to listen to for a number of reasons.

Michelle Fine drew from her extensive experiences with girls in urban education and was a most helpful and enthusiastic consultant. Teresa Bernardez brought her knowledge of group dynamics, her culturally sensitive analysis of women and anger, and her many years of clinical experience to the retreat process and was most generous with her time in discussing the Women and Race retreats with us. We would like to express our appreciation also to Jane Attanucci and Elliot Mishler for careful reading of earlier drafts, to Marcia Hall and Dorothy Austin for insightful comments, and to Joan Sullivan for her thoughtful questions and suggestions. We owe a special thanks and acknowledgment to George Horner for his significant and ongoing contributions throughout the process of our research and writing. His psychological insights, engagement with the central questions of this work, and innumerable careful and critical readings and rereadings of drafts have been extraordinary.

As in other work of the Harvard Project, the research reported here was conducted in the context of ongoing relationships and conversations among women and men involved in the studies of women's psychology and girls' development. Lyn Mikel Brown and Annie Rogers provided vital links and insights from their work as directors of, respectively, the Laurel School Study and the Strengthening Healthy Resistance and Courage in Girls Project. We also thank Lyn for her careful reading

and responses to earlier drafts of the first chapters. Niobe Way generously brought the insights and findings of her work with urban adolescents into many conversations with us. Our research method and our
way of thinking about women's psychology and psychological development in general reflect a process of collaboration that has gone on at
Harvard over a period of many years. The voices and ideas of many of
our colleagues are woven into our present thinking, and we also wish to
thank Dianne Argyris, Jane Attanucci, Betty Bardige, Mary Belenky,
Kathryn Geismar, Dana Jack, D. Kay Johnston, Holly Kreider, Sharry
Langdale, Nona Lyons, Laura Maciuika, Jane Margolis, J. Michael Mur-
phy, Natasha Mauthner, Lisa Machoian, Kate O'Neill, Dick Osborne,
Susan Pollack, Anna Romer, Steve Sherblom, Ellen Snee, Beverly Slade,
Catherine Steiner-Adair, Lori Stern, Niobe Way, Grant Wiggins, David
Wilcox, and Birute Zimlicki. To Barbara Miller and Mark Tappan, members of the Harvard Project, and to Sarah Hanson, an outstanding project
assistant, we owe special thanks. Sarah transcribed the retreat tapes and
also assumed responsibility for making the retreats happen.

Our discussion of voice is indebted to ongoing collaborations and
conversations with women who work in the theater and to whom voice
means the speaking voice. We are grateful to Kristin Linklater for exploring the relationship between her work on voice and the research of
the Harvard Project in the collaborative Company of Women/Company
of Girls Education and Theater Project. Our thanks to Normi Noel, who
collaborated on the Strengthening Healthy Resistance and Courage
Project and brought her analysis of resonance, and the relationship between voice and resonance in girls' development, into our work. Tina
Packer has talked with us about this book at critical junctures, bringing
her unflagging interest and enthusiasm, her ideas, and the encouragement to "speak our passion."

We thank Virginia LaPlante, our editorial consultant in the early stages
of this project. She helped to turn a final report into a book. Our thanks
also to Linda Howe of Harvard University Press for her vigilance, her skill,
and her extraordinary patience. To Angela von der Lippe, our editor, we
are most grateful for inspiring and encouraging our boldest visions.

Contents

Silence

Too many women
in too many countries
speak the same language
of silence.
My grandmother was always silent—
always aggrieved—
only her husband had the cosmic right
(or so it was said)
to speak and be heard.

They say it is different now
(After all, I am always vocal
and my grandmother thinks
I talk too much).
But sometimes, I wonder.

When a woman gives her love,
as most women do, generously—
it is accepted.
When a woman shares her thoughts,
as some women do, graciously—
it is allowed.
When a woman fights for power,
as all women would like to,
quietly or loudly
it is questioned.

And yet, there must be freedom—
if we are to speak.
And yes, there must be power—
if we are to be heard.
And when we have both
(freedom and power)
let us not be misunderstood.

SILENCE

XII

We seek only to give words
to those who cannot speak
(too many women
in too many countries).
I seek only to forget the sorrows
of my grandmother's
silence.

Anasuya Sengupta
Lady Shri Ram College, New Delhi

Between Voice and Silence

Prologue

In this book, we enter a landscape that is strangely silent—where girls for the most part are not heard in public, or if heard are generally spoken about in the third person. These girls have voices, they are perfectly capable of first-person speech, but as they will say repeatedly, nobody listens, nobody cares, nobody asks what they are feeling and thinking.

This common adolescent plaint becomes compelling when it has the ring of truth. In the study we will report in this book, we asked twenty-six girls who were designated "at risk" for high school dropout and early motherhood what they were feeling and thinking about themselves, their relationships, their lives, their futures, their experiences in school, and their decisions around sexuality. Our purpose in initiating these inter-view conversations stemmed from our conviction that the inclusion of these "at-risk" girls is essential to understanding women's psychology and girls' development. Most of the girls are poor and working class; many are members of the groups that compose the "ethnic minorities" of this country.

In the course of our research, we discovered the magnitude of their contribution. From a small group of twenty-six girls, interviewed annu-ally over a three-year period, we learned to ask "Who is listening" as well as "Who is speaking" and to see more deeply into the psychological and political implications of this joining. We found that it was in fact a risky business, this listening to girls.

Women have always been listening and not listening to girls, caring and not caring about what happens to them, because women have al-

1

ways been in the company of girls, if only of the girl they once were themselves. In the course of our research with this small group of girls attending an urban public high school, we discovered that it was the women in these girls' lives who seemed most often to listen, to care, to be interested in knowing them. Many of these women were themselves at risk, and the girls sometimes spoke of the women who listened and spoke with them as "crazy" or different.

We will struggle in this book with the word *different,* mainly to hold it apart from its common mistranslation, "deficient." Our group of twenty-six girls was so informative in part because of the cultural and racial differences among them: eight are African American or Caribbean; four are Latina; eight are Portuguese; and six are Irish or Italian American. All are from working-class or poor families. In the course of the project, six girls dropped out of school and five of them became mothers; twenty graduated from high school and five went on to college; fourteen entered the job market after high school at a level that suggested a continuation of their poor or working-class status.

Difference, in our understanding here, is the essence of relationship. In our efforts to come into relationship with girls who differ from us in ways that are potentially profoundly illuminating—who live in many respects in different cultures and in some ways speak a different language—we quickly realized our own limitations. In this project, as in all of our research with women, we would depend on an interpretive community to create a place where women's and girls' voices could be re-sounded without serious distortion, and where we could listen and try to hear without being distracted by premature judgment, by dismissive-ness or idealization, or by the pervasive stereotypes that surround girls (see Gilligan, Brown, and Rogers, 1990; Gilligan, Rogers, and Noel, 1992; and also Jordan et al., 1991).

In our study with the twenty-six "at-risk" girls, the composition of the interpretive community became central. We quickly discovered that we had to learn new ways of listening, become attuned to different voices, different cultures, and different languages even when English remained the spoken tongue. The question "Who is listening" now be-came an integral part of our voice-centered, relational method—integral to our understanding of both voice and relationship. We realized that our previous emphasis on "Who is speaking" reflected in part our own and our research participants' class and cultural location. Girls who by virtue of their class position, their cultural status, or their educational privilege have been led to believe that people are interested in who they are and what they have to say, worry about jeopardizing these relationships by revealing what seem like unacceptable parts of themselves. They will often modulate their voices to blend in or harmonize with the prevailing key. In short, girls who believe that the world of relationships is open to them and that they have access to the bounties of the world—to honor, riches, marriage, and blessing, which the goddesses offer Miranda, Prospero's daughter in *The Tempest*—will often be persuaded, as Miranda is in Shakespeare's play, to change their voices and give up their questions in order not to jeopardize their chances. This is what Virginia Woolf once called "committing adultery of the brain" (Woolf, 1938).

The girls in our study were not living under similar constraints. They could speak, but for the most part felt that few cared or listened to what they had to say. Having a "big mouth" often got them into trouble, but silence, the slow slipping into a kind of invisible isolation, was also devastating.

A main finding of our present research is that the vitality and psychological brilliance we have encountered in our previous studies with girls in more privileged school environments, and also among public school girls who were not identified as being "at risk," were also evident in our interviews with these "at-risk" girls at the time when they were roughly thirteen and in the eighth grade—in the first year of our project. Over the three years of the study, we observed a fight for relationship that often became dispirited as girls experienced betrayal or neglectful behavior and felt driven into a psychological isolation they and others readily confused with independence. Girls' descriptions of their increasing isolation and psychological distress, including their experience of having no effective voice, regularly preceded overt manifestations or symptoms of psychological trouble, highlighting the opportunity for prevention and also guiding preventive strategies. In contrast to other girls whom we have studied, there were few safety nets available to these girls when they made mistakes, took wrong turns, acted on impulses that turned out to be misguided or foolish or simply unlucky, or sank into a kind of depressive lethargy and withdrew from the world. It was here that the combined effects of race, ethnicity, and class were so powerful.

Women were perhaps the best protection against the risk of disconnection and psychological dissociation. A resonant relationship with a woman, meaning a relationship in which a girl can speak freely and hear her voice clearly resounded as a voice worth listening to and taking seriously—a voice that engages the heart and mind of another and calls forth response—was associated with psychological health and development and what are commonly regarded as good outcomes for the girls in this project: no early motherhood, graduation from high school, for some, higher education and social mobility, and a continuing sense of psychological vitality and involvement in life.

It is important to note that the women with whom girls found it easy to speak their minds and their hearts were women who spoke from their own experience. Because adolescents lack first-person experience in the worlds of adult sexuality, relationships, and work, they tend to rely on second- or third-person voices. These voices are at times misleading or confusing in the sense of speaking at a far remove from, or in direct contradiction to, what girls and women know through experience. Then the voice of women's experience affords a crucial resonance for girls, providing girls with an echo—a compass or gyroscope for centering themselves in what can otherwise be a disorienting and dangerous time.

Analyzing this phenomenon, we have come to the following formulation. At adolescence, girls in general are at risk for losing touch with what they know through experience, in part because the changes of puberty and adolescence may render girls' childhood experience seemingly irrelevant, in part because women's and girls' experiences tend to be idealized or devalued or simply not represented within patriarchal societies and culture, and in part because girls often discover in adolescence that their relational strengths and resilience (their ability to make and maintain connection with others and to name relational violations) paradoxically begin to jeopardize their relationships and undermine their sense of themselves (see Gilligan, in press; see also Miller, 1988). When girls' experience comes into tension with what are called "relationships," or girls' sense of themselves is at odds with images of good or valuable or desirable women, then women's voices can be psychologically life-saving in providing an internalized counter to what otherwise becomes an almost necessary process of dissociation that drains girls' vitality and energy. When women can stay with girls so that girls do not have to absent themselves in order to be with other people, relationships between women and girls can be of immense value in providing girls a place for sorting out and thinking through their responses to confusing and complicated realities. Because experiences of sexuality, relationships, and work are all deeply imbued with cultural meanings and are affected by race, class, and sexual orientation, girls tend to name women who are similar to them in these respects as important in their lives.

The gap between what girls and women know firsthand from experience and what is socially constructed and institutionally held to be reality or truth or common knowledge becomes starkly apparent in public discourse about "teenage pregnancy"—a discourse frequently raised when speaking of the poor. In a recent study based on a survey conducted by the National Center for Health Statistics between 1989 and 1991, researchers discovered, from interviewing 10,000 girls and women, that "half of the fathers of babies born to mothers between 15 and 17 were 20 or older, and that 20 percent of the fathers were six or more years older" (Steinhauer, 1995). Commenting on these findings, David Landry, a co-author of the study, observed: "To most people, these numbers are counterintuitive . . . This research highlights that teen-age pregnancy is not just limited to teenagers, but that in fact adult males bear a lot of the responsibility." To some people these numbers may be counterintuitive, but to half the girls and young women who become pregnant, the numbers simply reflect their experience and perhaps, more to the point, convey a prevalent, although unspoken, reality.

The present work is part of an ongoing effort to give voice to a fuller range of human experience within psychological research and theory. A central step in this process has been to bring women and girls into psychology as first-person narrators so that women's and girls' voices can directly inform theories of human development. The joining of women and girls lies at the heart of our research. This joining symbolizes and encourages our belief that the future experiences of women need not be bound to the past in a process of endless repetition, and that psychological understanding can contribute to change. Difference and relationship contain the seeds of the new, the potential for transformation, and in exploring cultural and racial and class differences, and relationships between women and girls, we often find ourselves standing at the threshold of that potential.

Our study here of girls who are at risk for early motherhood and school dropout—the Understanding Adolescence Study—is a crucial part of a series of studies through which we set out to learn from girls about girls' experiences and to explore the psychology of girls becoming women in North America at the end of the twentieth century. The research, itself a deeply collaborative effort, was carried out by members of the Harvard Project on Women's Psychology and Girls' Development.[1] The Understanding Adolescence Study was initially supported by a start-up grant from the Mailman Foundation and then, following the joining together of our research with girls and a series of retreats with women who were teaching girls in the Boston Public Schools, funded substantially by the Boston Foundation.

In preparation for these retreats with a culturally and racially diverse group of women teachers, counselors, and principals, we held a preparatory retreat for ourselves, inviting white women and women of color to join in exploring relationships among women and also between women and girls across politically and economically significant racial and cultural differences. First conceived as a single weekend retreat, this initial meeting expanded into six weekend meetings over a two-year period. This second project, the Women and Race retreats, overlapped with the final year of the Understanding Adolescence Study, and ultimately involved eleven women: five black, five white, and one Latina. The retreats took their impetus from a question that was spurred by our attention to girls: will women—will we—perpetuate past divisions among women into the future, including the racial and class divisions that have been so psychologically and politically divisive and painful? As we sought to create a psychology that carried the full range of women's and girls' voices, including the voices of those who are commonly thought of as not worth listening to or as having nothing important to say, we found that our research widened into a political inquiry: can women act in concert to end a racist and sexist society?

Tensions within feminism over the last twenty years have become heightened over the question of difference. Women who are white and privileged have been criticized by both black and white women and called "essentialist" for speaking about gender without also addressing race, class, cultural, and sexual differences among women (hooks, 1984; Spelman, 1988; Collins, 1990; Hirsch and Keller, 1990). It is a mark of a racist and class-driven society that those who are in a dominant position can easily remain blind to the experience of others and thereby to the reality of their own domination, and this blindness extends to women as well (Freire, 1970; Miller, 1976; Martín-Baró, 1994). At the same time, women often hold a higher standard for other women and are more forgiving of men (see Miller, 1986; Martin, 1994). The implication that women must speak of everything or keep silent is one of the many constraints on women's voices that characterize and maintain a patriarchal society and culture.

Inevitably, the argument about differences has deepened divisions among women along the lines of race, class, culture, and sexuality, and these divisions have had the effect of maintaining the status quo by keeping women separated from one another in a series of minority groups. Tensions among women are frequently explained in psychological terms and taken as evidence that women are by nature envious and competitive and therefore unable to work effectively together. But as our own and many other women's lives attest, there are strong working alliances and friendships among women across race, class, culture, and sexual difference: *not* being able to work together is itself a stereotype.

At this time, there are urgent calls for unity and cooperation across racial and ethnic lines (Guinier, 1994; Lerner and West, 1995; West,

1993), as well as for a more central inclusion of people of color and poor people in studies of human development and psychology (Dornbusch, Petersen, and Hetherington, 1991; Reid, 1993). It may well be, however, that the vision or the experience of women actually working together and forming a politically effective majority is so radical in its implications that it becomes profoundly unsettling and leads to attempts, witting or unwitting, to reinstate the familiar, the status quo. Racial divisions among women have been rekindled by the recent revival of debates over educational and economic equity, affirmative action policies, and intelligence as measured by IQ tests (see, for example, Jackson, 1995). And just as these tensions have been rising on a societal scale, women from different racial, ethnic, and social class groups working together have often been actively discouraged by other women, who accuse the black women in such collaborations of "selling out" and the white women of being hopelessly blind to their own race and class privilege (see Mud Flower Collective, 1985; hooks and Childers, 1990). Latina, Asian, and Native American women regularly see themselves disappearing from these binary black-white conversations, ignored by both black and white women. These dynamics all came up in the course of our projects and became part of our research and the retreat process.

In writing about women and girls, race and relationship, then, we enter a difficult conversation. This book offers a record of a long-term collaborative effort in which black and white women worked together over many years in the course of designing, funding, and carrying out the Understanding Adolescence Study and writing the final report of that project (see Gilligan et al., 1992). Black and white women (Katie Cannon, Judith Dorney, and Carol Gilligan) also worked together in conceiving and convening the Women and Race retreats. These retreats, which brought together women of different races and cultures and class backgrounds, were a logical extension of the Women Teaching Girls retreats that began at the Laurel School in Cleveland in response to the findings of the Harvard Project research there (see Brown, 1991a, 1991b; Brown and Gilligan, 1992; Dorney, 1991). The women who participated in the Women and Race retreats did so without compensation; retreat expenses were funded by royalties from previous Harvard Project books.

The voices of the women who took part in the retreats and the girls who participated in the study are at the heart of our voice-centered, relational research. Speaking here in counterpoint with the voices of women and girls of color as well as other white women and girls, we are three white women entering into a conversation about women and girls, race and relationship. In doing so, we wish to state clearly that while we have learned from and with women and girls who are of color, who are of cultures different from our own, who live in different economic circumstances, we do not in any sense attempt to speak for them or hear our voices as anything but open-ended—as starting or continuing a conversation. In writing this book, then, we speak for ourselves, saying what we have come to know through this research and collaboration.

The relational dynamic of our research process has become increasingly clear in the course of this work. To our original question about voice, "Who is speaking," we have added the question "Who is listening." To the original title, "Women Teaching Girls," we have added "Girls Teaching Women" to reflect the relational dynamic of the retreat process. In the Women and Race retreats we would amplify the voices of the economically disadvantaged, racially and ethnically diverse girls from the Understanding Adolescence Study and explore the resonances of girls' voices in relationships with women who were from similar and different racial, cultural, and class backgrounds. Five of the women who participated in the Women and Race retreats—Lyn Mikel Brown, Katie Cannon, Judith Dorney, Carol Gilligan, Joyce Grant, and Jill Taylor— were also involved in the Women Teaching Girls, Girls Teaching Women retreats with women from the Mary E. Curley Middle School and the Lewis Middle School in Boston.[2] The knowledge and experience gained in these retreats were a starting point for future work with girls and women and also for conversations with other psychologists and educators, parents, community workers, and politicians who were also seeking ways of supporting psychological health and preventing trouble.

Just as the voices of girls proved essential to the Women and Race retreats, spurring memory, undoing dissociation, and creating an atmosphere of hope and possibility, so the voices of the women in the retreats provide resonances that greatly enhanced our capacity to listen to and hear the girls. For this reason, we have interwoven excerpts from the retreat transcripts and descriptions of the retreat process with excerpts from interviews with girls and our discussion of the research findings. In the Women and Race retreats, the five white women were Lyn Mikel Brown, Judith Dorney, Carol Gilligan, and Jill Taylor, psychologists and educational researchers associated with the Harvard Project, and Kristin Linklater, a voice teacher and actor, and director of the Theater Training Program at Emerson College; the five black women were Katie Cannon, a theologian; Joyce Grant, an educator and administrator; Wendy Puriefoy, an administrator in a philanthropic foundation; Christine Robinson, a public health and policy analyst; and Janie Ward, a researcher and university teacher who was associated with the Harvard Project. Teresa Bernardez, an Argentinean woman, a psychiatrist and a teacher and supervisor of psychoanalytic candidates, was also a member of the retreat group and broadened the racial and cultural spectrum.

Almost everyone came to all six retreats, which were held between September of 1990 and August of 1992. Wendy, Joyce, Christine, and Katie each missed one retreat, as did Kristin, who joined us in the second retreat. During this period several women moved to positions in other parts of the country and one gave birth to a son. The location of the weekend retreats, the relationships among the women, the responsibility for various aspects of the weekends, and how all these were negotiated, played out, talked about, or covered over were as significant as the formal agenda, which was to explore relationships among women and between women and girls across racial and cultural and social class differences. Bringing in girls' voices encouraged women to move with one another through past bitterness and entrenched racial and cultural and class divisions and toward creating something new. It was this experience that compelled the women in the group to set aside six weekends. Four of the six retreats were taped, although at times the taping was stopped by request for particularly personal discussions. But the taped sessions and formal meeting times were only part of the weekends; the group walked and swam, did breathing and voice exercises, cooked, ate together, cleaned up, and continued talking.

At a crucial point in the retreats, the reading of a book written by an eight-year-old girl from Afghanistan (who was attending the Laurel School)[3] brought into sharp focus what women in one sense know and have often forgotten: that conflict and fighting are parts of relationship, that it is necessary to speak openly about difference and race and anger, that relationship means connection, and that being friends means working through problems. Girls' voices frequently encouraged women to become more lively and to speak more directly from their experience, in part because they disrupted what had become habitual ways of speaking among women, evoking strong childhood memories related to race, ethnicity, and class and also recalling a voice and a world of relationships that had become a lost time for many women—a time of clarity and courage at the edge of adolescence when girls tended to "hone to the truth" (Woolf, 1938).

In writing this book, then, we will attempt to hold differences by maintaining the distinctness, the individuality, and the cultural tonality of people's voices, and thereby to sustain relationship. When women from different racial, ethnic, class, and sexual orientations come into relationship, they are in the presence of what Patricia Hill Collins (1990) calls "interlocking systems of oppression." At the same time, women coming together create what is potentially a politically effective majority, since women are currently 51 percent of the population in North America. Exploring our relationship to these systems of oppression and opportunity means speaking about privilege and power, anger and conflict, hurt and violation, betrayal and isolation, as well as about friendship, love, joy, and generosity of spirit. Connection between women and girls means in part an open exploration of women's potentially central role as citizens in a democratic society and culture and also of women's currently central role in raising children, whether as mothers, othermothers, *comadres,* teachers, therapists, counselors, muses,[4] sisters, grandmothers, aunts, neighbors, or friends. Exploring women's relationships with other women and girls, as well as women's relationships with men and boys, leads us to ask how and whether these relationships can be or become transformative, be more effective in working toward a just and caring society and in preventing systematic as well as personal injustice, neglect, violation, and violence.

During the second of the Women and Race retreats in January 1991, Katie Cannon raised what was to be a persisting hope: "Is there something about the way we, as black, white, Hispanic women, relate in these retreats that can be transferred to girls? Can there be a generation of girls who are not racist? Can there be a generation of girls of color who will not internalize racism?" It was the psychological, and potentially the political, power of connecting women and girls that joined our two projects, and this joining of women and girls across race and culture and class differences proved to be more disruptive, more difficult, and more hopeful than we had imagined.

1

Holding Difference, Sustaining Hope

Anita, an African American adolescent in eighth grade, sits at a table in a small, sunny room off the library in her elementary school talking about her life in and out of school. Dressed for this winter day in a dark, baggy sweatshirt and black jeans that emphasize her small frame, Anita twists her hair and speaks animatedly, laughing often and unselfconsciously with her interviewer, Jill, a white woman from New Zealand. Information about Anita's life emerges during the interview: she lives in a housing project with her mother, stepfather, a younger sister, and two of her three brothers, and she continues to see her father frequently. Anita seems to be an adolescent with a great deal of energy and curiosity, asking Jill questions about her life, her accent, quickly adding after a question about age that she hopes Jill doesn't mind. The stories she tells portray a complicated relational world with her family, her boyfriend, and her teachers.[1]

Jill is drawn to Anita's sense of drama and vitality. Listening to Anita's stories, Jill becomes more conscious of her own very different experience of growing up in a suburban environment, attending an all-girls school in another country and at an earlier time. Looking at Anita, Jill becomes aware of how tall, how conservatively dressed, how like many other white women in the school she must appear.

The many differences between Anita and Jill—those of race, nationality, social class, family background, age, to name but a few—and how these relate to the interaction between them in the interview became central in the Understanding Adolescence Study, a three-year study with poor and working-class white, black, Latina, and Portuguese girls deemed to be "at risk" for school dropout and/or early parenthood. A narrative account is produced interactively, depending not only on the questions of the interviewer and the experiences of the narrator, but also on the "social location" of both.[2] Hence, any telling of "a story" may be affected by race, ethnicity, gender, class, age, sexual orientation, religious background, personal history, character—an infinite list of possible factors that form the scaffolding of relationships between people.

Attention in research to who is listening as well as who is speaking defines a relational approach to psychological inquiry, in which cultural as well as psychological differences directly enter the research process. In *Meeting at the Crossroads* (1992) Lyn Mikel Brown and Carol Gilligan, observing the effects of different interviewers on girls' responses, noted in particular how an African American girl's interview conversation differs when an African American woman is listening rather than a white interviewer, and also how a playful interviewer can elicit a very different girl from the one who takes a more formal approach.

Our voice-centered method of psychological inquiry means that we build theory from listening—in this case, listening to girls. Listening to girls speaking, we also listen for the unspoken—places where there is no voice or where girls may have silenced their experience or have simply not been heard—either in the interview itself or later, in the course of interpreting the interview. We structure this process in two ways. The first is a method of interpretive analysis, directed by a *Listening Guide* (Brown et al., 1988; Brown and Gilligan, 1992).[3] This voice-centered method guides a careful record of different voices within girls' narratives in girls' own words. This method also guides the interpreter through a reader response process of making explicit and documenting how her own experience and personal history, including her cultural, social, and familial frame of reference, may shape how she listens and what she hears. In this way the Listening Guide provides a means of naming and holding the relational nature of psychological analysis.

Equally important to this listening process is the *interpretive community*. In the Understanding Adolescence Study, our focus on race, ethnicity, and class underscored the central importance of "who is listening." Initially, the interpretive community was comprised of a core research group, which consisted of Jill Taylor, Deborah Tolman, Amy Sullivan, Sarah Ingersoll, and Mark Schernwetter.[4] Although there is diversity in our cultural, social, and family backgrounds, all of us are white and within the spectrum of the middle class. It therefore became essential to widen the interpretive community.

Before beginning our third and final year of interviews, we reviewed our analyses of girls' eighth- and ninth-grade interviews, including Anita's, in order to reexamine our research questions and explore ways of refining or redirecting our inquiry. To this reexamination, we invited Michelle Fine,[5] a white woman noted for her ethnographic work in urban public schools, and Janie Ward, an African American woman who rejoined the Harvard Project group, bringing her experience in adolescent racial identity development. Both women had considerable experience as researchers addressing questions of race, ethnicity, and social class in their work.

Janie immediately observed that in her eighth-grade interview, Anita had attempted on three occasions to introduce the topic of race in response to a question about something that made her feel bad about herself in school. Anita had said, "Well, last year me and another teacher in this school didn't get along so well . . . And so one time we got into an argument and I said something very bad about her, or very rude, which I shouldn't have said and I felt kind of bad because I was thinking . . . how would I feel if that was me, if I would feel sad or angry, not angry, but what would I do, what would my actions be?" Asked about this incident, in the course of her explanation Anita said, "it wasn't a crude racial comment" and "it wasn't racial." Anita's negation, "it wasn't racial," may have cued Jill not to pick up on this thread in the conversation, and it also went unnoticed by the interpretive community in discussing the interview. Despite Jill's silence, Anita again mentions race as she continues to talk about this incident, adding that it made her feel bad "because you are supposed to give everybody respect . . . Respect is like, oh God, not talking behind their back, you know, saying racial comments."

In the course of the analysis we had been noting the various ways in which our experience and background were similar to, and different from, Anita's. We had been exploring the cultural dimensions of girls' development by comparing girls' responses across racial or ethnic categories, but we had not directly asked girls about race or ethnicity nor had we followed up on the spontaneous references, such as Anita's, that occasionally arose. Michelle followed Janie's observation with the suggestion that we interrupt the dominant cultural taboo on speaking directly about race by bringing our questions about race into our interviews with girls.

As we reviewed our interview protocol, we discussed how to introduce the subjects of race and ethnicity in our conversations with girls; we also asked how deeply we were willing to listen and speak about it ourselves. The questions added to the interview included how a girl identifies herself racially and culturally and what she needs to know as a black, Hispanic, Portuguese, or white (or however she described her racial/ethnic identity) girl in high school. When the interviewer's race or ethnic background was different from the girl's, we asked her what it was like for her to be interviewed by a woman who differed from her in these ways. As we asked more directly about race, we became more attuned to racial and cultural references that arose spontaneously in the course of the interview conversation.[6]

Coming into relationship more openly with girls around issues of race and ethnicity, we also took steps to enlarge our interpretive community. Pamela Pleasants, an African American woman who had completed her master's degree in the Harvard program in Human Development and Psychology, joined the core research team, and Beverly Smith and Jamelle Gardine, also black women, made ongoing contributions in a consultant capacity.[7] More informally, we asked Latino women and men and Portuguese women and men to discuss our interpretation of interview texts with us. We felt the absence of Latina and Portuguese women, as well as poor and working-class women, in our core interpretive community, and noted the sparse body of literature currently available to inform our analysis of social class (Reid, 1993). The Women and Race retreats became an important extension of our interpretive community. We brought girls' transcripts to the retreats and discussed how the issues girls spoke about—anger, trust, relationships with friends and family—resonated with the issues the women discussed.

In *Yearning* bell hooks asks whether it is possible to "produce work that opposes structures of domination, that presents possibilities for a transformed future by willingly interrogating [our] own work on aesthetic and political grounds. This interrogation itself becomes an act of critical intervention, fostering a fundamental attitude of vigilance rather than denial" (1990, p. 53). Moving toward an "attitude of vigilance" by bringing class and race—that of the adolescent girls and ourselves—to the center of our method of inquiry and analysis, we experienced the dynamic interaction of an interpretive community. Opportunities for discussion around interpretations from our different social locations vied with difficulties in speaking, and with class and racial tensions and silences. Where we have succeeded in developing culturally rich and multilayered responses to the voices of girls in this study, the diversity of our interpretive community was key.

In this book, we include excerpts from the Women and Race retreats. Keeping the girls' voices central, we join women's voices and experience with those of girls to highlight, elaborate on, or provide resonance for certain themes that were important in the girls' interviews. We have worked from the transcripts of the retreats as well as from memoranda, agendas, notes, memory, and discussions with the participants, all of whom have reviewed drafts, made suggestions, and requested changes. In writing about the retreats and drawing on the voices of other women, we have sought to deepen our understanding and interpretation of women and girls, race and relationship.

Reassessing Risk

The purpose of the Understanding Adolescence Study was to listen to and understand voices like Anita's that have been missing from or inadequately represented in theories of adolescent development and women's psychology. As part of the ongoing work of the Harvard Project to bring a fuller range of human voice to psychological theory and educational practice, this study focused on a diverse group of twenty-six urban girls considered to be at risk for dropout or adolescent motherhood. Our goal was to build carefully rendered psychological portraits of girls' development from eighth to tenth grade and to identify strengths that might be sustained as well as risks that might be attenuated in the context of relationships.

Descriptive research with urban adolescent girls, especially girls who are at some level of academic risk, is also of particular importance because, although numerous studies addressing issues of risk exist, they are typically cast in terms of deficit or deviance. Public discourse follows similar lines, generating considerable conversation about, but rarely with, students at risk. What Michele Wallace has characterized as a problem for women of color in the public sphere and popular media—"high *visibility* together with [an] almost total lack of *voice*" (1990, p. 5)— applies to poor and working-class urban girls as well. Their social location of class, gender, age, and for many, race or ethnicity, places them in a socially marginalized position that does not grant a public hearing of their experience, strength, or knowledge.

The margins, however, can also offer a potentially transformative perspective on institutional and social norms, beliefs, and practices—an epistemological privilege that allows for an awareness and critique of standards of behavior or attitudes that diminish, demean, or disempower individuals or groups (hooks, 1984; Collins, 1986; Smith, 1986). The critical perspective that can be gained from the margins, and for which we sought evidence in our analysis, might include a critique of idealized standards of beauty or behavior for girls and women, recognition and rejection of conventions that idealize or denigrate mothers and motherhood, or an awareness of the use and misuse of power in the school and larger social system. Closely tied with the concept of a critical perspective is that of *resistance,* a related process in which girls consciously or unconsciously resist psychological and relational disconnection that can impede development and threaten their psychological health. Seeking evidence of strengths gained and lost in the intersection of girls' coming of age with cultural conventions of femininity and womanhood, we listened for signs of resistance to unhealthy conventions or norms.

We designed an interview protocol that paralleled protocols used in other Harvard Project research and covered a range of developmental and relational domains in girls' lives. This protocol included how they felt about themselves in and out of school, their relationships with their mothers, their relationships with another important person in their lives, acting in the face of conflict, making decisions about sex (ninth and tenth grade), and thinking about their future.

The students who participated in the study attended school in a large urban area, came from diverse racial and ethnic backgrounds, and were economically disadvantaged. They were chosen by means of a Dropout Prevention Survey (Higgins, 1986) administered by the school to seventh and eighth graders, which identified those who were considered to be at risk for school dropout and/or early parenthood. We selected those who met three or more of the standard at-risk predictors—high age for grade, single-parent family (usually mother), English as a second language, poor school performance and attendance, ethnic or minority status, and low self-esteem on the Rosenberg Scale—and this, along with further information from teachers,[8] produced a final list of thirty-three girls. Over the three years of the study, seven girls left because they moved, changed schools, or no longer wished to participate. This book concentrates on the twenty-six adolescent girls in the final sample.[9]

Because the group size is relatively small and was not drawn by random selection, it is not a representative sample of girls at risk or of poor and working-class girls. Our aim here, however, was not generalizability. The size of this group allowed us to make an intensive analysis of interviews and to trace girls' experience over time. Our longitudinal and in-depth analysis also provided an opportunity to develop our understanding of and our approach to working with difference. This method also stands for us as a model for the individual attention and sustained listening to girls that is possible outside a research relationship.

In this study, and perhaps in most cases, the "at-risk" label is of limited use because of the wide range of students it encompasses and because it is more of a proxy for social class. Some of the girls in the Understanding Adolescence Study were, in fact, performing relatively well in elementary school but were included because they met several of the criteria for risk that are associated with low income, such as living with a single parent, generally a mother. The high school the girls in the study attended also has strong programs that address a wide range of student needs, has maintained a high retention rate of approximately 90 percent, and is not in an area of concentrated poverty that would put a disproportionate share of students at risk for dropping out. Many of the girls in the study, in fact, completed high school.

The urban public system in which these adolescents attended school has an extremely diverse student population that includes over sixty nationalities and twenty languages. Students were not systematically selected for the study from particular ethnic or racial backgrounds, but the final group reflects the largest racial and ethnic groups in the community, with the exception of Asian American students. The participants are eight black, four Hispanic (primarily from Central America), eight Portuguese, and six white adolescents, all of whom are from poor or working-class families. A simple naming of these students as "black," "white," "Hispanic/Latina,"[10] or "Portuguese," however, obscures important differences within each category. In the group of black students, for instance, some girls are immigrants from Jamaica, some are from Haiti, and others describe themselves as African American. These differences are important because they affect how children and adults are acculturated and assimilate into U.S. society (Ogbu, 1987; Gibson and Ogbu, 1991).

What unifies this particular group of girls is that they have all been identified as at risk, yet precisely what they are at risk for—and of equal importance, what strengths, skills, and strategies they develop alongside these risks—became key questions in our research. Two different notions of risk have framed past research on adolescence, one traditional and the other related to growing up female. An understanding of each is critical to this work.

Traditional notions of risk, which generated the funding for this study and defined the selection of girls who participated, focus primarily on material inequities rooted in the social realities of unequal opportunity and unequal outcome in educational and economic spheres, inequities that are largely structured by race, class, and ethnicity. Social scientists, educational and public policymakers, and the media have raised various degrees of alarm about "children in crisis" or "youth under siege," citing the existence of widening circles of concentrated poverty, disproportionate school dropout rates among low-income youth, and increases in drug-related violence. Adolescent pregnancy and motherhood have continued to cause concern, not only from a health perspective in terms of child and maternal health, but also from an economic perspective. Decreasing economic opportunity, especially among those unable to acquire the necessary education and preparation for the job market, has also been identified as part of the increased risk many adolescents face (Orfield, 1994). These risks are defined largely in terms of physical and material consequences—low-paying jobs or unemployment, health problems, high infant mortality, inadequate education, incarceration—with all their attendant social and personal costs.

To the extent that this focus on physical and material risk has raised public consciousness and initiated the creation of programs geared to risk prevention and intervention, it has benefited many. There are dangers in focusing on risk, however, and these need to be examined if programs targeted to the affected students are to succeed and, more important, if concern for adolescents is to translate into effective social and educational change.

A primary danger of the "at-risk" label is its tendency to shift attention away from the social conditions that place adolescents at risk and locate the risk within the adolescents themselves. This shift places the burden of change on the adolescent and thus relieves the larger society of responsibility for addressing the inequities of race, class, and gender that create conditions of risk. It also emphasizes, often mistakenly, intellectual, social, or emotional deficit. This "within-child" deficit model, which attributes failure in school to "deficits the child brings to school," fails to account for the larger context of the child's or adolescent's life (Treuba, Spindler, and Spindler, 1989, p. 3; see also Fine, 1991; Fine and Rosenberg, 1983).

The stereotype of at-risk students can itself become a self-fulfilling prophecy, for "the school experience early on defines them as potential failures or even learning disabled" (Treuba, Spindler, and Spindler, 1989, p. 13). Students of color and those from poor families are more likely than other students to be tracked into nonacademic or special education high school programs, and teachers who expect little of their students are likely to find these expectations well met (Rose, 1989; Wheelock, 1992). One of the girls in the Understanding Adolescence Study characterized the self-negating impact of an adult who "didn't have any confidence" in her plans to go on to college: it made her feel, she said, "like I'm nothing."

Working from a notion of deficit also tends to diminish the value placed on adolescents' perspective. This consequence is demonstrated by the absence of the voices of adolescents themselves from most studies on students who are considered at risk. This absence was noted by the social psychologist Klaus Hurrelmann, who observes that we need to take account of the at-risk "adolescent's own perceptions, expectations, goals, and capacities . . . in a much more fundamental way than has been done before" (1989, p. 109). As one of the girls in the Understanding Adolescence Study remarked: "A lot of people don't ask . . . I think a lot of people should ask more questions . . . [people should be asking] what do we think about something?" Listening to the voices of adolescents—to their concerns, their experiences, their insights—and listening for their strengths and resources as well as their weaknesses and liabilities, we heard evidence of a range of competencies that are at odds with prevailing characterizations of deficit.

Finally, as is the danger with most labels, "at-risk" obscures the differences among those so labeled and suggests that those who are likely to suffer the material consequences of risk are a homogeneous group. However, economic, educational, or social risks often differ according to race, ethnicity, and economic class. Variability in school performance and retention among different racial and ethnic groups continues to be a central issue in public education (Rothstein, 1993). Data on school retention and completion show that, overall, black and Hispanic students are less likely to persist than white and Asian students. Hispanic students drop out of school at more than three times the rate of white students and twice the rate of black students. These discrepancies diminish or disappear when class is considered, however: among low-income families there is no statistically significant difference in dropout rates between black students and white students. Rates for low-income Hispanic students fall to approximately twice that of white and black low-income students (National Center for Education Statistics, 1993).[11] Most middle-class Hispanic children, however, fare well to reasonably well in American schools, due largely to the fact that their parents know how to negotiate the education system (Valdivieso and Nicolau, 1994).

Not all studies of risk have located it within the children and adolescents involved. Research on "resilience," the ability to weather adverse psychological, social, or economic conditions, focuses on the psychological and relational resources of children or adolescents deemed at risk. This work has contributed to our understanding of the internal and external resources that serve to protect children and adolescents in the face of stress. An important finding from studies of risk and resilience is the key role of supportive, confiding relationships in mitigating the effects of stress (Takesheni, 1992; Anthony and Cohler, 1987; Garmezy and Rutter, 1983; Rutter, 1980; Garbarino, 1992).

The other dimension of risk informing this work is that identified by previous research of the Harvard Project on the psychological and developmental risks of growing up female in a patriarchal culture. In the Laurel School Study Lyn Mikel Brown, Carol Gilligan, and Annie Rogers found that, prior to adolescence, many young girls demonstrate a strong sense of self, an ability to know and voice their feelings and thoughts and to give authority to their experience (Brown, 1989, 1991a, 1991b; Brown and Gilligan, 1990, 1992; Gilligan, 1982, 1990a, 1990b; Gilligan, Brown, and Rogers, 1990; Rogers, 1993). The sometimes unsettling directness and clarity of young girls' descriptions of the human world reveals a detailed knowledge and careful rendering of psychological realities.

At adolescence, however, a shift takes place for many girls as they experience a relational impasse and a developmental crisis. To be in relationship at this juncture often jeopardizes "relationships." Girls are under pressure from without and within to shape themselves in accordance with the dominant cultural ideals of femininity and womanhood or of maturity and adulthood. This creates a tension when the ideals of womanhood and femininity are those of "selflessness," and the ideals of maturity and adulthood are those of separation and independence (Gilligan, 1982). Girls experiencing this initiation into dominant cultural ideals and values often perceive that, either way, they will lose relationship: either they will give up their voices to others, learning to think, feel, and say what others want them to think, feel, and say, or they will give up their relationships with others and learn to be self-sufficient, entire unto themselves. In the face of this relational crisis, a preadolescent resilience can give way to an increasing uncertainty, a hesitancy in speaking, a tendency toward self-doubt that questions the validity of their feelings and dismisses the value of their experience (Gilligan, Brown, and Rogers, 1990; Gilligan, 1990b; Brown, 1991a, 1991b; Brown and Gilligan, 1990, 1992; Rogers, Brown, and Tappan, 1994).

Voice and relationship were complicated and nuanced for the writer bell hooks, an African American woman who grew up in a Southern black community. Reporting on her own experience she says: "I was never taught absolute silence, I was taught that it was important to speak but to talk a talk that was itself a silence. Taught to speak and beware of the betrayal of too much heard speech, I experienced intense confusion and deep anxiety in my efforts to speak and write" (1989, p. 7).

The anthropologist Signithia Fordham (1993) describes the complex interaction of voice, silence, and race in her work with black adolescent girls in a high school in Washington, D.C. She presents a cultural-specific route to womanhood among African American women that she sees as inevitable in a country stratified by gender, social class, culture, and race. "Those loud black girls" is a metaphor, Fordham notes, "proclaiming African-American women's existence, their collective denial of, and resistance to their socially proclaimed powerlessness, or 'nothingness'" (p. 10). The "loud black" girls, whom teachers recognize so well, are underachievers with common characteristics that include "striking visibility and presence"—everyone in the school knows them. There is also a lack of congruency, Fordham notes, between their grades and their standardized test scores, the latter far outstripping the former. "They are doomed, not necessarily because of academics, but because they will not comply with the view that as young women, they become silent." In Fordham's words, they resist " 'gender passing' or becoming like [most] white, middle-class girls at school," resisting at the same time disconnection from their peers and significant adults and from "the black egalitarian (i.e. fictive kinship) system" (p. 11).

In contrast, the high-achieving black girls in Fordham's study have adopted "a deliberate silence, a controlled response to their evolving, ambiguous status as academically successful students." This allows them to deflect both the underlying hostility and the anger that would become apparent from their peers and teachers if they were to be highly visible and academically successful. Like the actions of the "loud black girls," this too is resistance or defiance, but it may cause isolation and loss of relationship for high-achieving black girls, and lead to an abandonment of their efforts to succeed (Fordham, 1991; Fordham and Ogbu, 1986).

For middle-class white girls, under cultural pressure to conform to the dominant conventional image of the ideal, perfect girl—who is always nice and good, who never hurts other people's feelings, who either lacks or can control hunger and sexual desire, and who contains her feelings, especially anger—healthy resistance to disconnection in childhood can become at adolescence a resistance to knowing one's feelings, to knowing one's body, and to being in an authentic relationship with oneself and others (Tolman and Debold, 1994). Brown and Gilligan (1992) have called this process "psychological resistance," by which they mean "psychological dissociation," and we will use this latter term.

Dissociation has profound consequences for psychological health and development. Epidemiological studies repeatedly cite adolescence as a time of psychological risk and heightened vulnerability for girls (Petersen, 1988; Minnesota Women's Fund, 1990; AAUW, 1991). Of this period, Gilligan observes: "Suddenly girls feel the presence of a standard which does not come out of their experience and an image which . . . calls into question the reality which they have lived in—the moving, changing world of thoughts and feelings, relationships and people. Feeling the mesmerizing presence of the perfect girl, girls experience the imposition of a framework which seemingly comes out of nowhere . . . What once seemed ordinary to girls—speaking, difference, anger, conflict, fighting, bad as well as good thoughts and feelings—now seems treacherous: laced with danger, a sign of imperfection, a harbinger of being left out, not chosen" (1991, pp. 32–33).

Gilligan (1991) contrasts psychological dissociation—loss to the conscious self of knowledge or feelings that have become dangerous to know and feel—and political resistance. A healthy resistance and courage lead girls to take action against social or cultural conventions that encourage them to disconnect from themselves and others. This political resistance challenges the idealization of relationships and images of bodies that require girls not to experience their feelings and desires, or not to know what they know.

Political resistance can take two forms. It can be covert, as when a girl goes underground with her feelings and knowledge. Aware of the consequences of speaking out, she outwardly appears to comply with the conventions but does so as a conscious strategy of self-protection. This strategy poses a danger when there are no confiding relationships because knowledge that remains out of relationship with others can easily become lost to the girl herself, and the act of compliance may evolve into a habit of acceptance of harmful conventions of social behavior. Political resistance can also be overt, as when a girl either speaks out or acts against relationships that feel false or acts against conventions that require self-sacrifice or silence. Political resistance includes rejection of racial, ethnic, class, and sexual stereotypes as well as those conventions that equate separation from others—complete independence—with maturity. The primary danger in this kind of resistance lies in the reactions it may elicit from other people or from social systems that are threatened by such protest. Thus, there are psychological and political costs to both political resistance and psychological dissociation. As Gilligan explains: "If girls know what they know and bring themselves into relationship, they will be in conflict with prevailing authorities. If girls do not know what they know and take themselves out of relationship, they will be in trouble with themselves. The . . . difficult problem of relationship [is] how to stay connected with themselves and with others, how to keep in touch with themselves and with the world" (1991, p. 43).

Like the individual focus inherent in the traditional notion of risk, acknowledging these risks and dangers can readily sound like blame or cast girls or women as victims. Just as difference is often interpreted to mean deficit among poor adolescents or adolescents of color, so too has clinical and empirical evidence of losses among women and adolescent girls been construed as signaling inherent weakness or deficiency. But the developmental story of girls in adolescence is not simply a story of risk and loss; it is also one of strength and resilience. What the poet Audre Lorde has said of her own experience in "the war against the tyrannies of silence" is also true for girls in adolescence: "I am not only a casualty," wrote Lorde, "I am also a warrior" (1984b, p. 41). Girls' active attempts to maintain connection with others, and with their own thoughts and feelings, are acts of resistance and courage. That these actions often result in psychological distress or land girls in trouble with authorities—or both—points not to deficiencies in girls but to the need for social and cultural changes that would support healthy development in girls and women.

Tuning In: Method

In the first two years of the Understanding Adolescence Study, each student was interviewed once from forty-five to ninety minutes; in the third year, each girl was interviewed in two separate sessions of sixty to ninety minutes. In the first year, when girls were in eighth grade at the elementary schools, the interviews were conducted in cafeterias, libraries, or classrooms. At the high school space was provided in speech and physical therapy rooms. Every effort was made to have the same woman interview the same girl over the three years. All interviews were taped and transcribed for later analysis.[12] Students also filled out the Washington University Sentence Completion Test (Loevinger and Wessler, 1970). Difficulties in test administration in two of the grades preclude a systematic analysis of the sentence completions, but we have looked at individual responses for evidence of common patterns and themes.

We used two methods to carry out the interview analysis. One is an interpretive method described earlier in brief and again in more detail below. The other is a method of content analysis in which we created matrices to code and organize girls' descriptions of their experiences and to chart the progress of themes over time (Miles and Huberman, 1984). Most content categories were specified in the interview protocol: relationships with friends; relationship with mother; feeling good/bad about self in school; sexual decision-making;[13] future plans; and in the third year, discussions about race and ethnicity. Other categories, such as connections with women other than their mothers, emerged from readings of the interview texts for important topics that girls raised themselves.

For each content category, we created charts or matrices for each girl over the three years of the study, summarizing "within girl" themes. The next step allowed for comparison "across girls" by creating matrices for each content category that summarized information for all girls in that category, organized by race or ethnicity, across the three interview periods. These matrices created descriptive summaries for each content category that highlighted racial and cultural differences. The themes within each category were further organized into conceptual categories: for example, in the case of relationships with women other than mothers, categories included relational roles (such as aunt or neighbor), types of shared experiences (such as being the oldest sibling or running away from home), duration of relationships, uniqueness of relationship, types of interaction (such as listening or talking), and content of communication (school problems, dating, sexuality, future plans).[14]

Central to our interpretive analysis is the Listening Guide (Brown et al., 1988; Gilligan, Brown, and Rogers, 1990; Brown and Gilligan, 1992; Rogers, Brown, and Tappan, 1994), a voice-centered, relational method. In the Understanding Adolescence Study the method was expanded in response to the need for a more diverse community to provide resonances for racially and culturally different voices. In becoming an interpretive community we explicitly rejected the model of individual interpreters seeking to obtain reliability with other individual interpreters on the assumption that, ideally, everyone will hear the same thing. Listening, speaking, taking in, and interpreting "the words and the silences, the stories and the narratives of other people" (Brown and Gilligan, 1992, p. 22), we hear psychological truths embedded in language and culture.

Beginning with Kant's realization that the categories of our knowledge do not inhere in the nature of things, psychologists have sought to develop a means of doing research which recognizes that meaning is made rather than found, and "the means by which meaning is made are social and conventional and therefore limited by the institution or community of which the interpreter is a part" (Fish, 1980; cited in Tappan and Brown, 1992, p. 121; Mishler, 1986, 1992). As an interpretive community we share values concerning development and we share a method. Our differences are also crucial. As we came to find through working in an interpretive community—closely and collaboratively, with the same texts—it is precisely our differences that lead us to interpretations that take our understanding forward.

The Listening Guide method specifies reading through an interview at least four separate times, each time listening in a different way. The first listening attends to the overall shape of the narrative and the research relationship: to the questions asked, the story or stories being told, and the researchers' responses. Researchers record their first impressions, identify recurring themes, contradictions, and images, and track their intellectual and emotional responses to the person and the story. We were particularly attentive to how our own culture, race, ethnicity, and social class affect our responses and our understanding. A worksheet separates the evidence of the narrator's voice and silences from the interpretations of the researcher. This leaves a trail of evidence and makes explicit the relationship between the interviewee's voice and silences and the researcher's voice, silences, and interpretation. In this way, the voices are differentiated. This interpretive practice is explicitly feminist. It deliberately takes women's and girls' experience as constitutive of human knowledge; it provides a way to analyze the psychology of voice and resonance within patriarchal societies and attends to the differences in power that exist in the interview and in the analysis by requiring those in positions of greater power to reflect on and reveal their personal circumstances. Power differences constitute the social reality in which psychological development occurs, and these affect both development and how developmental research is carried out. This reflexivity introduces into our interpretation what bell hooks calls "a politics of location" (1990, p. 145).

The second time through the interview, researchers listen for the first-person voice, the *I*. Listening to the *I* is crucial: researchers hear how a girl speaks about herself—how *she* thinks, what *she* feels and does. They also notice what she does not say, where she sounds sure of her words, and where she sounds tentative or confused. Before speaking about her they record how she speaks of and for herself, including the cultural dimensions of her voice. The second listening is crucial to learning racial, cultural, and class differences as these differences affect the way a person speaks of or represents herself.

Important in the reading for the narrator is an understanding that the worldview of white, middle-class heterosexual male culture may contrast strongly with other voices and worldviews (Gilligan, 1977, 1982; Miller, 1976; Stack, 1974; Mbiti, 1969). In African worldviews, for example, the individual's frame of references may include "an extended definition of the self as 'we.' Embedded in this 'extended self' is an individual's connectedness with others" (Robinson and Ward, 1991, p. 92). In Chicana cultures, Gloria Anzaldúa explains, "the welfare of the family, the community . . . is more important than the welfare of the individual. The individual exists first—as sister, as father, as padrino—and last as self" (1987, p. 19). A similar theme is present among other Hispanic families, who are not a homogenous group but who do share general linguistic and cultural characteristics derived from shared ethnic origins. Interdependence and cooperation as well as the importance of the immediate and extended family are cultural values that strongly influence the socialization and identity formation of children (Carrasquillo, 1991). Portuguese people share many of the values and beliefs that Hispanic families hold, particularly those relating to the primacy of the family (Moitoza, 1982; Smith, 1980). Native Americans also view people as interdependent, not only with each other but also with nature (Silko, 1994; Schulz, 1994).

Research and clinical practice with women and girls across race and class have highlighted the centrality of relationship and interdependence in healthy development and, in the process, reframed psychological theory (Belenkey et al., 1986; Chodorow, 1974; Gilligan, 1977, 1982; Miller, 1976, 1986). This understanding of an interdependent "self" has frequently been interpreted as deficit, however, as Victoria Steintitz and Ellen Solomon found in their study of promising white working-class youths in three communities in the Boston area. Steinitz and Solomon note the strengths of interdependence and community among working-class people have been "conventionally portrayed as constricted by their unwillingness to free themselves from their relationships" (1986, p. 6).

After the second listening the researchers listen for contrapuntal voices—different ways of voicing the relational world. In this study we listened for signs of psychological health and development and also for psychological risk and loss. Using colored pencils—green for the *I* voice, red for signs of psychological resilience, and blue for psychological distress, we visually organized the counterpoint and relationship of voices within the text. There are many ways to arrange narratives for analysis, but the sociologist Catherine Reissman suggests that decisions about displaying talk are "inseparable from the process of interpretation." "By displaying texts in particular ways," Reissman asserts, "we provide grounds for our arguments, just like a photographer guides the viewer's eye with lenses and by cropping images" (1993, p. 51). The "layering" of our approach allows the reader/interpreter access to the narrator and makes it possible to "see" when, for example, the reader understands that the narrator is resisting conventions of femininity and when the narrator is dissociating from her thoughts, needs, and desires. It also makes it possible to locate the first-person voice in relationship to these different kinds of resistance.

Underlining the *I* statements, we find that when we excerpt them and place them in sequence, we gain a strong impression of how the person speaking experiences herself in relation to the world in which she lives. The following are the "*I* statements" of Anita's eighth-grade response to what makes her feel good about herself in school:

> I felt good . . . I made the basketball team . . . I made the honor roll . . . I was doing real good in school . . . and I really felt good about myself . . . I always wanted . . . I had thought very low of myself . . . I would make it or I wouldn't cheat . . . I wouldn't pass the test . . . I did and I was so happy . . .

As the narrator, the thinking, feeling, active *I,* Anita is at the center of her explanation of what makes her feel good about herself, as she is in other narrative accounts of school, of making decisions, of resolving a hypothetical dilemma. The following year, however, when Anita is in ninth grade in the high school, she cannot think of anything that makes her feel good about herself:

> Oh, I'm never happy. I don't know . . . I don't know. I guess I can do great, I don't know, I don't know, I'm never happy . . . When I know . . . I don't know . . . I'm never feeling good, I don't know . . . I don't know.

Following the *I* throughout the interview each year we hear and see changes in the ways Anita represents herself and we note that "I don't know" increases from six times in Anita's eighth-grade interview to sixty-five times in a ninth-grade interview of comparable length.

In tenth grade, Anita's unhappiness alternates with good feelings about her efforts to succeed at different school activities ("I don't know" appears twenty-one times in two long interviews). She begins by repeating the theme of her ninth-grade response:

> When I felt happy . . . I never feel happy . . . I don't know . . . when I, you know, try . . . I can . . . I feel happy . . . I may not succeed . . . I've tried . . . I feel this good, I feel this great confidence, I mean . . . I can do it . . . I may not succeed . . . I mean . . . I give myself . . . I probably won't get it . . . I mean . . . I can't do . . . I think I can do . . . I try . . . I try to do . . . I try to do . . . I can't swim for beans! . . . I try . . . I try . . . I try . . . I mean . . . I put in . . . I push myself . . . I mean, I may not always . . . I may not learn . . . I mean . . . I feel good 'cause I tried . . . I don't feel stupid . . . I have this good, I have good confidence for myself . . . I can do it . . . I mean, I don't really succeed all the time, you know.

In using the Listening Guide, the specific nature of the relational voices (the third and fourth readings) depends on the questions being asked in the research; hypothetically, any number of readings is possible, and any dimension of relational experience may be followed. Throughout the Understanding Adolescence Study we listened first for evidence of psychological health and development, and then for evidence of psychological distress or loss.

The third reading for girls' psychological health and resilience includes a listening for healthy resistance to disconnection from their own thoughts and feelings and from others.[15] This can include a girl's political resistance to the silencing or debilitating conventions of femininity and womanhood in the dominant culture and in the girl's own culture. Psychological health can entail a struggle against internalizing or taking into oneself negative messages about one's value, as well as resistance to the idealization of relationships, which overrides what the girl knows from experience. Examples of psychological health also include narratives of relationships in which girls feel free to voice the range of their thoughts and feelings. Increases in these capacities over time would be noted as evidence of psychological development (Gilligan, Brown, and Rogers, 1990; Brown, Tappan, and Rogers, 1993; Rogers, Brown, and Tappan, 1991).

In eighth grade, Anita describes a situation in which not being listened to by people "up there at the high school" was a cause of frustration for her. Although keeping specifics out of the story, Anita is self-reflective in thinking about how to solve the dilemma: "If they don't agree with what I am saying, or telling them, then I would get a little mad because no one would listen to me, but at the same time I would fight to get [them to listen]." Reasserting her claim that "I don't think they would listen as much as we [my mother and I] want them to" and at the same time continuing her attempt to be heard by school authorities, Anita persists in her desire and struggle to speak and be heard, resisting pressure to "just leave it alone, you know."

After telling this story, Anita reflects on what she has learned, foreshadowing developmental changes that we will hear as we follow her over the three years of the study. What she learned was, "I think not to go back and say things . . . but like, you know, try to keep other people out of your problems." Anita seems to be relinquishing her connection to her thoughts and feelings, and her struggle to stay in relationship with others, and to be moving to increasing isolation. Her psychological resilience and strength seem at once in evidence and at risk.

In the fourth and last reading, we listen for evidence of psychological distress or loss. We listen for signs of dissociation—girls' separation of themselves from their experience, their feelings, their thoughts, their desires. Evidence of psychological distress includes confusing stories, missing pieces of stories (such as no mention of anger or sadness when anger or sadness seem merited), and language such as a repeated "I don't know" or "I don't care," indicating uncertainty or confusion or numbness, particularly when they pertain to feelings or thoughts that were known by girls in their previous interviews. Increases in psychological dissociation over time are marked as possible evidence of developmental loss.

By Anita's tenth-grade year, concerns about being listened to and talking through problems have given way to stories of fighting to protect herself, showing others "not to mess with you . . . people don't really mess with me like they used to." Her faith in the possibility of talking to solve problems has been transformed by what Anita sees as necessary in her social world, where "people just talk about me, or touch me in a certain way I wouldn't like, you know what I mean?"

When psychological strengths and resilience lead girls into conflict with those in power, the attempt to maintain psychological health (a healthy resistance to psychological trouble) often turns into a political resistance or struggle. Frequently, political resistance or outspokenness leads to retaliation, which may take the form of isolation (ostracism, exclusion, not being listened to, not being heard), or may involve various forms of betrayal, violation, and violence. In this case, the same portion of the text may be marked as an example of psychological health (political resistance) *and* psychological distress.

The final step of the Listening Guide method is the case summary of each set of longitudinal interviews. These include a written record of our reader responses, examples from the various voice readings, notes on how prevalent they were in the interviews over time, and an interpretation of how each girl had changed over three years.

Discerning the differences between political resistance—not telling—and psychological dissociation—not knowing—became more complex in the presence of racial and ethnic differences. Making this distinction, or knowing when we could not, was greatly enhanced by asking girls if they thought the interview might have gone differently with a woman of the same rather than a different racial or ethnic background. In answering the question of what it is like to be interviewed by a woman who is white, for example, Anita in tenth grade first responds breathlessly, "Oh, no problem. No problem. I don't have a problem. I mean, I don't know. It's all right, no problem. I love it. It doesn't matter." When asked if it would be different if she were interviewed by a black woman, Anita replies: "Not really, but she'll, like, bug out, because everything I told you, you know, I think she'll laugh at everything I said, you know, because like, you know, this, we understand this stuff, you know what I mean? It doesn't really matter."

Anita's response taps into the central question in all psychological research—can one understand another whose life experience is different? She rejects the "you can't understand anything" position with respect to racial difference, but she also suggests that the interviewer's understanding of "this stuff" is limited because of her racial difference. "This stuff" has a number of possible meanings, and as Anita elaborates further, many of them are related to race and racism. Asked by the interviewer, *Can you give me an example where you felt I didn't understand and someone else would have?* Anita refers to an earlier part of the interview when the interviewer possibly did not "get" what Anita was talking about: "boys and things like that, in school, and you know, how we're dressing and stuff . . . Because, like, you'll see us, like, on the streets if you were black, especially if you lived in [the city] or something, you'll understand how we dress." *Is there anything else that you think I'd understand if I were the same as you, the same background as you?* Anita draws on her knowledge of race and class differences, and what the sociologist Patricia Hill Collins (1990) calls "the controlling images" of black adolescents held by the dominant culture, to explain what she thinks a black interviewer would understand: "What we want to achieve in life, yeah. I mean, what I want to be, because there are a lot of us black kids that are, like, falling back and they're dropping out of school and getting into, you know, getting arrested and going to jail and all this stuff, but I guess, you'd probably understand where I'm coming from and what I want to do and what I want out of my life, you know what I mean? There's a lot of people that I know that don't want a black kid to be somebody . . . I know you understand, but . . . ."

The controlling images or negative stereotypes of black adolescents that Anita names—falling back, dropping out of school, getting arrested and going to jail—are those that dominate the nightly news and daily newspapers and prevail in the minds of many white people. Anita knows the images and assumes that her interviewer understands some, but not all, of what she is saying: "But, if you lived where I lived, you'd probably, you know, see me, you know, you get what I'm trying to say, like, you'd probably understand what I'm trying to say." Anita's comparison of how her interview with Jill might be different from a discussion with a black woman interviewer underscores the need for a diverse interpretive community: different women will hear her narrative differently.

In addition, "who is listening" may also influence what Anita chooses to say. Adolescents may choose a form of political resistance—that is, choose not to speak about what they know and feel—to people they see as representing or aligned with unresponsive institutions and authorities, people who are for the most part from the dominant culture in the United States (see Friere, 1970; Miller, 1976; Martín-Baró, 1994). The degree of Anita's protest that it is "no problem" that her interviewer is white may point to the fact that she chooses not to or feels it would *not* be safe or wise for her to say what she really thinks.

Having an interviewer of a different race has limitations, but it also has advantages. The advantages of being an outsider have been well elaborated by anthropologists, since this position may elicit explanations that are assumed to be known by someone with insider status. This may have been true when Anita was asked in tenth grade, *What might it be good to know as a black girl in this school?* In responding, Anita describes instead what it is important for Jill to know *about* black girls in her school (the transcriber marks overlap because Anita begins to speak before the end of the question):

> ———That we *don't take no crap!* We don't take no kind of b.s. from nobody! That's how we are. We, we don't care who you are, black girls don't take no kind of trash from nobody! I mean, I know a lot of girls, I mean, I know a lot of my girl friends that are white, they take a lot of trash from a lot of people, and I sit there, like hmm, what's your problem? What are you taking that for, you know what I mean, but I mean, we're very outspoken, you know, we're very blunt, okay, we would tell you, you know, what's on our minds, if we don't like you, or whatever, you know what I mean, 'cause we don't bite our tongues for anybody, you know.

Anita sounds like one of the "loud black girls" that Fordham (1993) describes in high schools, and she is heard at first by white researchers as outspoken, blunt, her actions resisting the white, middle-class conventions of her more "quiet" and "polite" interviewer. As we progressed with this analysis, however, the different perspectives of our interpretive community led to a more complex reading. Voice is central throughout Anita's interviews over the three years as she describes speaking up and speaking out. Because she dares to argue with a teacher and describes black girls as "very outspoken," Anita resists mainstream conventions of femininity and silence. Yet speaking out gets Anita into trouble both in and out of school.

Although concerned by Anita's description of her frequent and sometimes physical fights with her mother and her friends, Jill responded positively to Anita's insistence on speaking up and saying what she thinks and knows. For Jill, who grew up in New Zealand and attended an all-girls school (whose motto translates "So That We May Serve"), and who for many years obediently followed the conventions of femininity in a colonial culture that "subliminally gives girls a message of compliance,"[16] Anita's ability to resist being a "nice," "good" girl who keeps silent about things that are not usually spoken of (including sex) seems a strength. Aware of the possible costs of such outspokenness in an educational system that demands conformity and in a society that is racist and sexist, Jill nevertheless hears psychological resilience and political resistance in Anita's description of black girls: "We're very blunt, okay, we would tell you, you know, what's on our minds, if we don't like you, or whatever, you know what I mean, 'cause we don't bite our tongues for anybody."

As Jill voiced her interpretation of Anita's interview, she was interrupted by Pam Pleasants and Janie Ward—two African American women—whose responses were very different from hers. Pam, who was working with adolescent girls in an urban public school system, read aloud to the group her initial response to Anita's eighth-grade interview: "As I read Anita, I find myself becoming agitated by her attitude. She strikes me as probably being like the students that I least look forward to dealing with in the schools . . . brash, opinionated, cocky and just a pain because they constantly challenge you. Perhaps [this is] because she dared to say and do things I never would have done and only does things that I associated with the wild crowd [in my high school]."

As a group, we talked about the interaction between race and class: how class differences between Pam and Janie, who came from middle-class backgrounds, and Anita, who was poor, and race and class differences between Jill and Anita, resulted in different interpretations. To Janie, Anita's statements could be heard as excessively assertive and unyielding, almost belligerent, an example of "resistance for survival," a reaction against destructive elements in her social world and in the larger sociopolitical context of the United States (Robinson and Ward, 1991). Janie and Pam pointed out something that may have been less obvious to the others in the interpretive community—that Anita may have carried her outspokenness too far, that she seems to have moved from an effective political resistance into a counterproductively aggressive manner of conducting herself that was getting her into trouble, damaging her relationships, and causing her confusion and distress. The outspokenness that may be healthy and viable in some cultural settings may be psychologically and politically too costly in others, and in those settings may even be belligerent and self-defeating. In fact, we heard, and Anita herself is aware of, the vulnerability under her seemingly tough exterior. By tenth grade, when she is asked to describe herself, her first words are "Fine, sexy, and beautiful," at which she and Jill both laugh. Anita continues: "Well, it's uh, I don't know, no, I describe myself as a little, sweet, sensitive person, I mean I hurt really easily, you know what I mean? Like, I always have like this wall up in front of me, like, no one can bother me, you know what I mean? I mean, I just walk around like (makes disdainful sound), you know, you don't (disdainful sound), I don't care what you say, you know what I mean. But like, I hurt really easily, and I hate people to hurt me." Anita's image of a wall as protection against being known and therefore potentially being hurt in both a psychological and physical sense reframes her fighting as a way of guarding against this risk and protecting herself. The costs of this protection become more fully evident in the context of a culturally and racially diverse community.

2

Girls, Risk, and Resilience

What gets me into trouble is—my big mouth!!
—Bettina, Portuguese American, tenth grade

Writing in large, rounded letters punctuated with double exclamation points, Bettina underscores a problem well known to many girls: speaking up leads to trouble. Among the girls who filled out the sentence completion task "What gets me into trouble is . . . ," the majority describe speaking out as a problem. Remarkably, more than half use the same words—"my mouth" or "my big mouth"—to name the source of their trouble, as if repeating a mantra given them by some higher authority.

The responses to the sentence completion test highlight a central paradox and a major challenge to girls in adolescence. Alongside girls' desire to voice their thoughts, their feelings, and their experience is the equally compelling knowledge that such actions often lead to reprisals—which for the girls in the Understanding Adolescence Study include the material consequences of disruption in school as well as the psychological costs of disruption in relationships. Eighth-grader Carla, for example, describes a key element of psychological health when she completes a statement that begins "A girl has a right to . . . " by claiming the right to "speak for herself and tell . . . what she means." Yet Carla also knows that speaking can lead to trouble: "When I talk [too] much, some of my conduct grades are going down and my mother is getting kind of mad." In grade ten, she abbreviates this statement by identifying the trouble as simply "my big mouth." Similarly, in tenth grade Maria also asserts a

39

girl's right to "talk and express her feelings," but she, too, finds that what gets her into trouble is her "big mouth."

At adolescence, relationships with self and others can be placed at risk as girls negotiate the often competing needs for self-expression and staying out of trouble. But if there is uniformity among girls in equating speaking with trouble, the specific dynamics of risk and resilience vary. Understanding the risks faced by different girls, as well as the resources and strategies available to them in managing these risks, requires an understanding of the cultural contexts in which they live and of the multiple and often contradictory conventions they learn.

The Palette of Risk

Cultural conventions, patterns of socialization, school standing, and relational resources all contribute to the varying psychological strengths and vulnerabilities among the girls in the Understanding Adolescence Study. Both the black girls and the white girls in the study tend to maintain their ability to express disagreement or anger, and many demonstrate a willingness to speak about sexuality. There is little evidence that the majority of these girls experience pressure to conform to the idealized standards of femininity so prominent in the dominant culture. These commonalties are consistent with the clinical psychologist Jewelle Taylor Gibbs's (1985) suggestion that low-income and working-class white adolescent girls may share more with black girls of the same class than they do with white girls in middle-income groups. For many of the more outspoken girls in the Understanding Adolescence Study, however, maintaining a strong voice throughout adolescence carries with it distinct risks. By the time these girls reach tenth grade, "being strong" or "self-confident" may also mean a covering over of their desire for relationships and a lessening of their willingness or their ability to voice fears and concerns. For girls close to dropping out of school, the need to "stand alone" or keep their feelings to themselves not only seems to bring them closer to leaving school but also puts them in danger of increased isolation and psychological distress.

For Latina and Portuguese girls, cultural conventions of femininity and being a good woman center on maintaining loyalty to their families and adhering to cultural and familial restrictions in speaking about sexual interest or engaging in sexual activity. These conventions may actually protect them from becoming teen mothers or dropping out of school, since only one Latina girl and none of the Portuguese girls had a child or dropped out during the course of the study. By tenth grade, however, a number of the Latina and Portuguese girls appear to display signs of depression or self-silencing, which may be related to their efforts to comply with family restrictions, particularly sexual restrictions, or to resolve the conflicts between the expectations of their cultures of origin and the dominant culture.

The stories of Ruby, Mary, Ana, and Christina that follow demonstrate patterns of development of voice and relationship among this group of African American, white, Latina, and Portuguese girls. Their developmental stories do not imply, however, that each girl represents a fixed pattern for her racial or ethnic group; within each group we encountered a variety of individual styles and temperaments. We interviewed soft-spoken black and white girls along with outspoken Latina and Portuguese girls. What we found were trends that seemed to be shaped, at least in part, by a girl's relationship to her culture and class.

Standing Up, Standing Out, Standing Alone: Ruby

Ruby is an African American girl, the oldest of seven children. Born when her mother was herself a teenager, Ruby meets the criteria of risk by virtue of living in a single-parent household supported by public assistance. She is also considered at risk for dropping out because she was held back one year in elementary school. Ruby's narrative reveals evidence of cultural conventions of voice and power that shape her development. Her story describes a double trajectory of developing strength and intensifying loss.

In her first interview, in eighth grade, Ruby presents a portrait not of risk but of psychological resilience and health. There is an appealing heartiness about her: she is solidly built, her voice is pleasant and her speech punctuated with frequent laughter. Her narrative has a strength and clarity, a directness, which suggests that she feels herself to be on solid ground. At the same time, her openness projects a sense of innocence and vulnerability. She engages herself fully in conversation, speaking forthrightly and without guile, conveying a simplicity of spirit that immediately draws us in.

Ruby demonstrates that she cares deeply about connections with others by framing her stories of satisfaction and disappointment within the context of relationships. She says, for example, that she felt good about herself when she was elected to a special team in her history class, taking pleasure not so much in the academic achievement as in the votes she received from her classmates: "The kids are all—I guess they accepted me for that, so maybe they like me . . . You know you're wanted. That's all I can say." At home she describes a circle of support and connection with the women in her family. Asked to whom she can talk about the future, she says, "My mother. She says if I want something, I can always accomplish it. I believe that, too. And my aunt and my grandmother. There's lots of people."

Ruby's openness and her desire for connection in eighth grade are signs of a healthy psychological resilience, which she shares with many of the preadolescent girls from the Laurel School Study. Like them, Ruby speaks frankly about the complexities of relational life at school, including some of the harsher realities of school politics that co-exist with her desire to be "accepted" and "wanted." She is critical of the unkindnesses meted out by those in her class who "know they are tops"; she names and censures the practices of exclusion and lack of care that she observes. Complaining about the popular girls, who "always pick on everybody else" and "put people down," Ruby says that they should "learn to respect each other more." She directs most of her concern to the effects of teasing and meanness on others, describing a girl in her class who is incessantly teased and a "quiet group" that is similarly victimized. Ruby implies that she herself is immune to the negative attention of the popular girls when she says that her own group is "in between" and "could fit in any group," and that it is her choice not to be a part of their entourage: "I could be with them sometimes . . . [but] it just doesn't suit me."

Yet she also hints that she has in fact been hurt by their actions, including herself when she says, "They don't care about other people's feelings, like us." This concern—about the lack of respect and care among her peers—becomes a persistent, ongoing theme throughout the three years of interviews.

What Ruby does not share with most of the girls from more privileged settings is the pressure to meet idealized images of femininity that many begin to face at this time. Concerns about not expressing anger or hurting other people's feelings, which become prominent from early adolescence onward among many girls from middle-class backgrounds, are not issues for Ruby. When she discusses conflicts or dilemmas, for example, she speaks about fairness, respect, and care, yet she does not excessively deliberate over whether or not she has hurt someone else's feelings. During the interview Ruby describes a fight her cousin started with another girl, who in turn "said something to aggravate me" and drew her into the conflict. But she expresses regret over the fight, which escalated into a physical skirmish, not because she felt that fighting was untoward behavior for a girl but because she "sort of liked this girl" and "we didn't have to fight just to prove that we were bad or anything."

The socialization of African American girls is often described as less stereotypic than that of white middle- and upper-middle-class girls, since it puts less emphasis on cultivating the qualities of idealized femininity, such as restraint from displays of assertiveness or anger (Binion, 1990; Ward, 1990). Like most girls, black girls are raised to assume the traditional female role of nurturing and child care, but they are also encouraged to be strong and self-sufficient and to expect to work outside the home—as have generations of black women before them (Ladner, 1971; Reid, 1991; Stack, 1974; Wade-Gayles, 1984; Wilson, 1986; Wolfman, 1984).

Child-rearing practices have also traditionally encouraged black girls to stand up for themselves and fight back—essential survival skills when racism is a pervasive reality. The sociologist Kesho Yvonne Scott documented this in her research and her personal life: after profiling four black women and chronicling the common survival strategies they had developed and passed on to their daughters, Scott was moved to ask her own daughters what they had learned from her. Her eleven-year-old daughter responded that she had been taught "to stand up for myself . . . to get right back up and fight. You have taught me so many ways to fight" (1991, p. 191). The sociologist Linda Grant (1994) identified this dynamic among younger girls, finding that, although black girls in first grade "rarely instigated physical or verbal aggression," they "fought back verbally or physically against more than half the aggression they encountered" (Zinn and Dill, 1994, p. 58). This sense of strength, combined with a positive sense of racial identity, is an important contributor to healthy development (Tatum, 1992; Cross, 1980).

Ruby maintains her strong voice throughout the interviews, but there is evidence that her need to be strong begins to eclipse the desire for connection that was so apparent in eighth grade. As she enters high school, Ruby shows evidence of cognitive and emotional development, but losses in relationship and in her sense of well-being also become increasingly present. She describes a new perspective, one of being seen, heard, and talked about, perhaps a cognitive move to more abstract, self-reflective thinking. Ruby's more reflective stance is evident in her description of learning to measure her words more carefully and how this change affects her behavior in the interview: "Last year I was pretty into it. I wasn't as mature. Last year I didn't think about it, the interview, I just said everything, blurted everything out. Right now I think about it more, what I am going to say." In this year's interview Ruby chooses to withhold certain information "about my personal life . . . and maybe my thoughts," which may in part account for the doubling in the number of her "I don't know" responses to questions. She often gives the impression that she really does know but simply chooses not to say. As she says, "I guess it's more my business. When I was littler, last year, I would have just said that. It was really dumb. This year I'm not."

It is at this point, when they begin to pay more attention to being the object of others' awareness, that many girls go "underground" with their feelings, that public silence about their thoughts and feeling begins. In the Laurel Study, the phrase "I don't know" peppered girls' language at this time, marking the point where they either chose not to speak or began to lose the knowledge of feelings and desires they had known before. For Ruby, the use of the phrase "I don't know" can be tied to her choice not to speak, but it also reflects some loss of knowledge of her need and desire for connection with others. Interviewed by someone she has just met for the first time, a white woman whose education, culture, and economic background are at some distance from her own, Ruby expresses a justified caution about sharing personal information. Her ability to assess what she can and cannot safely say, and her knowledge that she is free to reveal or conceal things that are "[her] business," are signs of psychological and political strength. This decision to withhold personal material from her interviewer is a useful and appropriate strategy of self-protection. Yet it quickly becomes evident that Ruby has grown similarly guarded at school as well. The reason for this change appears to be her discovery that the social landscape of high school can be dangerous.

Describing her first year in the new school, Ruby says, "It's fun I guess. I guess it's fun." Clarifying this faint praise, Ruby describes her experience: "It's sort of like trying to fit in with everything, with people, and I don't know. I just stay to myself . . . I'd rather do that, no problems." When asked to describe the problems she avoids in this way, Ruby responds: "I don't know, when you are in a crowd, there's the 'he said,' 'she said' stuff and, I don't know, just rumors and fights and arguments. I don't like that. I just try to stay to myself." Ruby's solution, keeping her own counsel, was one arrived at by many others in this study.

For most girls, by ninth grade rumors and gossip had become a predominant concern, and were reasons for many girls to move out of relationship with others in order to protect themselves. While this move may be an appropriate response in these circumstances, it does have a psychological cost. Psychological health and development, as previous research has shown, are grounded in one's relationship with self and others. Too great a loss of relationship poses a serious threat to healthy development. For Ruby, what had been a few stories of exclusion and disconnection in the eighth grade becomes a prominent theme in the ninth. She seems to be at much greater psychological risk for disconnection from others and from her eighth-grade desire to "know you're wanted." In response to repeated betrayals of her trust by others, she moves away from the judicious use of self-protective strategies and toward a consistent pattern of cutting herself off from others at school. "Staying to herself" may be an effective solution in the short term, but Ruby's cautionary stance, while perhaps the only option, puts her in jeopardy of long-term isolation.

Ruby seems to recognize the danger of her isolation. She admits that, while she cannot change the "other kids," she could "try to communicate with kids more, instead of just staying to myself." Yet her social environment continually works against her. At one point she tells a story of betrayal: "I like this school . . . it's just some of the kids that I don't like . . . I don't know, all the troublemakers, I guess. I used to be friends with this girl, and me and her stopped being friends, so she went around telling everybody rumors about me, and just, like, everybody started to turn against me. But that's about all I knew. I mean, they are the same people she talked about, and now she's friends with them. I don't get it. She's really confused. I don't know" (laughs). In this story, Ruby's repeated "I don't know" and closing laughter may constitute some resistance to acknowledging her loss and hurt. And attributing her former friend's behavior to "confusion" may cover over her sense of deliberate betrayal.

But Ruby does not withdraw into silence, as some girls do; she fights back, and she recounts these stories with obvious pride. When the interviewer expresses sympathy for the pain of having others talk about her, Ruby counters by saying, "But I like it," because "I can walk by with my head up in the air and it makes them even madder." While in one sense her remark carries an air of bravado that may to some extent be a defense against her feelings of rejection, Ruby also experiences genuine delight in getting back at her tormentors. Enjoying a sense of her own power in this case and, at another time, feeling pleasure in successfully competing with her peers are positive and acceptable experiences for her.

Ruby associates her strength and her resistance to the epidemic of gossip at school with maturity: "I think I am very mature for my age . . . Well, I could say that 'he said,' 'she said' stuff, but . . . if someone says something about me, I'm like, 'So what, I don't care' . . . Or just, I don't know, lots of things. It could be talking, all of a sudden they start talking about a certain person, and that's not right. I am going to tell them that's

not right. That's why I think I'm a lot more mature than some teenagers."
Ruby says she will "stand up for whatever I believe in." Her maturity
comes at a cost, however, since "standing up" often means "standing
alone": "It's probably because I stand alone . . . Like, I don't know, a lot
of people could just be in a group and they're talking, but I don't just go
over and join in like that—I just like to keep by myself. I like to be
different, I think that's more better."

Thus to her stated desire to stand alone, Ruby also adds that of being
different, standing out: "You get a lot more attention that way than seeing everybody dressing the same, looking the same. Come on, it's boring." Ruby's desire to stand out contains elements of both strength and
loss. Her resistance to conforming to the hurtful conventions of her peers
is certainly a strength, but Ruby's emphasis on standing alone and standing out seems to have obscured her knowledge of her desire for connection, which was so evident a year earlier. In eighth grade Ruby felt good
when her classmates "accepted me . . . so maybe they like me." In ninth
grade, her dismissal of being part of the group—"Come on, it's boring"—may mask the loneliness of being left out.

By tenth grade, Ruby's response to what she has learned about herself
in the interview shows her grappling with the contrast between her
strong self-image and the precarious reality of her life: "I discovered
(laughs), I don't know, I think I'm self-confident. I don't know, I seem
like I am, yeah . . . Because I seem like I know what I want. I mean, I
want, you know." In one way Ruby's voice sounds even stronger this
year, conveying a sense of maturity and confidence. She speaks repeatedly of how she values the sense of having "a mind of [her] own" and
of how she respects other people who are the same. Yet alongside this
strength is a tripling of her "I don't know" responses and evidence
of increasing school failure. Ruby is frequently late for or absent from
school and reports that she is failing at least one class.

This year Ruby speaks even more pointedly about power issues in
relationships and defies the conventional dictates of femininity by claiming power of her own. She speaks a number of times of how she vies for
"leverage" in her relationships with her boyfriend and her peers. As she
did the previous year, Ruby experiences pleasure in standing up for her-

self: "Yeah, it gives me the leverage to walk down the hall and shake my booty, you know, and then they get all upset about it. That's their fault. I mean, they can walk down the hall all they want and any way they want, I am not going to be intimidated, you know, I don't care." Ruby's enjoyment of power over others is beneficial to her in an environment that generates the ongoing threats of betrayal and abandonment she describes. Her desire for power, however, may also reflect the messages black girls receive that they "can deny pain by the experience of power" (hooks, 1993b, p. 141). Like many of the girls in the Laurel Study, who seemed to lose their knowledge of strength and anger—a loss often flagged by an increase in "I don't know"—a companion phrase, "I don't care," enters into Ruby's narrative in the ninth and tenth grades. Its increased frequency suggests that she may be covering over or denying the painful losses of relationship she has experienced.

In tenth grade Ruby says she feels bad about herself in school because of the failure that seems imminent: "Everybody tells me I could do better, and I know I could do better. For some reason I just don't do better. I just give up altogether. Not yet, anyway, but I am giving up. I have no choice really, I'm going down" (laughs). Although hearing that she can do better, Ruby does not seem to believe it. She is at a loss to explain her behavior, and her laughter underscores the psychological distance and resistance she experiences because of it.

Ruby's disengagement from school sounds distressingly final: "I don't want to be in school. School can be fun sometimes, too, but I don't know, maybe it's just the time in my life. Maybe I'll look back on it and laugh one day, but still, I don't know." She could turn things around, she says, do "homework, try to understand the teachers, maybe. I don't understand them. They're at a different stage, I don't know (laughs). They're at the stage where they want to bother us, you know (laughs). They're like that, they can bother me all they want. It doesn't do anything. It doesn't mean I'm not going to think about what they say, you know. They must be doing something. Because I'm talking about it. I'm worried about it. They don't know that, though" (laughs).

The reality of her precarious position in school must be painful to Ruby, and just as she works at keeping this knowledge from other people, she may also be working to keep it from herself. By continuing to keep her concerns to herself—as may be true for many black women, "who cannot imagine asking for help, who see this as a sign of weakness" (hooks, 1993b, p. 144)—she is at risk for ultimately losing sight of her academic crisis and failing to take the steps necessary to deal with her problems at school.

In the context of a stressful social and academic climate, then, developing strengths may be accompanied by the psychological risk of covering over the need and desire for connection with others. In the ninth grade, Ruby's pride in her ability to "stand alone" is offset by evidence of her increasing loneliness and isolation. Gone are her earlier acknowledgment of vulnerability and desire for attention. Over time, relationships seem to have disappeared. (An aunt, for example, whom she named as important in the eighth grade, barely receives mention in the tenth.) The cost of standing alone is especially evident at the end of her final interview, when Ruby says that it has given her a chance to "get to talk to someone . . . 'Cause I really don't talk to nobody." Lorene Cary, in describing her own experience as an adolescent in a prestigious, primarily white New England preparatory school, reports that she learned this convention of strong womanhood early on: "I'd been afraid to admit, even to my mother, how much I'd wanted to lie down somewhere and hide. Black women, tall and strong as cypress trees, didn't pull that. Pain and shame and cowardice and fear had to be kept secret" (1991, p. 191).

Being tough, strong, or outspoken are common survival strategies in a culture where racism is a historical reality and in a school environment where rumors and gossip pose a daily threat to relationship (Robinson and Ward, 1991). In resisting the debilitating effects of racism, bell hooks explains, "over time, the ability to mask, hide, and contain feelings came to be viewed by many black people as a sign of strong character. To show one's emotions was seen as foolish" (1993b, p. 133). John Ogbu (1987) has called these resistance strategies "secondary cultural differences," characteristics that are not part of the primary culture but develop in the context of racism. Kesho Scott's careful accounting of a small but diverse group of black women led her to note the personal costs of such survival strategies and the need to create a place where black women can feel safe enough to express and share pain. And bell hooks, too, calls on black women to begin "sharing with one another ways to process pain and grief" and to "challenge old myths that would have us repress emotional feeling in order to appear 'strong.' " This is crucial, she says, because "bottled-in grief can erupt into illness" (1993b, p. 104).

Ruby certainly seems to be carrying her share of "bottled-in grief." By the end of her freshman year she is in academic trouble. Over and over in the interview she notes that she keeps to herself at school. And although she claims that she likes staying by herself, when asked if there was a time she felt good about herself outside of school, she says, "I don't know if I felt good outside of school." In fact, she tells her interviewer, she feels "bad about a lot of things." Her distress continues to be evident in tenth grade, when she answers the question about when she felt good about herself in a similar way: "Hmm, I don't know, I can't remember any, but I know there must have been times when I felt really good." "There's probably more bad than there is good," Ruby adds, "but I don't know." The following year, in eleventh grade, Ruby dropped out to have a baby.

Dealing with It Herself: Mary

Mary is an Irish American girl, the youngest of three children. She lives with her divorced mother, stepfather, and two older brothers in a housing project not far from her school. In eighth grade, Mary's teachers express concern about her future, primarily because her brothers have already dropped out of high school. During the course of the study, Mary does in fact drop out for a time in the ninth grade, but she returns to school again in the tenth.

In contrast to girls socialized in middle-class settings, Mary speaks openly of fights she either gets into or attempts to avoid. But she gains no pleasure from her battles, and in ninth and tenth grades she strives to keep herself from speaking her mind in order to avoid getting into trouble or getting hurt. In many ways, Mary's experience is much like Ruby's. She faces similar risks, not just of dropping out but of isolation and disconnection from others. Over time, she increasingly aligns with conventions of separation and independence, remarking that she does not talk to anyone about her problems because she "should be able to deal with [them]" herself.

In eighth grade, however, Mary, like Ruby, does not seem to be at risk either academically or psychologically. Shy at first, she becomes talkative and animated after she and her interviewer have spent some time together. Mary is on the honor roll in eighth grade and draws strength and support from her family, friends, and teachers. She names a resource for every contingency: "If I have a school problem, then I'd go to my father. If I have a boyfriend problem, then I go to my mother . . . And when my stepfather and mother are not home, I always have my best friends to go to." She also says that she and her classmates take problems to two male teachers: "Our science teacher . . . every time we felt we had to talk to someone, we go and talk to him and feel comfortable with him . . . So we pick Mr. Miller or Mr. James to talk to, because these are the teachers we feel comfortable with."

Mary seems open and engaged in eighth grade. About her relationship with her mother, for example, she says: "I don't think you should hide anything from your mother. I think you can just sit down and talk to your mother about anything you want without having to be ashamed." By tenth grade, however, this has changed dramatically: "I do not tell my mother nothing about what I do, how I do it, or whatever. There is so much she don't know about me, and there's some reason I don't want her to know . . . I feel like, I don't know, 'You raised me, you did a good job, you did your job, but now it's time for me to raise myself.' " Although change in Mary's relationship with her mother is by itself not unexpected, these conventions of separation and independence appear in various guises throughout her ninth- and tenth-grade narratives and suggest that she has adopted these as general strategies of behavior.

By tenth grade, Mary relabels her desire for connection as dependency and a burden, and she increasingly cites the need to do things on her own. In contrast to her eighth-grade description of being surrounded by people to whom she can turn, Mary in tenth grade stakes an unquestioned claim on independence. She says there is no one at school to whom she can, or should, go for help with problems: "I really don't tell anybody about anything. I just try to deal with it myself . . . I don't like telling people my problems, because I don't feel like, I don't want to feel like I have to depend on other people to do things for me. You know what I mean? They have their own problems, why do they need to listen to mine? You know what I mean . . . But I don't know, I think throwing your problems on somebody else's back is, you should be able to deal with it yourself. Because I figure I'm here, I got the problems, I should be able to take care of them and get rid of them. What makes me feel good is when I can do things by myself and not having to depend on other people."

The words "you should" and "I should" are flags that signal a convention Mary has learned and adopted. Her added "You know what I mean." reflects her assumption that her listener shares her knowledge of these rules of self-sufficiency. Mary's eighth-grade desire for connection and support have metamorphosed, in her estimation, into an abdication of responsibility, or "throwing your problems on somebody else's back." Believing that talking to others about her problems would be a sign of dependency and weakness, Mary chooses to keep her problems to herself.

Like Ruby, Mary in tenth grade emphasizes the need to be "strong," which she equates with being able to suppress or repress feelings. She criticizes herself for being "too emotional" and compares herself unfavorably with those who are better able to control, or even to avoid experiencing, their emotions. "Some people," she says, "are stronger than others. Like my friend Sharon. Her boyfriend left her, and she thought it was like nothing. I would be sitting there crying and everything else. It's like she can handle it."

Mary also experiences being hurt at school, but unlike Ruby, she does not seem to gloss over or dismiss these experiences. She describes an incident in tenth grade in which a boy she did not know insulted her by saying to a group of students, "I don't talk to white girls," and then he "looked at me." Instead of following her first impulse to respond, Mary decided to "pretend . . . I didn't even hear it, and I walked away." She observes that the "old" Mary probably would have said something to him: "See, back then I used to speak up when it really wasn't necessary, you know what I mean? I used to, I don't know, it would just come out, and I'd open my mouth at the wrong time and say the wrong things. But now I got like control over what I do and what I say. Like I can stop myself from saying something."

Mary's revised strategy, considering the possible effect of her words before she speaks, may represent a cognitive and social advance over the previous year. Indiscriminately speaking one's mind is a dangerous and inadvisable strategy. Girls do have to watch what they say in the presence of racial tension and in the "he said," "she said" environment of the high school. What becomes a problem for Mary, however, is the extent to which she carries this strategy of self-restraint and "stopping herself from saying something" beyond those situations where it is wise or necessary.

According to Mary the incident with the boy who insulted her is typical of what goes on: "There's tons of that stuff going on in school." The kids treat each other "unfair. Very unfair." Her sense of the school climate as hostile and threatening echoes Ruby's, but unlike Ruby, who says she likes to retaliate by walking by "with my head up in the air and it makes them even madder," or "walk down the hall and shake my booty, you know, and then they get all upset about it," Mary responds by silencing herself. She learns to "control" what she says and does or pretends that she does not hear the insults. Later, Mary remarks that remaining silent keeps her out of trouble and suggests that, because she experiences so much "unfairness" at school, speaking out against it is simply too taxing. Although ignoring hurtful comments seems a sensible way to cope with them, Mary is in a no-win situation, since not responding to insult also has its costs: "I've had that on my mind all day yesterday, all last night. I went to work, and I had it on my mind . . . I don't know why it bothered me, really, so much." Mary's new philosophy about being strong does not seem to include room for accepting her feelings of injury at the harsh words of others. Nor does this philosophy encourage her to find ways to resolve her hurt by talking about her experience with someone else.

Although Mary judges herself for getting hurt and being "too emotional," she does not deny experiencing these feelings and seems aware of the losses she has experienced since eighth grade. In tenth grade Mary describes her loss of openness when she explains how the interview has affected her: "Well, probably in the future it will help me be more open and honest and everything . . . See, I am not really a very open and honest person right now. So maybe, like this interview, when I go out to get a job or when I'm working or I have another relationship, I'd be, like, open about it, tell them how I feel straight out, and play down the line and everything." Mary says this change has been a self-protective move, because "I've been hurt in relationships and stuff so many times that I just can't be honest or open anymore. I'm afraid that if I just open up to everybody, I'll end up getting hurt again. Like, I am an affectionate person, and the simplest things can hurt me. Some kid can tell me he doesn't like me, and then I'd be hurt so." While there is wisdom in not "opening up to everybody," Mary's strategy of not opening up to anybody is a psychologically dangerous solution.

Like many of the girls in the study, Mary has also learned that speaking up gets her into trouble. References to "trouble" become more frequent over time, although she does not describe the specifics, when, for example, she talks about feeling bad and good about herself: "If I was outside of school and got into trouble . . . I would feel bad about myself and hate myself. I feel good if I stay out of trouble and keep busy." This appears again in describing a time when she felt bad about herself outside of school: "When I get into trouble and fights, I feel real bad about myself. Like, if I fight people bothering me and stuff. Like, sometimes it is not my fault, but I still feel bad because I could have walked away and ignored it, but I didn't. I had to, like, stay there and argue and get in trouble and stuff like that."

It seems to Mary that the only way to stay out of trouble is to stay away from other people: "When I get into the fight . . . I feel bad, I wish that I had stayed home and stayed in my room all day, and maybe if I don't go outside, I won't get into no fights. I know I can't do that, but I wish I could sometimes." Since Mary "cannot stay in my house twenty-four hours a day" to avoid a fight, her solution is to mind her own business: "If you see two people fighting, don't try being a hero and going in and breaking it up, or if you see two people arguing . . . just like keep your own business, you know. Don't go around trying to start any trouble." Still, it is hard for Mary to avoid trouble: "Sometimes if you are walking down the hall and you bump into some girl and say you're sorry, but she won't accept your apology, she'll want to fight you, stupid stuff like that." In ninth grade an embattled Mary voices a wish for an end to fighting, where "no problems would happen": "I think if all this fighting stops in this school, everybody would be like better friends, people would look forward to coming to school, people like would have, like everybody would be friends and no problems would happen or anything. All the fighting would stop."

Mary's concern for keeping out of trouble becomes more understandable in tenth grade when she describes having dropped out of school in the middle of the previous year. What was at stake for her became clear at the moment she made her decision to return to school in tenth grade: "I don't really know what made me come back to school. It wasn't my parents. It wasn't my friends—well, my friend Kate kind of pushed me a little, you know what I mean? She led me the way to the door . . . She brought me to school and she was like, 'Mary, there's the door, you can either go in and make a life or turn around and lose your life,' and I just went in. I don't know what made me come in. I just walked right through the door and reenlisted . . . I guess something really scared me when she said, 'There's your life, if you walk through the door, and if you don't walk through the door, you go that way and your life's gone.' I guess that kind of like scared me 'cause I don't want to be one of those people working at Burger King, living in a raggedy old house, you know what I mean? No life. No nothing."

Mary had left school in ninth grade because of "all the pressure and everything all at once, you know, like you held it all in from one day, it's just like everything went wrong, nothing went right, and it just, I felt like I couldn't take it anymore, so I just left." Mary was in a dilemma then, since she got into trouble when she spoke out or stood up for herself, yet when she kept her feelings to herself and "held it all in" the "pressure" became too much for her to bear. Being out of school, however, proved to offer no relief. "I was out for a while, and I realized how boring it was, I mean you just sit around and do nothing. You can't get a job because you just quit high school, and it's boring. Then people, you talk to people and they're like, 'Well, are you still in school?' and you know, 'No, I quit.' And they're like, 'Well, you're a loser, you're a loser.' So, I mean, if you can't handle school, then you can't handle life. And then I have no future."

Mary's act of leaving school seemed, for a time, to bring her satisfaction, perhaps because it was an act of defiance, an act of speaking out against a situation she "couldn't take . . . anymore." If so, this soon became a pyrrhic victory as she came to think of herself as a "loser": "Last year when I quit school, I used to brag about it, and now I think about it and I feel like just hitting myself. How could I sit around and brag about quitting school? Because I was . . . when I was talking, bragging about quitting school, I was really bragging about being a loser, you know what I mean? Because that's what you feel like when you quit school. You feel like once you quit school, you can't accomplish anything in life. Everything you start you will not finish." Michelle Fine (1991) describes a similar pattern among young women who, when they first drop out of high school, feel energized and empowered by taking action on their own behalf and making a political statement about the school system. Later, however, these feelings change to hopelessness and despair when they discover that there are few or no options available to them after they leave school.

Frightened by the potential of having "no life" if she does not finish school, Mary returns at age sixteen, but she is aware that she is paying a price: "[Dropping out] is like a big thing to do, that could totally change like, quitting school totally changes your life. And when you come back to school, it's like you got it back, but the thing is it's a little stronger, you've got a little bit more stronger feeling about everything. But like I lost the ability to do some things." One important loss for Mary is her writing: "I used to be a good writer, write great stories. But now, I read my stories and I'm like, you know . . . I don't really know what happened . . . They don't feel the same. When I used to read my stories, no matter what, . . . I was a mess-up, but I wrote some damn good stories, let me tell you . . . Oh, they were about my feelings towards other people and a whole bunch of that stuff, and now I, I'd write a story and

I'd read it, you know what I mean. It's not as good. Or as good as I want it to be, as the others were."

Mary connects being "a mess-up" with being "a good writer"—knowing her feelings toward other people and being able to give voice to those feelings in a creative, spontaneous way through writing. The creative flow she experienced has been interrupted; whereas previously Mary would "automatically . . . have a story in my head. I don't plan it. I just write . . . so it comes down, just like that on paper," now she thinks "of nothing, and it takes me a long time to write down a story."

Although Mary claims she does not know "what happened," she reveals some clues about the loss of her ability to write. She could, in fact, still write good stories if she could write about her feelings instead of what she is assigned. Her teacher asks her to write stories about "vacations, you know, Thanksgiving, Christmas. Talking about other people because she wants description in it. I could give her a damn good story with description about myself, you know what I mean?" Trying to conform to her teacher's wishes, Mary says, "is like I look at a piece of paper, it's like this. Blank. I see nothing. I think of nothing." Mary's efforts to follow her writing assignments rather than express her own feelings, and to "control . . . what I say" rather than "open up my mouth" and let her thoughts and feelings "just come out," are demanding a high price of her creativity and psychological well-being.

Mary may be back in school, but in tenth grade she seems at greater risk than before. Having left school because of too much pressure, she now experiences even greater stress. She works after school five days a week, which is still too difficult a schedule, even though an improvement over her recent seven-day work week. Feeling that her future is at stake, Mary works to stay in school, keep her after-school job, and stay out of trouble—all on her own: "It's hard, because it's, like, everybody depends on me to do this much and so much, and they don't realize that they're putting too much pressure on me, like seven classes . . . And I have, I'm on a contract now, I have to be in 80 percent of the time, you know. And it's like everybody expects too much out of me, this person expects that and this person expects that . . . and it's just like it was before, but just a little bit more pressure."

Mary's dilemma is that, on the one hand, attending school, doing homework, and making critical decisions such as whether or not to stay in school, are all issues she feels she must decide and act on for herself. Yet the story of her longtime best friend's role in her decision to return to school and in helping her face the possible consequences of leaving school permanently makes clear the essential place of relationship in these decisions and these actions. And the intense pressure that Mary experiences is likely to remain unrelieved if she continues to avoid talking to anyone about her feelings or seeking help with her situation. Given this additional pressure, Mary will have a hard time sustaining her motivation to stay in school if she insists on doing it on her own: "Everybody says you could do it, and sometimes I feel like I can do it. But other times I'm just like, I don't even have enough energy to carry this school bag through the day." Again, Mary's words echo Ruby's—"everybody tells me I could do better"—and like Ruby, Mary questions this assessment.

Mary's tenth-grade struggle to remain in school illustrates how the strategies she has developed—to depend on herself, to stay out of conflict, and to control what she says and does—work for her and against her. When these strategies work for her they keep her out of trouble and thus enable her to remain in school. When they work against her they weaken her connection to her own feelings and her own voice and diminish her relationships with others. They also work against her by pushing her to try to maintain an impossible schedule: "[I feel happy outside of school] when I'm able to finish work without passing out, that makes me feel good. By the time I get home from work and I do my homework and it's still early enough to go to bed, then I think that's real good, because I finished everything today without collapsing or screaming or cutting my head off. That makes me feel good . . . Half of my friends are like 'Oh, want to go out?' 'I can't, I've got to work. I can't, I've got homework to do' . . . And I end up staying in all day and doing homework. Sometimes I feel like my brain is going to fly right out of my head."

If instead of dismissing Mary's remarks as overly dramatic, we take her words seriously, we hear evidence of real psychological distress. Her example of times she feels good or happy is when she ends the day "without collapsing or screaming or cutting my head off." This description suggests, none too subtly, that she is in or is approaching a crisis—despite outward signs of "progress," such as returning to school and conforming to the expected codes of behavior.

Although Mary says "I really don't tell anybody anything," in the presence of someone who is genuinely interested in her she is well able to articulate the difficulties she is experiencing and why she has made the choices she has. She asks to be taken seriously, to have the gravity of the decisions she faces understood: "I think, um, quitting school really puts, like, a lesson on you. It really teaches you a lesson. You know what I mean? . . . I mean, you've got this big choice, right? I'm sixteen years old, and I had this choice, either go back to school, stay a bum, or go out and get a job working in Burger King, and there's my life. So if you think about it, I had, you know, a pretty big choice."

Having made this "big choice," Mary continues to face daunting challenges in tenth grade. Her wish to be supported in such challenges is clearest in eighth grade; by tenth grade her desire for connection is less readily apparent, yet her need for it remains clear. The pressure Mary experiences cannot be sustained over time, and certainly she cannot face it alone without jeopardizing her psychological and physical well-being. Despite her claim in tenth grade that she will not go to anyone for help, she nevertheless voices a desire for support from her homeroom teacher: "I don't think [she] is giving me as much credit as I deserve. You know, some days, she knows I got a job, she knows I work 'til nine-thirty and I do homework and don't go to bed 'til, like, two o'clock and I get up at six to get ready to go to school. And she don't realize, I don't think she realizes, all the pressure I'm under . . . You need to hear good things, especially when I just quit school, and I could do it again."

In their study of twenty white working-class students, both male and female, who dropped out of school, Robert Stevenson and Jeanne Ellsworth suggest that the experience and interpretation of dropping out may be different for white students than it is for black students. Just as Mary spoke of "being a loser" when she left school, Stevenson and Ellsworth found that the students in their study "had internalized the popular media image of the dropout as incompetent or deviant" (1993,

p. 267). While some "alternated between blaming themselves and blaming the school," all "eventually reclaimed for themselves the blame for their inability to graduate" (p. 266). This self-blame not only had a powerfully detrimental impact on the students themselves, it also worked to silence any legitimate critique they may have had about the school's role in their decision to leave. Stevenson and Ellsworth note that "without the working class' having a clear oppositional identity, the culture of individualism, which already dominates the social fabric of white America, becomes a more powerful influence on the white working class as well. In the case of dropouts, since individualism means that everyone has an equal chance to succeed irrespective of their personal or family circumstances, failure can only be attributed to deficiencies in the individual" (p. 270). As Stevenson and Ellsworth's formulation might predict, Mary seems indeed to have embraced the "culture of individualism," and thus may be more likely to ascribe the blame for her difficulties in school solely to herself.

In her junior year, despite all that she knew about the consequences and about how she would feel because of it, Mary dropped out of school.

A Clash of Demands: Ana and Christina

Ana is a Latina American girl who lives with her parents and three brothers, one older and two younger, in a city housing project. Her parents, émigrés from Central America, understand but do not speak English. Christina, who is Portuguese American, has two older brothers and, like most of the Portuguese girls in the study, lives with both parents—until the death of her father when she is fifteen years old and a freshman in high school. Although they are of different ethnicities, Ana and Christina share many of the same concerns and risks. Their cultures, too, share many traditional values and patterns of socialization. In both Hispanic and Portuguese cultures girls are raised to be respectful, conforming, dependent, obedient, and virtuous; their families protect them and in return expect loyalty to their values (Bernal, 1982; Falicov, 1982; García-Preto, 1982; García-Coll and Mattei, 1989; Moitoza, 1982; Vásquez-Nuttall and Romero-García, 1989).

In eighth grade Ana displays evidence of psychological health and energy like that of Ruby and Mary at the same age. Her responses to the sentence completion test reflect her engagement with the world; being with other people, she writes, "makes me feel alive. I do not feel left out or alone." Ana also writes about her feelings of connection and mutuality with her mother, saying that the two of them "are really good friends, well, at least we treat each other like friends. I tell her private things and she tells me things."

Ana is likewise cognizant of the demands of conventions of femininity, which she both criticizes and tries to accommodate. The worst thing about being a woman, she writes in eighth grade, is that "you have to act like a woman at all times even when you're having fun." Ana describes a strict environment at home, where acting "like a woman" includes being discreet about her interest in boys. She often gets into trouble when she talks to her mother about boys: if her mother "feels all grouchy," she will get angry and "start saying, 'All you think about is boys.' " In fact, all the Latina girls in the study describe partial or complete injunctions against such conversations, unlike many of the African American and white girls, who say they can talk with their mothers about sex or dating.

Ana's experience is in keeping with the socialization of girls and women in many Latin American families, where strictly defined sex roles are transmitted through traditional cultural values. One such tradition is *marianismo,* which is based on worship of the Virgin Mary. This tradition holds that women are morally and spiritually superior to men and thus creates exacting standards of behavior for girls and women to emulate (Stevens, 1973). Associated with *marianismo* are the values of *decente,* referring to virtuous and proper behavior, and *verguenza,* referring to modesty or embarrassment about the female body and the notion that girls should not know about sexuality (Scott et al., 1988). The association of virginity with family honor thus places restrictions on female sexual behavior (Espin, 1984). Although sex roles are becoming less rigid as a combined result of acculturation in this country and increased levels of education and labor force participation by women (Comas-Diaz, 1987), these traditions and values remain strong influences for girls, especially first-generation daughters like Ana.

Many Latina girls encounter difficulty with the difference in values and the "clash of demands in the transition from home to school" (García-Coll and Mattei, 1989, p. xiv). Ana, for example, wants the same freedom as her peers to speak about her interest in boys and the same freedom as her brothers to go out with friends, but both of these desires conflict with strict rules at home, which define these as inappropriate for girls. In other ways, however, Ana's culture of origin and the dominant culture amplify each other—both embrace similar ideals of femininity and self-sacrifice for women and girls—so that living in two cultures magnifies demands to adhere to feminine roles and behaviors. Lilian Comas-Diaz also describes how, "like Anglo women," Latina women "receive multiple cultural messages prohibiting their expressions of anger" (1987, p. 466); thus Ana is doubly encouraged to be polite and restrained, "even when she's having fun," and to limit her interest in sexuality and her expressions of anger or power.

Dealing with competing values as well as those working in synergy may be causing Ana distress in ninth grade. When asked about a time when she felt happy or good about herself outside of school she begins by speaking about "problems . . . at home." Even her younger brothers are allowed to "go out everywhere," Ana says, but "if I wanted to go out somewhere, it will be like this big thing . . . I'm like, 'Why can't I go?' . . . And they're like, 'You're a girl.' " Although she objects to this double standard, she also frames these rules as evidence that her parents care about her: "I feel good that they care, you know." While recognizing that her parents' concern for her safety and reputation may indeed offer her some comfort and security, Ana's acknowledgment of her parents' good intentions may be overshadowing her objections and diminishing her connection to her own feelings and desires.

Language barriers add another layer of complexity by making it difficult for Ana to communicate her experience to her mother: "My mother doesn't know about school things, she's, she doesn't hardly even know English, okay. It's different from her country . . . It's different now, you know, she doesn't know what pressures we're going [through] in school, what temptations, a lot of problems, you know. So let's say, um, we can't really talk . . . about it, you know. Because [my parents] don't understand it. Like my mother doesn't know English. It's hard to tell her. And if I tell her in Spanish, it won't come out so good, you know, how it really is in English."

In ninth grade Ana keeps her concerns about school out of her relationship with her mother; when asked to whom she does talk about these pressures and temptations, she replies, "I mostly don't talk to anybody." Over time, Ana, like Ruby and Mary, has developed a practice of keeping her thoughts, feelings, and experiences out of relationships. And also like Ruby and Mary, despite her self-imposed exile, she continues to describe a need and a desire to speak. She liked the interviews, for example, because "you feel like this is a lot off you": "It just helps you talk out, like bring out some things, like you know, like you asked me about my mother and my father, sometimes you don't talk to people like that . . . You feel good because you feel like this is a lot off you, you know." Like Mary, who describes the buildup of "pressure" from holding things in, Ana acknowledges the corresponding relief of being able to speak and having "a lot off you."

By tenth grade, fifteen-year-old Ana appears alienated from her family and from those at school. In response to questions about her relationship with her mother, she describes the distance that has come between them. "We don't . . . talk so much," Ana says, "because I am hardly home." When asked how she feels about this, she replies, "I don't feel anything, I'm used to it." Ana sounds depressed, and her claim that she has no feelings about her disconnection from her mother seems further evidence of her distress and her disconnection from her own feelings.

Being in two cultures can produce intrapsychic or interpersonal stress according to the degree to which a girl or woman tries to adhere to strict traditional values while at the same time adopting new and conflicting values (Soto, 1979). Clinical work with Latina girls who have attempted suicide suggests that they share two common characteristics: "considerable parent-child conflict, principally around the girls' friends, dating and sexuality" and "being a first or second generation adolescent from a family that is strongly tied to Hispanic culture" (Zayas, 1987, p. 5). For Ana, added to these stresses is the burden of rumors and gossip at school, where she finds little opportunity for connection: "When I leave this school I don't leave happy, I don't . . . I feel like, I know that somebody must have talked about me today . . . I don't know, it must be the people, I don't know." Ana sounds much like Ruby and Mary in her concern about the pervasive and painful frequency of gossip in school. Like the other Portuguese and Latina girls in this study, Ana is particularly concerned about rumors and gossip of a sexual nature and about protecting her reputation.

These cultural characteristics—strict family rules and an emphasis on safe-guarding their reputations—may serve as protective factors against school dropout and pregnancy. Ana, like all but one of the Latina girls and all of the Portuguese girls, neither drops out of school nor has a child. Strong connection with family is also an important resource for these girls. But national statistics show that Latina girls living in conditions of concentrated poverty, who do not have stable and protective extended families like those of most of the Latina and Portuguese girls in the study, do not seem to be protected by these cultural norms. For these girls, high school dropout exceeds—at sometimes twice the rate—that of black or white urban girls (Vásquez-Nuttall and Romero-García, 1989; U.S. Bureau of the Census, 1994).

The strong emphasis on cooperation and compliance they experience at home may also leave some Latina girls unprepared for a competitive school environment if they encounter sharp contrasts "between the traditional socialization patterns of [their] culture and the school's values and expectations" (García-Coll and Mattei, 1989, p. xiv). Lack of attention from teachers and, for some girls, language barriers compound their psychological risks: "Teachers and other adults expect very little of them, the limited amount of feedback they receive is discouraging, and their needs as bilingual, bicultural females are not acknowledged or addressed" (Vásquez-Nuttall and Romero-García, 1989, p. 74). Distressed girls like Ana, who "mostly don't talk to anybody," may be too easily overlooked. At the end of her tenth-grade interview, Ana says the interview was a positive experience because it gave her the opportunity to speak about things that are "inside": "I like speaking it out, because I have it all inside here, and you know, if I don't speak it, I don't think if you weren't asking me, that I would be talking to anybody."

Portuguese culture, although different from Hispanic culture in many ways, maintains similar beliefs and values. The Portuguese girls in this study describe some of the same concerns as the Latina girls: double standards at home, with brothers having greater freedom and fewer responsibilities; strict rules about dating and speaking about sexual matters; and concern about rumors and gossip at school, particularly around their sexual reputation.

Christina, who is Portuguese, writes in her eighth-grade response to the sentence completion task that "What gets me into trouble" is "my mouth." She returns to this theme again later in the exercise, when she uses these same words to complete the sentence that begins "My *main* problem is . . . " Like many of the Latina and other Portuguese girls, Christina also complains in her interview about the greater privileges accorded her brothers, saying that they "count more than I do."

Christina does not, however, seem to feel bounded by restrictions about expressing anger. Throughout the three years of her interviews she speaks freely of having had fights with her boyfriend, of being angry with teachers "who yell," of "getting mad" at her father for grounding her, and of times when she and her best friend get "a little bit angry at each other." She maintains her ability to speak out and stand up for herself, and in tenth grade says that, although she does not seek out arguments, "if it comes to it, I will fight."

Evidence of psychological health and resilience are also present in Christina's description of her relationship with her mother. She describes how her mother "helps me through everything . . . Like if I have a problem that I can't solve, she'll help . . . She'll come and pick me up from school . . . if I need her . . . She makes me talk, like if I am not in the mood to talk, she understands and she goes away and then comes back later . . . Anything I need, like money, or anything, she'll be there to give it to me." Christina does not, however, idealize this relationship, and says: "Sometimes she is [an ideal mother] and sometimes she isn't . . . She is when she cares and everything but sometimes when she gets on my nerves she isn't."

After her father's death, Christina speaks more frequently about how she feels it is up to her to take care of her mother. In ninth grade, she first complains that her mother yells at her for things that are not her fault: "[one of my brothers] didn't work before and she'd yell at me, 'Oh, he doesn't do nothing,' and she'd start screaming at me about it. And, you know, I didn't do nothing and I have to hear it." But she also hears this anger as evidence of her mother's reliance on her: "My brothers are never there for her, so I guess I am the only one left." She continues this theme the following year, explaining how "it's hard after my father died" and "my mother's real lonely . . . so she always, she needs me there with her." Christina adds that she feels good about herself when she makes her mother proud, because "I'm the only one in the house who gets good grades."

Christina's positive identification with her culture is a source of strength and gives her, she says, a sense of "heritage." In tenth grade, she remarks that "my grandfather was born in Portugal and my grandmother, and, like, all my friends, almost all my friends, are Portuguese . . . I like that." But she also says that, as a Portuguese girl, it is important to learn "how to be quiet in certain situations," to know when intolerant attitudes make it unwise or dangerous to speak, to "know when to keep your mouth shut, you know. Like sometimes when I see things that are wrong, you know, I don't want to say anything, because I don't want to get myself in trouble. I just leave it, you know . . . Because some people hate Portuguese people, you know, they don't like them at all . . . So I stay away." Maintaining this "double consciousness" about one's heritage—being able to look "at one's self through the eyes of others"—is an essential skill (Du Bois, 1989, p. 5). For Christina, as well as for others at risk for discrimination or oppression because of their ethnicity, race, class, sex, or sexuality, this awareness is critical when making decisions about when—and whether—to speak.

Christina recognizes when standing up for herself is "not worth it," when it may perpetuate a cycle of fighting, "start violence," and "add more to this world's problems": "When someone is like, 'I don't like Portuguese people,' I'm not going to stand up for myself and say, 'I'm Portuguese,' you know. You know, you can't do that. I wouldn't do that. Because, like, if she starts fighting, I kind of think fights are, like, always continuous. Like you start a fight with one person, then another person, and it's always going to be going on. And then their family is going to get into it, and then other people are going to fight because of it."

Over the three years of interviews, Christina demonstrates the ability to develop sensible strategies in response to prejudice and maintains her connection to feelings of anger as well as to a desire for support, respect, and care from her mother and from her friends. Despite these strengths, over time she also seems to be at increasing risk for psychological distress because of decreasing opportunities for connection. In ninth grade she loses her father, and in tenth, a long-term relationship with a boy (who was first a good friend and then a boyfriend) ends abruptly and without explanation. Christina speaks less of being cared for by her mother and more about having to take care of her. And in the third year Christina complains about having gained weight, a change her interviewer also notes with concern as a possible somatic manifestation of distress.

Christina says in ninth grade that she liked the interview because "you could talk to somebody, somebody listens to you for once." In tenth she says that the interview was good for her because "talking about things makes me feel better." Alongside these remarks, and after two significant losses, the risks she faces in tenth grade are evident when she says: "I usually keep my feelings bottled up. You know, I don't usually say anything, but when something bad happens, like if I get into a fight, it all comes out, knocks against me. If I don't talk about it, it all stays inside, all my feelings stay inside, and I don't really say anything about them."

Voice and Silence

Girls use both voice and silence as strategies in navigating the multiple and sometimes contradictory conventions they learn at home and at school. Each strategy has its advantages and, when the pendulum of voice or silence swings too far in either direction, each poses a risk. As Kesho Yvonne Scott has written of the stories of the women she portrays in *The Habit of Surviving*, girls' stories "can give the rest of us examples of great courage and perseverance as well as new perspectives on habits of survival that may—or may not—work well for us" (1991, p. 36). Along-side evidence of their courage and perseverance, the girls in the Understanding Adolescence Study demonstrate some survival strategies that, while intended to protect them, paradoxically also result in putting their relationships at risk.

The outspoken girls in this study are likely to find themselves in conflict with parents and peers or in trouble with the authorities at school. The costs of speaking out and getting into trouble can be considerable for girls from poor or working-class families, when already limited access to opportunity in the workforce is even more sharply diminished if they do not complete high school. In addition to the educational and economic costs, we also see in this study what is at stake for them psychologically. Efforts to be strong, self-reliant, and outspoken can be reasonable and effective survival strategies in a difficult, and sometimes hostile, environment. These efforts can cease to be adaptive, however, when they move to a position that precipitates disconnections from others, covering over vulnerabilities and the desire for relatedness.

As so many girls indicated in the sentence completion exercise, speaking out can and does get them into trouble. But as their interview narratives demonstrate, silence presents its own dangers. Girls who learn to silence their voices or desires so that they can stay in school or to stay connected to their families and their cultures may also find themselves out of connection with important psychological and relational needs. Even if their efforts succeed at keeping them in school, their "good conduct" often results in their being overlooked or unnoticed.

Whether girls choose a strategy of public voice or public silence, the interviews reveal a clear and disquieting trend toward psychological isolation—disconnection from their own feelings and from relationships with others. Even among those who feel more free to express their anger, power, or sexual interest, the overriding move is to "stay to myself," "not talk to anybody," "keep my feelings bottled up," and "not tell anybody about anything." This is quite different from the eighth-grade confidence of having "lots of people" to talk to about important concerns and the pleasure of connection with others that "makes me feel alive." The girls in this study voice a tremendous need for an experience of connection in which they feel safe and can speak the truths of their lives without fear that they will lose relationship or endanger their place in school. That they are willing and able to do so is evident in their interviews. That these opportunities become increasingly rare for most as they enter into womanhood, however, is also painfully apparent.

While preparing a talk on silence, Audre Lorde reflected on the obstacles to speech: "Of course I am afraid, because the transformation of silence into language and action is an act of self-revelation, and that always seems fraught with danger." Lorde's daughter reminded her about the consequences of remaining silent: "My daughter, when I told her of our topic and my difficulty with it, said, 'Tell them about how you're never really a whole person if you remain silent, because there's always that one little piece inside you that wants to be spoken out, and if you keep ignoring it, it gets madder and madder and hotter and hotter, and if you don't speak it out one day it will just up and punch you in the mouth from the inside' " (1984b, p. 42). Her daughter's image has the force of psychological truth, one equally well understood by some of the girls in our study, who knew they would "blow up some day" if prevented from talking about their feelings.

Voice "is a powerful psychological instrument and channel, connecting inner and outer worlds" (Gilligan, 1993, p. xvi), and its expression or suppression has important psychological consequences. This does not mean that psychological health is served by speaking out all the time or by indiscriminately saying whatever is on one's mind; as the girls' narratives here so clearly illustrate, this can be psychologically and politically risky for girls as well as unnecessarily hurtful to others. What is important is being able to speak one's experience, to say what is true or psychologically true, and being able to do so in safe company.

The choices made and paths taken at adolescence have the potential to be pivotal, setting a course for the educational and vocational direction—and the psychological and relational character—of adulthood. The conventional paths set before many girls, often "fraught with danger," make adolescence a complex and consequential journey. It is not a journey that should be undertaken alone.

3

Cultural Stories:
Daughters and Mothers

I don't know. I don't know how I would describe an ideal
mother. Nice . . . I don't know, I don't know what I should
say about an ideal mother. Be like mine . . . she's not perfect,
but she does the best she can . . . That's all I'd say, to do the
best that they can do . . . No one's perfect.
—Diana, African American, eighth grade

Across race, ethnic group, and social class girls learn cultural conventions of femininity and womanhood from their mothers and from other
women. In the Understanding Adolescence Study, girls' accounts of their
relationships with their mothers are imbued with these cultural traditions and meanings. There are greater differences in the way the black,
white, Portuguese, and Hispanic girls describe their relationships with
their mothers than in the way they describe other aspects of their lives
that were covered in our research. For this reason, mother-daughter
relationships become central to our analysis of cultural and racial differences in this group of poor and working-class girls.

Tension and conflict about being bicultural or multicultural are perhaps most apparent in mother-daughter relationships. Women may
serve as the bearers and guardians of culture, yet in educating girls to
simultaneously "fit in" and "be themselves" they may revisit their own
development and face their own relationship to culture in an intensely
personal and often conflicted way. Mothers, teachers, and other women
directly involved in girls' lives can be caught in the tension between
educating girls to fit in and, at the same time, to be themselves. Some
mothers, particularly those not born in the United States, are in the

difficult position of attempting to uphold cultural beliefs and traditions while speaking little, if any, English and not knowing, as Ana says, "what pressures we're going [through] in school, what temptations, a lot of problems, you know."

Across cultural contexts, both the adolescents in the study and women in the retreats described being taught by women to live in a world where men play dominant roles. Women remembered the negative messages that as girls they received from adult women: that it is better, as Katie Cannon said she had learned, to have "a man who is abusing you than no man at all" and that it is probably your fault if a man does not stay in relationship.[1] Teresa Bernardez spoke of wishing that her mother had told her what life as a married woman was really like, the difficulties as well as the positive aspects. Jill insisted that Teresa, as a young woman, in love and ready to marry, would not have listened, but Teresa's point was that in attempting to talk frankly to her daughter, a mother would be interrupting a cycle of idealizing marriage and covering over the difficult truths of adult women's lives.

Black women also spoke about being socialized to work to be independent, not as an alternative in terms of relationships with men, but as a reality of their lives. In all cultural contexts in the United States, conventions of femininity and masculinity reflect sociopolitical realities, which include, centrally, access to education and paid labor. Maxine Baca Zinn and Barrie Thornton Dill, summarizing the economics of gender, class, race, and culture, write that "historically, opportunities in the labor market are influenced by who people are—by their being male or female; White, Black, Latina, Native American, or Asian: rich or poor" (1994, p. 5). Although Civil Rights and Affirmative Action legislation has to some extent redressed this discrimination across racial and ethnic lines, many inequities persist.

In most cultures, masculinity includes the roles of provider and protector of family members and sometimes of extended family members and fictive kin. For many men these roles have been difficult to fulfill due to the structural effects of race and class. Access to education and employment opportunities has been limited and the possibility of fulfilling role expectations diminished or denied altogether. This has been particularly true for African American families, where the legacy of slavery and continuing discrimination along racial lines have led to high unemployment rates for black men (Jones, 1986; Wilson, 1986; Hacker, 1992). The strength of black women in part reflects these realities and has led to a certain kind of egalitarianism among black men and women (Greene, 1990b).

For Hispanic families living in the United States, patterns of employment have also provided more opportunities for Hispanic women in urban areas than for the men in their families (Comas-Diaz, 1989; Carrasquillo, 1991; Fernandez Kelly, 1990). As is true for other immigrant women and African American women, available work has traditionally been exploitive and poorly paid. The lack of access to education and adequately paid employment has brought about, in the writer Gloria Anzaldúa's view, a change in the meaning of cultural concepts like *machismo*. Anzaldúa argues that by aligning aggressively masculine, sexist, sometimes violent behavior with *machismo,* the current meaning is "actually an Anglo invention . . . an adaptation to oppression and poverty and low self-esteem" (1987, p. 83). Originally *machismo* included courage, honor, and respect for others, as well as protection of and provision for one's family. For men like Anzaldúa's father, "being macho meant being strong enough to protect and support my mother and us, yet being able to show love." Through loss of the ability to provide, Latino men may move to exaggerate other aspects of masculine strength.

Lilian Comas-Diaz and Beverly Greene (1994) also believe that the complexity of the values associated with *machismo* and *marianismo*, once linked to strictly defined roles of Hispanic male dominance and female submissiveness, have changed over the years. Latino children and adolescents attending school in the United States are inundated with messages about individualism from the mainstream culture so that growing up is filled with contradictions. The cultural values enforced and rewarded in the family frequently differ from those presented in school, in social groups, and at work (Darder, 1994). This also holds true for Portuguese children, whose culture embodies strong values of respect for family members and those in authority that may run counter to the expectation of speaking up at school (Pepler and Lessa, 1993). The cross-fertilization of frequently returning to Puerto Rico and the Dominican Republic and of being visited by family and friends makes acculturation more difficult for some Latino children than for other immigrants to the United States (Boyd-Franklin and García-Preto, 1994).

The harsh social and economic realities of many poor African American, Latino, Portuguese, and white families place them in a complex relation to the ideals of family life in the dominant culture. Despite changes in family structure over the years, the fantasy of the perfect mother—one who is ever-present, devoted, and self-sacrificing—persists (Rich, 1976; Chodorow and Contratto, 1982; Debold, Wilson, Malave, 1993; Bassin, Honey, and Kaplan, 1994). In the public sphere, the idealization of motherhood finds expression in a sentimental political rhetoric about mothers and children and families that goes hand in hand with a denigration of mothers and motherhood and an economic squeeze on families. The hypocrisy and political expediency of current social policy has led in the eighties and nineties to virulent mother-blaming and to reduced support for mothers and their children, particularly single mothers, who are more likely than married women to be poor (Mulroy, 1988; Funiciello, 1993). The blame is even more severe when mothers are black and Hispanic and receiving Aid to Families with Dependent Children (Amott, 1990). Although the aggregate number of white women and their children receiving AFDC far exceeds that of any other group, "welfare immediately conjures up images of black female-headed families" (Higginbotham, 1992). In the political context of the midnineties, as debate about welfare reform becomes more vitriolic and cuts in programs and funding become law, the so-called "family values" rhetoric continues to excoriate mothers who are without male partners.

In the psychoanalytic literature, the language used to describe the relationship between unmarried adolescent mothers and their own mothers exemplifies mother-blaming, and also reveals the underlying assumption that separation and individuation are the developmental tasks of adolescence. Mothers are often described as "enmeshed with their daughters," "unable to separate" or "to observe boundaries." Likewise, their adolescent daughters, by having children, are described as "avoiding separation" or making "infantile efforts of separation."[2] The blame, however, is not limited to the mothers of adolescent girls who have so obviously transgressed. Mothers in general are held responsible for many of society's ills (Ehrenreich and English, 1978; Debold, Wilson, and Malave, 1993). The tragedy is that this view, according to which women have so much influence yet so little power, is believed and internalized by many women, who then see themselves as "bad" mothers if their lives and the lives of their children do not measure up to an image of perfection that is in fact impossible to achieve.

Over a three-year period, as the girls in the Understanding Adolescence Study described their relationships with their mothers, the openness and closeness they spoke of in eighth grade often gave way to wariness about speaking openly in ninth and tenth grades. As eighth graders, most girls had strong opinions about these relationships with their mothers as well as those with their friends, their teachers, and the school. They were curious about our study and why we were asking them questions; some asked questions back. Many spoke of conflict with their mothers and of arguments over restrictions or what they perceived as different, and preferential, treatment of brothers or younger siblings.

As the girls moved into ninth and tenth grades, we heard changes and more obvious differences across cultures in how the girls spoke of their relationships with their mothers. The black girls were more likely than the white, Latina, and Portuguese girls to keep talking openly to their mothers throughout these three years and to perceive their mothers as talking openly to them, telling them about their lives—the problems as well as the positive aspects. Openness as an ideal for the white girls became more difficult to maintain as their thoughts, needs, and desires came into conflict with their mothers' beliefs and concerns and perhaps also with their religious background. The Latina and Portuguese girls spoke more often about not telling their mothers what they were thinking, hiding feelings of hurt, and accepting restrictions they had previously chafed against as "being for my own good." They spoke of resigning themselves to a family double standard based on gender, and took in and held potentially harmful messages of femininity and womanhood in the dominant culture and in their own. Despite being deemed "at risk" in eighth grade, three of the four Hispanic girls, and all of the eight Portuguese girls graduated from high school, suggesting that the restrictions the girls complained of were also protective. In the Portuguese families, both parents were present, although during the years of the study, two fathers died.

Learning what subjects are appropriate to speak about, as well as to whom it is appropriate to speak and who is trustworthy, is part of adolescent development—part of girls' initiation into womanhood. During this period, cultural expectations for girls often come into acute conflict with changes in their developing capacity to think and feel and with their desires, including their desire to have a voice that is heard—to be in relationship.

Shifting the Center

During the three years of the study we asked each adolescent girl to tell us with whom she was living; if her response included her mother, we asked open-ended questions about the relationship.[3] We also asked questions about an "ideal mother" to draw on girls' understanding of cultural values and cultural images of mothers. Some girls either misunderstood the question or resisted it by asking interviewers what they meant or responding, "I don't know," which was the reaction of six of the eight black girls and four of the six white girls in the study.[4] Diana's response in eighth grade, quoted at the beginning of this chapter, is a good example.

As we read the interview transcripts, we were at first surprised by the confusion and the apparent difficulty adolescent girls seemed to have with the ideal mother question. In cognitive terms, Diana's thinking can be characterized as "concrete": she refers to her own mother and her mother's experiences rather than to a general or abstract concept of "mother." Reframing Diana's response according to Mary Belenky, Blythe Clinchy, Nancy Goldberger, and Jill Tarule (1986), it exemplifies "connected knowing"—a knowing achieved through empathy and experience. In this interpretation, the difference in Diana's response does not signify lack of development but rather the development of knowledge of mothers based on experience, including the experience of her relationship with her mother. As Elizabeth Debold notes, the development of girls' connected knowing is still not generally recognized and named as evidence of psychological strength and health (1990; see also Debold, Wilson, and Malave, 1993).

Diana acknowledges that there may be a correct answer to the ideal mother question when she comments, "I don't know what I *should* say," but she goes on to speak from her own experience, describing the kind of relationship she and her mother have and explaining "how we got to being so close":

> We talk a lot every time together. There's nothing we keep from each other, like, if I'm having trouble with one of my friends or in school, I can talk to her, and if she's having problems, any kind of problems, we can rely on each other to talk . . . Just about anything, just about mother-to-daughter things, about like, if I was to like a boy, I could talk to her about it. Or if she was having trouble at work, she could talk to me about it, things like that. But we're real close . . . She always told me if I had anything to say, that I could come talk to her, and that's, that's about how mainly we got to being so close . . . is that she always told me that I can rely on her to talk to me, to talk about things, and I suppose that's about it.

As Diana speaks not of the ideal mother but of what is ideal in her relationship with her own mother, she emphasizes the importance of speaking and being listened to, of hearing about the problems as well as the good things in her mother's life. In her study of African American women and girls, Suzanne Carothers (1990) named this the "free flow of information." The mothers in her study did not attempt to cover over or shield their daughters from the realities of their lives; they chose instead to prepare their daughters for an adult life in which problems, including racism and economic concerns, would be ongoing.

Diana's experience of her relationship with her mother, like all relationships, occurs in a particular context of race and social class, one in which women have traditionally held multiple roles as economic providers, mothers, wives, lovers, community and church organizers, and workers (Higginbotham and Weber, 1992; Mullings, 1994). The black and the white working-class adolescent girls in our studies call into question a middle-class—white—image of an "ideal mother" (see also Brown and Gilligan, 1992). In contrast, the "Super Woman" image, a contemporary rendition of the Victorian "Angel in the House," is an image that several girls describe vividly when they speak about the future. Both images, when analyzed, however, turn out to be images of sacrificial isolation. The ideal mother, although involved in relationships, is portrayed in selfless separation from her voice, without a sense of self; the "Super Woman" is independent, self-sufficient, able to manage everything by herself.

The theme of openness and free speaking with her mother that Diana introduces is also mentioned by Valerie, a curly-haired Jamaican girl, engaging but reserved, who has lived in the United States for ten years. She reports: "[I am able] to talk to her about things and I like that, because I like for her to know what's going on with my life. And I don't keep anything from her, and she doesn't keep anything from me or my older sister." In tenth grade, when the interviewer, an African American woman, asks how Valerie manages to have such a close relationship, since "not everybody does," Valerie explains: "My father hasn't, isn't around, so she has to, like, play both roles, and she, when we were small, she always used to tell us never to be afraid to tell her anything and she's always there when we need to talk to her and stuff like that. She encourages us to talk to her. So it makes it much easier."

The relationship is different for her younger brothers and sisters, Valerie goes on to explain, who are afraid "that they might be punished if they do anything, but I think they will grow out of it . . . I did." Valerie and her older sister now have a different relationship with their mother than the younger children in the family, and they hear about the difficult as well as the good aspects of their mother's life. Valerie speaks of feeling particularly close to her mother when they visited Jamaica: "She was taking the time to tell me things about her childhood. We were just there talking and having fun and laughing and enjoying ourselves." Valerie, in talking about her relationship with her mother, also describes times when both she and her mother get angry, depicting a relationship that seemingly can weather a range of feelings, including pleasure and anger.

Pauline, tall and athletic, who identifies herself as Haitian American, is in the first year a little hesitant about the interview. In eighth grade she says that what is important about her relationship with her mother is that "I have a mother, because some people don't have mothers that can be living with their fathers or something," and she repeats almost the same words in ninth grade. Pauline elaborates on her ability to talk to her mother: "Like, if I have a problem, I'll just ask her and we'll talk about it, or if she has a problem, she will just talk to me." In the ninth grade, Pauline cites the fact "that we're together" as the reason their relationship is important, "because if I was away from my mother, I don't know what I would do." She and her mother are close "in some ways, like getting along, going shopping and stuff like that." They argue, "but not that much."

Pauline's relationship with her mother, in her view, includes hearing about her mother's problems as well as speaking about her own. Pauline values the fact that she has a mother to whom she can say anything. Yet in tenth grade, when she says of the relationship: "Well, it's fun. We're best friends, kind of," we hear the same qualifier we heard from other black girls, hinting at an acknowledged "condition" in this friendship: saying anything may not mean saying everything, since some things would signify a lack of respect. Pauline draws on her experience, implicitly acknowledging the effects on families of the need to work long hours, separations caused by legal and illegal immigration, substance abuse, death, and poverty, explaining that it makes her feel good to be with her mother because "some kids don't really get a chance to spend time with their mothers, and every time I spend time with my mother, I just . . . I just say whatever comes to mind."

Gloria Joseph and Jill Lewis (1981), who observed the conflict of openness and respect between black mothers and black daughters, found it also among working-class whites. Black mothers, often described as strong disciplinarians and overly protective, raise daughters to be self-reliant and assertive (Wilson, 1986; Greene, 1990a). As Gloria Wade-Gayles says of this contradiction: "Black mothers . . . socialize their daughters to be independent, strong and self-confident. Black mothers are suffocatingly protective precisely because they are determined to mold their daughters into whole and self-actualizing persons in a racist society" (1984, p. 12).

Respect, and at times fear as well as admiration, for their mothers was expressed by the African American women in our conversations in the Women and Race retreats, often in conjunction with socialization toward racial identity and an awareness of racism. Katie Cannon spoke of her mother's reaction when, as an eight-year-old and star pupil at her elementary school, she wanted desperately to be in the town spelling bee. She practiced and practiced, but by law in 1958, her all-black school could not compete. Katie's mother took action, organizing a spelling contest in her school, but she made Katie promise not to cry—to be strong—if she did not win, a lesson that carried over into adulthood. Third-grader Katie came in second and telephoned her mother at work, crying because she was so happy.

Black mothers often feel that they must teach their daughters about the realities of racial discrimination and limited resources, and many black girls experience their mothers as strict and overburdened. Gloria Wade-Gayles observed that mothers in black women's fiction are often portrayed as "strong and devoted, [but] they are rarely affectionate" (1984, p. 10). For a black daughter, according to Patricia Hill Collins (1986, 1990), growing up "means developing a better understanding that even though she may desire more affection and greater freedom, her mother's physical care and protection are acts of maternal love" (1986, p. 127). Teaching black girls to be "strong, economically independent and responsible for family" is thus an integral part of the roles of mothers and other women in black communities (Bell-Scott and Guy-Sheftall, 1992).

Four of the six white girls in the study also speak about being open with their mothers, but not in the same way that Diana, Valerie, and Pauline do. They do not report a free flow of information between their mothers and themselves, although some allude to their feeling that their mothers have become "like sisters." In poor and working-class white families, conventions of femininity and womanhood are complex. On the one hand, Jean Anyon (1982) observes, girls are meant to be subordinate, even submissive, in the private sphere of home, where fathers are the accepted authority figure. This is often in contradiction to their behavior in public, where they can be outspoken and challenge implicit and explicit rules and regulations. What gets her into trouble, says Carla, is her "big mouth."

Twenty years ago, Lilian Rubin (1992) heard poor and working-class white women describe boundaries of acceptable sexual behavior, even as they exceeded those boundaries. Then, becoming pregnant meant marrying the father of the baby, since that upheld conventional and acceptable social mores. Fewer restrictions apply now, although working-class families are less liberal than middle-class families in terms of their children's sexuality. When Donna explains that she wants to leave home after graduating from high school, she describes her large family as "like a chain all around," keeping her in.

Barbara, who in tenth grade describes herself to her African American interviewer as "Irish, you know, red hair, freckles, like Howdy Doody," is consistent in characterizing her relationship with her mother as open. Over the three years of the study, their relationship undergoes renegotiation. During this time her mother and stepfather divorce. When she is in eighth grade, Barbara does not question her mother's authority, and her mother performs both parental roles: "Well, we talk when we have troubles and we go places with each other and we watch TV. She's a mother that's nice on occasion, and if you do something bad, she'll tell you that you're wrong and if you don't stop what you're doing, then you are going to be punished for it, so she's kind of like father and mother put together." Barbara's traditional view—aligning fathers with discipline—is similar to that of Valerie, whose mother also assumed both roles in the absence of her father.

In eighth grade, Barbara struggles to understand the image of the "ideal mother." When the interviewer rephrases the question to "the best way a mother could be," she responds: "Nice and kind and caring and lets you do things like stay out till eight o'clock P.M. See, I can't go outside because she thinks I am too young. So I wish I could go outside. My brother can. She's kind of, how would you say, overprotective, you know, she thinks that I'm too young and I can't do this because I will get hurt." By ninth grade, however, Barbara's relationship with her mother has changed, and being restricted and overprotected are no longer mentioned as problems. At the same time, Barbara takes a more critical view of the cultural image of the ideal mother: "Someone who's there when you have problems. Someone who, huh, that's a hard one. Maybe I should describe the 'Leave It to Beaver' mother. The high heels, dressed up . . . That she is all perky and all that, you know. She's happy when anything is wrong and she always has the answer for everything." When the interviewer asks if being happy and having all the answers is being an ideal mother, Barbara immediately identifies this portrayal of uninterrupted happiness and confidence as an idealized and false version of motherhood: "That's not true, though, that's on a show." To explain the kind of relationship she and her mother have, she uses language common among adolescent girls when speaking about mothers that describes a shift from an authoritarian relationship in eighth grade to one that is more egalitarian in ninth and tenth grades: "We get along good. We're like sisters, like. We tell each other everything, you know. Tell her, I tell her everything. Like I tell her the truth like, 'Oh Ma, I went out there.' And she'll like, 'Well, as long as I know where you're going,' you know, because she knows, like, wherever I am, I'm safe and all that, I'll call her wherever I am or something. So we have a good relationship. But we do have fights sometimes."

The fights Barbara mentions are provoked by issues ranging from a messy room to a more serious situation that illustrates the complexity of the mutual openness Barbara desires. Barbara is looking for her biological father, and this makes her mother apprehensive about "losing her." To explain why she and her mother cannot talk about this, Barbara draws on the televised image she has just critiqued: her mother "just brushes it off," as though there is no problem. Barbara, who is white, is the only girl to draw on a familiar (to Americans, particularly white Americans) television image of the ideal mother. The role of June Cleaver as housewife and mother combines cheerful domesticity—a woman's place is in the home—with an uncanny ability to solve her family's problems.

Barbara speaks of her strong religious beliefs and values, and these beliefs guide her response to questions about sexual decision-making in her ninth- and tenth-grade interviews, when she says emphatically that she will wait to have sex until she is married. Unlike other adolescents in the study, Barbara does not speak of sexuality as a source of conflict with her mother or a part of the renegotiation of their relationship.

Speaking about their relationships with their mothers, the four Latina girls in the study describe a change over the three years that is related to what they feel is possible—and safe—to speak about in their cultural contexts, where gender roles and expectations are both clearly defined and directly related to sexuality. The role of mother in Latino families is revered, and it is associated with *aguante,* meaning fortitude, endurance, patience, and resistance to toil or fatigue (Shorris, 1992). Mothers are seen as self-sacrificing and saintly, virtues embodied in *marianismo* (Anzaldúa, 1987). Implicit also in *marianismo* is the repression or sublimation of sexual desire and the idea that sex is an obligation. Premarital sex brings dishonor to the family, and there is a clear line between good women and bad (Boyd-Franklin and García-Preto, 1994).

A Latina version of "Super Woman" is captured in the concept of *hembrismo,* which Lilian Comas-Diaz describes as meaning "strength, perseverance, flexibility, and an ability for survival." A Latina woman fulfilling the multiple roles of wife, mother, and worker outside the home may act in a traditional *marianista* manner at home and in a more assimilated *hembrista* manner at work (1989, p. 35). Cultural traits related to appearance, hairstyles, wearing vibrant colors, and a cultural heritage of music and dance, lead non-Latinos to stereotype and label Latina girls and women (Santiago, 1993).

Pilar, a Hispanic adolescent, expresses the power of the negative image that "people," including perhaps her interviewer, hold of Hispanic girls. When she is asked in her tenth-grade interview what Hispanic girls in her school need to know, she replies: "People think of them as a girl who gets pregnant easy. And who just doesn't care or anything, who's just a loser, so they say, but then there is one thing they [Hispanic girls] have to watch is not to let people think they're like that . . . it depends on how you present yourself. If you can present yourself like what people think of you, well then they're not going to know who you are." Pilar astutely observes that by playing into people's assumptions you can prevent them from knowing you as you really are.

"Being Spanish," Ana says, "you've got to watch yourself, you've got to, because a lot of people misinterpret Spanish people. A lot of people have different, they have these ways of thinking about these people, they think they know about these Puerto Rican people and stuff like that, and Salvadoran people too, but I say, I mean a boy is talking about, 'Oh, the Spanish girl.' They will always say a Spanish girl." Ana, talking about the need to "watch yourself," elaborates on the negative stereotypes, indicating how acutely she has taken them in: "Some people think, they think Spanish people are really rude and they just came down here to be housewives and clean houses and stuff like that. I mean, people come down here just to make a living, I mean, you make a living anywhere . . . Just like my father told me, he said, 'I came down here to live a better life.' The same thing my mother told me, you know. But people have a different point of view, and until you're that person, you don't know. That's what I say to them. You're not Spanish, are you, so you don't know how it is. We do!" Arguing strongly against those who would categorize others when they "don't know how it is," Ana resists false and controlling images of Hispanic people. In telling this story to her interviewer, who is "not Spanish," Ana may be cautioning the interviewer and also assuming that because of her questions and her attentive listening she will understand and will not "misinterpret her."

In Oliva's interviews, there is a clear tension between her mother's cultural values and beliefs and her own thinking. Oliva, a Hispanic adolescent with dark, curly hair and pale skin, tells her interviewer that she looks different from other members of her family who are darker skinned, a fact that, when she was younger, caused her to imagine that she had been adopted, especially when her punishments seemed less severe than her sister's. With passion and a well-developed contempt for "falseness" in relationships, Oliva describes how her mother suffers because of her "niceness" and "goodness." In tenth grade she says that her mother is "like, the nicest person in the world . . . She's so nice to everybody and she does favors for everybody. Even though, like, when she asks them to do something, they'll say no. She'll do it for them anyway. She'll do a favor for them anyway." Oliva complains to her mother about this situation: "I'm like, 'Ma, but it's not right. It's not right. You're so nice to them and do everything for everybody, and it's like, you're not getting anything out of it.' " And when Oliva speaks her mind to those who will not return her mother's favors, "my mother gets mad at me because, like, when I tell them I'm like, 'Why are you doing that to my mother?' . . . And my mother gets mad . . . She says, 'Don't say anything to them.' " Oliva realizes there is no easy way out: if she speaks in defense of her mother, her mother gets angry with her; if she does what her mother wants, she silences herself and becomes an unwilling bystander while others take advantage of her mother.

Oliva points to the seeming inauthenticity of her mother's niceness: "All she does is complain to me, so there's no real relationship there . . . And she's nice to everybody else, that's what gets me mad, she's nice to everybody else . . . and she's not nice to us." Oliva's assertion that her mother is "not nice" to her daughters can be heard as part of an adolescent litany of complaints about mothers, but her mother's niceness and helpfulness to others can also be understood as an expression of the selflessness demanded of the "good woman" in both mainstream and Hispanic cultures. When Oliva speaks of "no real relationship," she reveals her experience and awareness of a central problem in women's psychology and girls' development—the impossibility of being in a real relationship when one person keeps her thoughts and feelings out of that relationship (see Gilligan, 1982, 1990a; Miller, 1976, 1988). In consistently subordinating her own needs, Oliva's mother seems to be concealing her feelings even though she might be expected to have many strong feelings: as Oliva tells us, her husband has left her for someone else, another daughter and her baby are living at home, and Oliva's earlier behavior caused her mother so much concern she sent her out of the country to live with relatives for a year. Meanwhile, as Oliva recognizes the toll that being nice exacts from her mother and other people's hypocrisy in taking her mother's help without reciprocating, she and her mother often come into conflict, signifying, perhaps, Oliva's fight for a "real relationship."

James Zimmerman (1991), a psychologist who works with suicidal Latina girls, identifies two central questions that capture the tension between psychological development and cultural norms and values, as well as the tension between girls' conflicting wishes for closeness with their mothers and economic advancement: How can a daughter be compliant and simultaneously fulfill her own unique potential? How can she go beyond her mother yet stay in relationship with her? The second question is as salient for low-income and working-class girls as it is for middle-class girls across different cultural groups, particularly as opportunities in education and employment open up to women. At the same time, mothers face questions about how to protect their daughters while encouraging freedom from the constraints imposed by the culture's norms of beauty and behavior—how women should look and how they should act.

The politics of hair and skin color ran throughout the retreats and interviews, particularly in the third year of the study when girls were asked about their racial or ethnic background and what they, as an adolescent from that background, thought it was important to know in the high school. In a memo sent out in preparation for the third retreat, Lyn Brown asked how we could teach girls to view with a critical "I" rather than with the "eye" of the culture and what this implies for girls' physical and psychological development.[5]

Bettina, a Portuguese adolescent who like many girls in her school has what is called "big hair" and is always surrounded by friends, describes the changes in her relationship with her mother over the three years of the study. During this time, Bettina says, her mother became increasingly concerned about her daughter's appearance and reputation. In the first year, her mother was an ally against her three brothers. "Sometimes when I want to be alone for a few minutes and my brothers are always bothering me when I am doing homework, she tells them to stop." Bettina also mentions a time when her mother bought her something: "It made me feel good, because my mother thought of me when she bought it and she wanted to buy it for me, not that she had to."

By the second year, however, when she is in ninth grade, Bettina tells Carol—who has a different kind of big hair—that she cannot remember a time when she felt close to her mother: "No, I don't remember, not over the past year, because over the past year I haven't talked to my mother that much. I am usually out with my friends, but I know when I was younger, I always used to talk to my mom. Sometimes when I have problems, I talk to my mom and my friends." The things Bettina cannot talk about with her mother include "boys" because her mother "is very old-fashioned," which means "that she believes if you're too young to date, you're too young to, well, it's not like you can't have boys that are your friends, you can have that, it's just that she believes you have to be a certain age to date, stuff like that."

Carol asks Bettina if she agrees, and Bettina says she does not. In asserting that she is old enough to make her own decisions and that her mother usually lets her, Bettina first speaks openly. Then she reframes her description of their relationship in terms of the conventional ideals associated with mothers in the dominant and the Portuguese cultures: "And then if she doesn't like it, she won't tell me she doesn't like it, she just like, it's a (*dismissive sound*), so." Carol is curious and asks, *Do you know when your mother doesn't like something?* "No, not really, she doesn't show it." *No?* "No. She doesn't show it." Asked if her mother does not show what she thinks, even in subtle ways, Bettina again responds that she doesn't. But further inquiry, *So you really can't tell what she thinks?* leads Bettina into what sounds at first like a contradiction: "No. Not when I, I know when I do something wrong, she tells me, like if I go somewhere and I don't tell her . . . I know she gets very angry, because she'll, when I get home she'll talk to me, she'll be like, 'Where have you been?' and all that, so." Although Bettina knows that her mother gets "very angry," she also seems to recognize that her mother covers up this anger because it is a transgression of the image of good womanhood and of the ideal mother: "Well, I think she's a very nice person." *What does that mean?* "She's a nice person, she talks to people, she understands, she likes to have fun. She talks to my friends . . . She has fun. She goes shopping with me, she does, and she helps me pick out my clothes, and then sometimes she buys me stuff and talks to my friends. She just, like, kids around with them, plays around."

Cultural restrictions on women's expression of what are considered negative emotions, particularly anger, play a larger role the following year, when Bettina is in tenth grade (Smith, 1980). Now she adds further details of her mother's daily life, explaining that her mother looks after

Bettina's grandmother and her whole family. She also observes that her mother "can be nice, you know, and she can be, like, mean." This year, "my mom gets on my nerves, and I get on her nerves. So either way, we're pulling and we're real nice to each other, I try to be." Their simultaneous "pulling" and being "nice to each other" is different from the assumptions Bettina holds of mother-daughter conflict. As Bettina notes: "I'm happy, because some mothers and daughters don't get along at all, you know, because I heard that when a daughter reaches a certain age, when they are teenagers, it gets more difficult for the mother and daughter to relate, so that hasn't happened with me and my mom, so I'm pretty happy about that."

Bettina names this disconnection as something that happens to *other* mothers and daughters in adolescence. Yet she is not completely sure: "I don't think she can do anything, you know, because it can just happen. I don't think you can do anything, but it just happens. I guess you can just keep on talking about things, about it, and try to communicate." Bettina's use of "it" and her shift from the first-person pronouns "I" and "we" to the second-person pronoun "you" suggest that she may not want to take on this topic—possibly because of the strong cultural value placed on family loyalty and also perhaps because of the strength of her own feelings. It is also possible that for some combination of psychological and cultural reasons, Bettina does not want to align herself with her wish to keep some things from her mother or take in her mother's warning.

Bettina has had a long-term relationship with her boyfriend, yet she says repeatedly that she cannot talk to her mother about boys. Eventually, however, Bettina disclaims her earlier description of her mother and herself as "getting on each other's nerves" and recasts their relationship in terms more in keeping with the cultural ideal of mother-daughter relationships: "Oh, we always, we usually always get along. It's no big deal. I don't know. We usually, we always get along, so I always feel happy. My mom's a nice person, I think, overall. Overall, she does and says, sometimes she tries to, you know, criticize, but it's for my own good, she has to. She doesn't like my hair when it's out to here, you know, thick, so she's like, 'Put it down,' and everything. It's for my own good, because she doesn't want people looking at me because people talk. It's like you always feel bad. She doesn't want me to feel bad or anything. She cheers me up."

The subject of hair seemed a universal theme between mothers and daughters.[6] In the Women and Race retreats one of the black women remembered her mother's tears of anger when she returned from college with her hair in a short Afro, a political statement of solidarity with other blacks and of nonassimilation. Her mother was sorrowful remembering her daughter's long hair, which she had braided when her daughter was young—her connection to her daughter as a girl with hair that was not only beautiful but specifically "black." She was angry because her daughter had done this to her hair without any consultation or permission: "And it was, she owned my hair and how could I do this to her?" For many years, this woman's mother would continue to ask about her hair when they talked on the phone. This story brought affirmation and laughter from other black women. Katie recalled her surprise when she saw white girls doing their own hair—being *allowed* to do their own hair—at age nine or so. Carol spoke of her mother telling her always to brush her hair, to get it out of her face, a refrain familiar to many white women in adolescence.

The protective and restrictive elements of mothers' concerns, whether about hair or reputation, are evident to Bettina at fifteen. She repeats her mother's wish that she have a good reputation, that she not have to struggle with feeling bad and being different—a wish that, in the context of a community in which to be Portuguese is to be a minority, encompasses its share of negative stereotypes. When Elena's interviewer asks her what she thinks it would be good for her, as a Portuguese girl, to know in the high school, Elena says: "The only thing that I can think of being Portuguese is that a lot of people, you know, have slang words, talk about ethnic backgrounds." Elena mentions a slang word but first explains that it might have a legitimate basis, that people "might not mean it in a bad way," and that it doesn't "really bother her." Another girl, Maria, tells of being warned by a friend not to give directions in her native language because "then they'll know you're Portuguese." But Maria tells her friend, "I don't care. I'm Portuguese and I'm proud."

Recasting their mother-daughter relationship in terms that are more in keeping with culturally sanctioned ideals was a common pattern in the interviews with the Portuguese and Hispanic girls in the study. For Bettina, criticism becomes something "for her own good," something intended to protect her and her reputation. She reframes her relationship with her mother in positive terms that leave out any direct reference to the anger or conflict or hurt she may feel. At the same time, during the ninth and tenth grades Bettina seems to lose some of her vitality and, like Christina, gains a significant amount of weight.

Oliva and Bettina both struggle with the tension between respect for their mothers and frustration and anger at not being able to speak openly about what bothers them. For Hispanic and Portuguese girls, as for white, middle-class girls, conflict has historically been difficult to deal with because showing anger runs counter to cultural values about femininity, although variations within these large groups are important to note.[7] Anger, rather than its cause, becomes the problem for girls within their families and at school. If they complain about unfairness and injustice they are labeled troublemakers. Just as black girls in the study talk about expressing their anger more and about their mothers expressing anger, Joyce Grant posed several questions in the retreats: "There is something about young black girls being able to have access to their anger, at least the girls in the Understanding Adolescence Study. Are they more expressive than the other girls? But in terms of really expressing anger and dealing with it, are the black girls more adept than other girls? Or is it just the expression, as opposed to dealing with it?" Her questions are important. Anita, for example, seems to express her anger toward her mother as well as toward others at school by frequent and sometimes physical fighting, a strategy that gets her into trouble and covers over the fact that she "hurts really easily, and I hate people to hurt me."

In the retreats, often when we became angry and hurt we also reached an impasse. Unconsciously—until Teresa Bernardez pointed it out—we employed various strategies to divert ourselves (eating, joking, breaking for walks or meals), which enabled us to skirt the dangerous territory we were heading into. Most dangerous was speaking about race and racism. Although there were many differences in the group—differences in class among the African American women, differences in race, class, ethnicity and nationality among the white women (Carol was the only Jewish woman in a group of Christians, Jill is a Pakeha New Zealander,[8] Kristin was born and raised in Scotland, and Lyn grew up in a working-class family in rural Maine. Teresa, the only Latina woman, whose fair skin makes her indistinguishable from white women until she speaks, is often grouped with white women)—the most explosive moment arose in terms of differences between black and white.

For our third weekend together we gathered on what really was a dark and stormy April night in a comfortable house that belonged to a friend of Teresa's in Wellfleet, on Cape Cod. Janie Ward and Lyn Brown had selected the voices of young girls, young women, adult women, and adult men to structure our discussion over the weekend, since there had been a desire to be a little more "structured and purposeful in the weekend's discussions, but at the same time, appreciating the spontaneity/ flexibility that had gone before, the spontaneous generation of ideas." We were trying to strike a balance between the two. As organizers for this weekend, Janie, Lyn, and Joyce brought interview transcripts and poetry and literature to raise a series of questions about power, about race, about gender and oppression, about psychological development, and about the relationship between girls and women.[9]

As a way of reconnecting with our thoughts and feelings from the January retreat, Janie, Lyn, and Joyce had asked us all to consider some questions that would begin the discussion on Friday night: What were our memories of the January retreat? What was most meaningful or important to each of us about that experience? What was surprising? What were our hopes for it? Was there any particular leftover business from that retreat that we thought or felt we needed to address this weekend? If so, how might we do that?

What came to be known as the "Wellfleet incident" was a tense confrontation that through time vied with strong positive memories and experiences of connection and cohesion in the group. The incident started after dinner on Friday night, when the group picked up on a conversation from the January meeting, and marked a turning point in the retreat process because it led to an impasse in relationship. The group was divided between a desire for more intense engagement, which seemed necessary for working through the problem, and wanting to disengage and dissolve. Perhaps the retreats had come to the point where people were beginning to raise real questions and risk relationships for the kind of relationship they had hoped for in joining the group. Wendy's absence was palpable. She had facilitated conversation during the January retreat when similar tension had erupted around a racial issue. On that Friday night in April, as one woman pressed for direct confrontation in response to what she perceived as an accusation of racism, the woman she confronted moved into silence, feeling herself racially attacked. Leaning her head back and breaking eye contact with the group, she removed herself from the conversation. A gap opened within the group as disagreement rapidly swirled around what had been spoken, what was meant, what was the intention, what was happening? The group did not divide simply by race, although race and racism precipitated the incident. Painful questions followed about who was and was not speaking, who was and was not listening, who was being spoken for, who should side with whom, who was hurt in the incident, and who was protected by the group.[10]

The core dynamics of the relational impasse many girls face in adolescence had erupted in the women's group. An atmosphere of tense discomfort gave way to a replaying of patterns that many women remember from the years around adolescence: exclusion, scapegoating, resistance, and a kind of self-abnegating capitulation that, according to the girls in our study, often forced them into isolation and false independence or into complicity with relationships they experienced as false.

Our hopes were shaken. We wondered both privately and in twos and threes about the future of the group and our commitment to the process we had begun.

The next morning was bright and clear, and we opened with voice exercises led by Kristin. Moving backward through developmental time, Kristin took us through different ages, and we experienced being in the time before the physical, psychological, and sociocultural changes of adolescence. As we felt these shifts in our bodies, we heard the difference in our voices. Returning then to the voices of younger girls from our research, Lyn, Janie, and Joyce posed three questions: What in the girls' voices and experiences do you connect with? What resonates in you as you listen to these girls? What do these girls know that they could bring to our conversation today?

Lyn had brought a book written by eight-year-old Lily, a girl from Afghanistan who was attending the Laurel School. It was entitled "A Friend" and dedicated by Lily to her friends. As Kristin read aloud, we were astonished to hear an uncanny naming of many of the issues that had come up between us and been so divisive and painful the previous night. The questions that came to every woman were: Had we forgotten what we once knew? How had we forgotten what in another sense we know?

Lily's book consists of five short chapters:

Chapter One: Making Friends
Making friends is easy with some people and hard with others, and you will have to be careful because anything can happen and you will have to cope with it.
Chapter Two: Fights
When you and a friend get in a fight, don't worry because it is normal. Everyone gets in fights, right?
Chapter Three: Race
When you want a new friend, do not judge people by race. Indians, English, Asians, anybody. Pretend you are from Afghanistan, and a year ago you moved to America. You have been living in America for a year but you only have a few friends, but the point of making friends has nothing to do with race.
Chapter Four: The End of Friendship
In a real relationship there is usually no end of friendship. Hey, it's up to you and your friend to keep your friendship together!
Chapter Five: My Opinion
I hope you have learned something from this story. Good luck in making friends, but remember, never judge someone by race.

Lily's book, the voices of other girls from interviews, and the questions on the agenda that structured the meeting now seemed to anticipate the previous night's conflict—the experience of fights as a normal part of friendship or relationship, an awareness of the power to end friendship. As we listened to eight-year-old Lily, we heard a simplicity and clarity in her presentation of powerful and passionate feelings—her own desire and frustration in making friends. Listening to Lily brought us to what seemed a dangerous remembering and to the central part of our retreat work: remembering is the second step in Maria Harris's sequence—the step between silence and mourning, "one that is dangerous and communal, as well as mythic and liturgical" (1988, p. 31). The ways in which we, as black women, white women, and Latina women have tried to make ourselves invulnerable to hurt and injustice often differ because of different cultural realities and values. The risks involved in being open in the retreat group, heightened by the events of the previous evening, also differ according to issues of privilege and power, skin color, social class, and professional standing as well as personal history and family background. Among the participants in the retreats, the black women were emerging as or were already established as leaders in their professional fields, while several of the white women (and one of the black women) had been students of Carol's and had only recently left graduate school.

That afternoon we continued to listen to the voices of women and girls, from Lorna de Cervantes's (1981) "Poem for the Young White Man Who Asked Me How I, an Intelligent, Well-read Person, Could Believe in the War between Races" to the interviews with an Indian, a white, and two black adolescent girls in the Laurel Study and the Understanding Adolescence Study. Our listening was framed by several questions: How do we stay with ourselves and what we know and remain in connection with others? What would we say to these girls about myth and reality? About survival? What gets in the way of the ability of whites to understand black experience? Who is responsible for educating whom and why?

At our last retreat, Carol pointed out that the question of trust among women, which became so central in the Women and Race retreats, was also the central issue among girls at adolescence: "Something happens and the issue of trust suddenly becomes like a cliff—one false step and the fall is irrevocable." As we now struggled with the open tension between staying together and going on with our work or disbanding, Carol continued: "The same thing we're talking about now starts to happen among girls at adolescence . . . I think that the wish to continue a relational life that grows past the edge we're talking about now, something that really could move forward, comes into tension with a feeling that betrayal is inevitable—this is how it always goes, you always end up sort of disappointed. There's always an edge of bitterness around this giving up the wish or the hope for relationship. This may be because of the sense that it could have gone differently."

In the same long final conversation in which we spoke about trust within our group, we also talked about anger. Katie, who originally planned to come to the final retreat, could not come when it was postponed and rescheduled because of Carol's father's death. Her absence left unresolved the issue of what had happened at Wellfleet. Jill said that in the Understanding Adolescence Study, girls gave evidence that their teachers—both women and men—"have a terribly hard time engaging with girls' anger." Adolescent girls typically get sent to someone like a counselor who then "copes" with their anger. Teresa observed that many women have a hard time "relating to each other in anger" and then asked, "When you talk about the adolescent girls, do we seem to represent [their future] in some ways, do you think that has something to do with the coming of adolescence? I mean, do the girls see what happens to them, do they have a preview?" To this, Carol responded, "Yes! That's what I mean."

4

Talking (and Not Talking) about Sexuality

> Me and my mother, we're real close. I mean we joke around
> all the time and we sit there and sometimes we wrestle and
> make fun, and we sit down and sometimes we bake—but I
> can't tell her what's happening to me, how it's happening to
> me . . . I never tell her what I'm thinking about . . . I never
> told a lie to my mother, but then again, I never really told her
> anything . . . I keep it all to myself.
>
> —Mary, Irish American, tenth grade

When girls in the Understanding Adolescence Study spoke about their relationships with their mothers, some, like Mary, said that they are close to their mothers but that they can't talk to them about anything that is really important. Pilar, a Latina girl, said that she can only "tell her [mother] things that don't really have questions." With their women interviewers, girls spoke about changes in their physical appearance, their interest in boys and going out, and how their mothers' responses had changed as they moved toward sexual maturity. Girls picked up their mothers' heightened concern for their daughters' reputation, particularly the Latina and Portuguese mothers, whose cultural beliefs and values relating to adolescent sexuality appear to be in direct tension with the expression of sexual feelings that girls experience in their bodies. It makes sense, therefore, for girls to keep sexual thoughts and feelings from their mothers, as tighter restrictions may follow if they speak openly about their desires and concerns. Six of the twelve low-income Latina and Portuguese girls in the study spoke in words almost identical to Bettina's: "There are things you can't talk to your mother about: boys!"

In the retreats, Teresa Bernardez, a Latina woman, remembered "discovering that she was bleeding, not knowing why, being terrified that she had hurt herself, and going to her mother": "My mother sat with me in a most somber mood . . . and gave me a talk with very few words." Yet she was the person "who had most encouraged my freedom, who helped me, and all of a sudden it's as if she had seen this imprisonment for the rest of my life, as a woman, I would sort of be condemned to live off this body for reasons that I couldn't fathom." Lyn Brown also felt betrayed by her body, getting furious when her mother explained menstruation: "I was not, this was not going to happen to me!" Aligning herself with the men in her family, Lyn explained "that it was part of reading the signs, knowing where the power was, knowing what I wasn't going to be able to do if I aligned with women."

Many of the women remembered instances in which the "freedom" and connection of preadolescence, the activities and creativity, and for some, even friendships with girls and boys of different racial, ethnic, and social class groups, were discouraged by their mothers as they became adolescents. Women's restriction of the expression of strong feelings, including joy and pleasure, can also extend to other women in a kind of "good women policing." Some women spoke of their reluctance to tell their friends about their own energy and joy after a morning of writing or thinking and working together, since they felt their friends "pulling them back into the role of wife and mother." The "erons," Katie Cannon said— the creative and powerful, almost erotic energy that is present when women work well together—are somehow too threatening to women as well as to men (see Cannon and Heyward, 1992). Carol observed that women seem more able to support one another's painful experiences than to join one another in pleasure: being able to support a full range of feelings, including honesty, passion, creativity, joy, jealousy, and anger, is much more difficult.

The difficulty of allowing and holding on to a full spectrum of emotions came to the surface when Kristin Linklater joined us in the second retreat. She spoke of coming to New York from Britain in the late sixties and teaching in the graduate theater program at New York University into the seventies, where she found working with black actors and actresses very exciting. As Janie Ward listened, she realized that she too had been at NYU—at the film school—when Kristin was there in the theater program. For Kristin this was a delightful coincidence and, while acknowledging to Janie that she did not know how it seemed from her point of view, she said that the student body in the theater program had been two-thirds black and Hispanic, the place wild, and everything enormously stimulating. At this point, Wendy Puriefoy called our attention to Kristin and to the fact that around her expression of joy, pleasure, and excitement she had started to retract some of her enthusiasm, checking with Janie who had become quiet and still, signifying that her experience might have been different. Kristin tied some of the reasons she wanted to be part of the Women and Race Retreats to the changes that have taken place in the theater: the excitement and energy she had always felt in "working with black people in the theater, kind of feeding off that, this is a life-giving thing for me, and I feel, but wait a minute, what is it for you? You know," Kristin continued emotionally to Janie, "that for *me* more and more in the theater, but more and more in the theater generally, we're less and less playing together, and that's why I want to get into some of that, to find out why."

Wendy pointed out that "pain is the ticket that gets us through race," but to experience Kristin's joy is much harder, so that we "cut it off, box it up, because someone else may not validate it." Tying this to the work of listening to girls, Carol elaborated: "The thing that is pushed down, stopped, squelched in girls is the exuberance, the joy, and," Carol continued, "I wonder whether we carry, I know I carry, memories of being told, it's too sexual, it's too this, it's too that . . ."

For Teresa, Janie and Kristin embodied some of the group's ambivalent feelings and tensions about race and difference. On the one hand, Teresa explained, "Janie was saying, 'I'd like to be cautious' . . . I mean, she's speaking for a part of us. Then Kristin speaks with great passion and we stop her! We do stop her. And I think the two are sitting together, and it seems to me that these are the two representations of the fear that we have: on the one hand, the caution represented by Janie, and silence, pain; and the joy, as you were saying, the joy that we repress, as represented by Kristin."

Kristin and Janie both expanded on their experiences, Janie as a young, black film student when there were few blacks in the NYU program, and Kristin from her perspective as a white teacher who found working with black people in the theater "an extra injection of energy, life, that I don't get from my own white heritage, I guess. So in that way you could call it a sort of vampirism, although perhaps that's going a bit far." Kristin wondered if it made any sense to think that "that might be, in the theater, why there's more separatism now." Appropriation by whites of the energy and creativity of black actors and their reaction to it could perhaps explain, as Kristin had suggested, why "we're playing together less and less." Even though at NYU they were in different places in their lives, as Katie pointed out, the exchange between these two women was a paradigm of what we were talking about—differences in perspectives and experiences because of who we are and our difficulty in talking and understanding across these differences.

Often, women are stirred by girls' energy and perceptiveness and then turn away, so that as Carol said, "Girls are ushered out of the room as they start to speak about what they know." Seeing and hearing what is often generally said *not* to be happening—in families, in classrooms, in schools, in the community—girls are literally and figuratively taught to "straighten up, and straighten the house up." But, as Katie observed, the message that girls need to "straighten up" came, in her experience, from women, "and who are those girls we are doing it to now?"

Speaking about their mothers, girls expressed a variety of feelings and described relationships that ranged from open, free-flowing communication and closeness to disconnection, reconnection, a struggle to stay in relationship, and at the extreme, no relationship. Terri Apter (1990), in her study of sixty-five mother-daughter pairs from diverse racial and ethnic backgrounds in Britain and America, describes how at first she listened for stories of separation. What she heard, however, were girls' efforts to renegotiate the relationship with their mother as they moved through adolescence. The girls and their mothers tried to maintain their connection through the messiness and unpredictability of "voice"— namely, through speaking, arguing, and explaining—as the daughters moved not toward separation, as many mothers had been led to expect, but toward a different kind of reconnection. Apter admits that she would have missed the renegotiation and redefinition of the relationship had she not included daughters in her study, since the mothers, relying on their own experience and expectations and echoing the various professionals that work with adolescents, interpreted conflict with their daughters as a sign of the daughter's need to separate from them.

Speaking about Sexuality

Some girls in the Understanding Adolescence Study may well underestimate their mother's tolerance for discussions of sexuality, but it is their perception of their mothers' ability to understand their sexuality that concerns us in this analysis. The interviews similarly reflect girls' perception and experience of what their older, predominantly white, middle-class interviewers can hear and tolerate. Girls may be projecting onto the interviewers a problem with other women or, conversely, attributing to their mothers feelings and beliefs they assume the interviewer holds.

In tenth grade, when Valerie is interviewed by an African American woman, she speaks plainly about sexuality, recounting how she and her boyfriend arrived at their decision to use birth control. The family doctor influenced this decision, and when the interviewer asks if the doctor talked to her mother, Valerie answers: "My mother knows. I talk to her about anything . . . She said to me, she said, um, 'I hope if you are having sex that you're protected and you won't get pregnant or anything.' And I started talking to her and I did all that stuff." Asked why the conversation was helpful, Valerie replies, "Because she was understanding, she was, she was letting me know if there was anything I needed that she was there."

Valerie's experience may be common. According to a number of scholars, black mothers, in keeping with a free flow of information, are more likely than white and Hispanic mothers to speak with their daughters about sex—although the interaction of race and class, along with the particular role and expectations attached to a specific daughter in an African American family, also influences these discussions (Fox and

Inazu, 1980; Scott et al., 1988; Scott-Jones and Turner, 1988; Geronimus, 1987; Ward and Taylor, 1991; Zabin et al., 1986). Anita and Ruby
also spoke of how their mothers asked them about their sexual behavior,
warning them of the consequences of unprotected sex. In eighth grade,
Anita tells Jill how her mother encouraged her to pay attention to her
own sexual feelings and to respond to them responsibly: "She will say,
'Anita, I always thought that you had a mind of your own and I want you
to use it.' And she said, 'If you do decide to do it,' she said, 'do it because
you want to do it, don't do it because he wants you to do it.' "

In contrast, Mary's communication and openness with her mother
change over the three years of the study. In eighth grade Mary said "you
should talk about anything without being ashamed." But in tenth grade,
describing her feeling about her relationship with her mother, she says,
"It's weird." Their closeness is vivid in her description of how she and
her mother spend time together, yet something has happened to Mary
and she "can't tell":

> Me and my mother, we're real close. I mean we joke around all the time
> and we sit there and sometimes we wrestle and make fun and we sit down
> and sometimes we bake and—but I can't tell her what's happening to me,
> how it's happening to me . . . I never tell her what I'm thinking about . . .
> I never told a lie to my mother, but then again, I never really told her
> anything . . . I keep it all to myself. I do not tell my mother nothing about
> what I do, how I do it, whatever. There is so much she don't know about
> me, and there's some reason I don't want her to know . . . It's weird, be-
> cause I want to tell her, but I, it's not like it's none of her business, I don't
> know. It's weird . . . I feel like she wouldn't understand, so I don't tell her.
> It's weird, I don't know.

What may be disconcerting and "weird" to Mary is what closeness
means, given the richness of her physical description alongside her experience of not telling her mother anything, of keeping it all to herself.
Her internal conflict is evident in her conflicting wishes: "I want to tell
her" and "I don't want her to know."

The "it" that Mary does not speak of seems related to sexuality. Intro-
ducing her relationship with her boyfriend, she talks about her decision
to have sex. She stresses that she decided when she felt ready: "I mean,

it's weird, it's hard to explain, but I mean, you'll say no if you really mean no. You know what I mean? That [other] kid, I really meant no." Explaining how she knew she was ready, she describes what she feels in her body: "It seems like something, I guess something like you feel inside. I mean butterflies, like that, you know when you're ready. Not just something, well he's pressuring me, I'd better do it. He didn't pressure me at all, he did not pressure me at all, it was all my decision. And it was just, like, I knew I was ready and this was the kid, and we'd probably be together today if I wasn't so jealous." Mary explicitly locates desire and feelings—"pleasure and danger"—in her body, connecting her decision to have sex to her feelings ("butterflies") rather than pressure from a boy.[1]

Michelle Fine (1988) points out that girls' sexual desire is frequently missing from discourse about adolescent sexuality and sex education in schools. As Deborah Tolman observes, when sexual desire is reinterpreted as girls' desire for relationship, which sexual intimacy will enhance and strengthen (Tolman, 1990, 1991, 1992, 1994), girls then have no language—and no safe place—to speak about sexuality as such, and they may consequently become disconnected from their "bodily knowledge" (Tolman and Debold, 1994). This disconnection, in the form of dissociation, puts girls in serious danger, as they can be mistreated and abused without acknowledging to themselves the extent of their hurt and loss through violation. Dissociation is characteristically the response of girls and women who have been sexually abused (see Herman, 1992).

When her interviewer asks Mary if she talked with her boyfriend about being ready, Mary says: "No. See, I really, I'm kind of like quiet about my business, you know what I mean? If I want people to know, I'd probably put it on the news." She returns to her relationship with her mother and her quietness in that relationship as well: "But see, like my mother, I can, there's something about it, I can never tell her anything. I mean, not that she'll chop my head off, or you know, put me on punishment or something else. She'd understand and she'd listen, but I just, I can't tell her. 'Cause I mean, I guess she raised me all my life for like respect, and some people say if you have sex before you are married it's disrespectful to your parents and stuff . . . So I won't tell her, because I have a lot of respect for my mother and I just, I couldn't tell her personal things about me . . . It's like if I tell her I'd like hurt her feelings or something."

Speaking of prohibitions on premarital sex, Mary attributes this not to her mother but to what "some people say," leaving open the question of her own and her mother's relationship to these "people." When the interviewer asks directly whether she herself thinks it shows disrespect to parents to have sex before marriage, Mary returns to her sense of her own inner conflict: "No, I don't think it is disrespectful to them, but it's, like, I just can't come down and tell her, you know what I mean? It's not disrespectful, I know it's not. But, it's, like, she thinks I am the innocent one of the family, you know, with the halo over my head. I do good, but then again, I do bad . . . It's, like, if I tell her I'd hurt her feelings or something."

Imprisoned perhaps in the image of the perfect Irish Catholic girl, one who is meant to have no sexual feelings, Mary faces an impasse: not wanting to hurt her mother or get in trouble at home, but at the same time wanting to respond to her own feelings.

Mary then describes her solution to this problem: leaving home. "But that's one thing I'm just going to have to deal with when I get older, I guess. I mean, I made this pact. Eighteen years old, I graduate from high school, and I'm moving out of my house. And I'd probably tell her then, because then, you know, she can't do nothing, she can't kick me out, because I'm in my own house . . . Because if I live under my mother's roof, I live under my mother's rules, you know what I mean? I don't want no curfew, and I just feel like my mother's done enough already."

Mary's proposal to move out after high school is contrary to expectations in poor or working-class families (Steinitz and Solomon, 1986; Rubin, 1994). And in "keeping my business to myself," remaining private and not revealing her inner world, Mary is no longer able to "write damn good stories" that flow onto the page. The pressure she is under to keep mind and body together becomes evident in the violence of her image of a successful day as one in which she has "finished everything . . . without collapsing or screaming or cutting my head off."

Carla, who identifies herself as an Italian American, speaks of her curiosity about sexuality, although she seems to comply willingly with her parents' wish that she not go out until she is sixteen and tells her interviewer that she wants to wait until after she is married to have sex. Carla has little to say about her relationship with her mother in eighth grade other than that it is "good." In ninth grade she reports that her relationship with her mother is important because "I can talk to her about anything. It's a really open relationship. We can talk about anything." Being with her mother is "almost like with a friend," a description she repeats in tenth grade in talking about when she and her mother went to a fair together: "She wasn't, like, my mother, she was, like, one of my friends, and we were just, like, having fun together. She wasn't trying to teach me a lesson or all this stuff, and it was just be together stuff." When the interviewer remarks on that description of her mother as a friend, Carla adds, "But sometimes she is like my mother." She makes a clear distinction: "My mother, she's, like, trying to teach me how to, like, grow up right and watch my grades and make sure I am not absent too much a semester, and when she's like my friend, it's, like, we have fun together and we just, like, go around together and stuff."

In tenth grade, however, Carla's conversations with her mother are not always of the "talk about anything" variety. Carla tells the interviewer a complicated story of being with a boy and "just leaving" when he wanted to do more sexually than she was comfortable with, a story she says she kept from her mother. She uses her mother's rule about dating as a way to avoid "all this stuff, it's, like, too complicated," to help her to exert some power in a difficult situation. Breaking her mother's rules would involve excuses and lies, and the consequences then may be as Carla has said, that her parents would not allow her to date until she is eighteen. At another point in the interview, Carla says that how she looks is a problem for her at the moment: "I don't like, sometimes I feel like, I feel clumsy about myself sometimes . . . I think I'm fat. I feel like I'm overweight. And it's like, um, I don't think people would like me because I'm overweight or something. That's like, I think, my parents think I'm fat. But it's like on a scale of, like, it doesn't seem like I'm fat, but the way I look in the mirror and stuff and see myself, I do." *And how do you feel when that happens?* "Sometimes I feel like, I couldn't stand it, like I try to go on a diet and stuff, but it just doesn't work. So I just like, just don't think about it then, and if I do, I just want to be comfortable around, around myself."

Carla's negative view of her maturing—and by today's standards, "overweight" body—is not unusual, and it is well-documented in the research literature.[2] Being overweight may be good protection against having to make decisions about sexual activity in a culture where being desirable is equated with being thin. Carla may also be using her mother's rules, and those of her cultural and perhaps religious background, as a protective strategy to delay going out, which for many girls starts when they are in high school. The delay can then serve to hold off what Carla calls "complicated stuff," decisions about the level of her sexual activity, and allow her time to become more comfortable with her maturing body away from the pressure that accompanies dating and negotiating family concerns.

Speaking about their relationships with their mothers, the four Hispanic and eight Portuguese girls describe values and beliefs about gender roles and sexuality that they both resist and feel protected by. Explaining the dynamics of their relationships with their mothers in the context of these rules and restrictions, the girls talk about how their thinking differs from that of their mothers and about the conflict they experience as a result, especially within the conventions of femininity in Hispanic and Portuguese culture and their interaction with working-class status. Girls speak of the irrevocable nature of a lost reputation if they should make a mistake.

Although Pilar says that she respects her mother, she also says her underlying fear of betrayal causes her to be cautious about what she tells her. Pilar, who describes herself in tenth grade as Hispanic, explains that "in Spanish families, usually you respect the mother more than the father, because the mother means more. She's the one who carries you and everything, and usually, like in South America . . . and even here . . . the mother is the one with all the responsibilities," a view aligned with the Hispanic cultural values and beliefs associated with the concepts of *marianismo* and *aguante*. As Pilar explains, she does not tell her mother everything because of the possible consequences: "It's close as mother-daughter, but I don't really tell her my private business, because I think if I tell her, she'll tell my father. So I just keep my stuff to myself or tell my best friend. I tell her . . . what is proper to tell her I guess, things that don't really have questions. 'Why did you do that? Why did you? . . .' you know."

In the third year of the study when Pilar is in tenth grade her parents send her to a parochial school. As she speaks about her family this year she seems again, like Mary, to be using a strategy of keeping to herself to deal with her difficulties, explaining that there is not a lot of communication in "families and elsewhere, just in general." Her interviewer asks if that is true in Pilar's family: "Well, not really. But to some people in my family, do you know what I mean? It's not, yeah, I think maybe there is a loss of communication." Pilar's interviewer asks her to explain it to her so that she can understand it better. Pilar replies, describing what is initially a conscious strategy that she and her family use: "That maybe, maybe if I, if I have a problem with something they tell me, I just say forget it, I'm not going to go into a big argument over it, just, you know, I'll just accept it. And I think they do that, too, with me."

Pilar begins to do this around the potentially dangerous subject of sexuality. In eighth grade, Pilar places girls and sex in a cultural framework and understands that girls must be careful not to do anything sexual because the result will be getting a bad reputation: "If she loves the kid, well, I don't know, but if she knows that she's going to go out with a lot of other boys, right, then if she does it with him then he's going to tell other boys, 'Oh, she's so easy, she's so easy, you've got to go out with her,' and then a lot of boys are going to go out with her and everything and if she does it on the first date, they are going to go back and say, 'Did you make it with her?' And even though they didn't, he'll say, 'Yeah, I did.' And it's just going to keep on going."

Pilar is well aware of the difficult place girls find themselves in when it comes to sexuality and offers a powerful analysis of a no-win situation: "[The girl] might enjoy it and if she enjoys it, she will get a bad reputation by letting them do it, if she enjoys it, and if she doesn't, she'll feel dirty inside and she'll feel like abused." Pilar knows the emphasis Hispanic culture places on goodness and virtue for women in the values of *ma-rianismo* and *decente*.[3] Like other girls in this study, Pilar is also well aware of the culture of school, which, she says, labels girls "easy" and a "slut" if they are thought to be sexually active outside a long-term monogamous relationship. By ninth grade, however, Pilar sounds as if she has aligned herself with her Hispanic culture and with the dominant culture in speaking of decisions about sex in relationships: "I'd say definitely no, because I don't want my husband to be like, 'you are already leftovers,' you know *(laughs)*, so I would want to be, I would want to wear white when I get married."

Given Pilar's description of the bind girls are in, it is not clear whether or not she is now keeping her "private business" out of the interview. She has a boyfriend whom she has kept secret from her parents. Like Mary, she raises the issue of pleasure, although more explicitly, but knows she cannot speak about sexuality and pleasure without putting herself in danger.

Sexuality and Danger

There is no joy or pleasure around sexuality in Sandy's interviews as she speaks about emotional abuse by her stepfather and hints at sexual abuse.[4] Sandy, who describes her background as European and Irish, speaks shyly and self-consciously, with her hand over her mouth, telling about her attempts to stay in school and to be listened to at home as she tries to talk to her mother and stepfather about her experiences. The recurring themes are of fighting to speak and be heard, and of being ignored and "getting a lot of yelling" from her stepfather.

In eighth grade Sandy links her reluctance to speak up in school to the way some of her classmates tease her: "because a lot of people in the class, they are always teasing me and all . . . well, they call me retarded and all." When the interviewer asks if Sandy can talk to her mother about this teasing, Sandy's explanation reveals a deeper struggle: "Yes. I talk about it with both my parents, but my [step]father, I don't really get along with him, so I just, I tell him things and he says just ignore them, if I take that, I am a baby and stuff." But Sandy resists her stepfather's advice to ignore the people who tease her and hurt her feelings and fights with a girl who has been annoying her and a friend, for which she is suspended from school for a few days. This action makes her feel bad but, at the time, it seemed the only option.

Although teasing is still a concern in the third year of the study, Sandy no longer mentions fighting back. Yet what on the surface sounds more appropriate and less costly in terms of school may exact a greater psychological cost. Sandy is learning to silence herself: "I don't know, they say they only joke around, but, I mean, I don't think it's a joke. I mean, it really hurts my feelings. I mean, for a while it doesn't hurt me, but after a while I just have enough of it." Her interviewer asks what Sandy does when she has had enough. "I just don't talk and just, I don't know, I just, I don't know, 'cause when I'm upset, I don't talk to nobody."

Loyalty to her mother and the possibility of losing relationship with her pose a dilemma for Sandy, since her counselors tell her she should get away from her house and her stepfather. In ninth grade Sandy highlights this conflict as she tells of attempting to leave home: "My mother called later on that day because she found a note in her drawer that I wrote to her, and she told me that I shouldn't have done that, that she wanted me home, and so I went home." The interviewer asks if her stepfather had been angry, but as Sandy reports that he didn't know about the incident for a month, she also reveals more about an emotionally abusive relationship with her stepfather: "He speaks to me, but if he's angry, he'll say stuff to me that I don't like, like swear at me and stuff, but I guess he didn't bother with me because he knew that I would do something like that. He was afraid that I would tell on him." Making an assumption that Sandy's stepfather may be physically abusive, her interviewer asks if her grandfather or mother get involved when her stepfather swears at her. "Yes, because my [step]father doesn't really treat my mother right also, and, like, she's usually on my side when things happen like that. If things get too bad, my grandfather will jump in."

Each year as Sandy explains what makes her happy, she mentions similar factors—having friends and being accepted—but her friends are unable to help her when in tenth grade she talks about trying to run away again. "I thought I would have a place to stay because my friends were with me and they were going to ask their parents, and, like, no parents wanted me to stay because they would get into trouble if they hid me, you know." As a member of a working-class family that is involved with social service case workers, who may suggest that the family be separated, Sandy lacks places to go and people to turn to.

In tenth grade Sandy is involved in a small vocational program at the school. She describes herself as still failing but says she is attending her classes and feels happy there. Sandy strives to stay in the school she likes, but, at the same time, she speaks about more conflict with her stepfather, who left, but has now returned home. This has led to profound changes in her relationship with her mother. During the first two years of the study, Sandy has spoken of their relationship as close. In eighth grade, "I like, I love my mother a lot, and we get along very well . . . See my mother's kind of young and she likes things that I like and I like what she likes and sometimes we get along like friends." What makes their relationship close is "just all the stuff that we do and how much we like and love each other." Sandy's mother talks to her about her stepfather, "She says he doesn't treat her very well either and she says she wants to divorce him, but she doesn't know how because I guess he'll try to take things away from her."

Sandy explains why she and her mother "get along great together . . . because she acts like, she's thirty-three, but she acts like she's younger, like she seems younger, she dresses younger, she looks it and she likes the stuff that I like and so I guess we have a lot in common. And when we're walking in the street or when we're together and we meet people, they say that we look just like sisters instead of mother and daughter." Their relationship is close because "we both help each other and stuff . . . Well, usually we help with my [step]father. We are both helping to get him out."

Sandy and her mother seem to be switching back and forth in their roles as mother and daughter, acting much like the sisters people sometimes think they are. In the language used to describe family members in alcoholic families, Sandy could be identified as the "parentified child," because she assumes responsibility for her mother and the household that takes a toll on her school attendance and the attention she wants from her mother.

In ninth grade, Sandy speaks with optimism of her mother's new boyfriend, and the possibility of change. But these hopes "to get a better life" have not been realized since, when she is in tenth grade, her mother and stepfather are reunited, and Sandy reports that her mother has aligned herself with her stepfather: "I mean she started getting into him and not paying any attention to me. I mean she cares about me, she pays attention to me, but not as much as she does when my stepfather's not around. I mean now, I mean before when they used to fight all the time, I mean she used to agree with me, but now she never agrees with me that much. She only agrees with my stepfather." Her interviewer asks if Sandy thinks her mother is afraid to agree with her, and as Sandy responds she draws attention to the fact that sexuality is not a one-way street in mother-daughter relationships, and that her stepfather has assumed a more powerful place than previously: "I don't know, I guess, she's pregnant now by him, so I guess he just got her to love him a lot more so now she listens to him a lot now. I mean, I don't know. I guess he doesn't drink like he used to. And, like, he doesn't do a lot of things that my mother hated before. So now my mother respects him and lets him live in the house and everything." Asked if it is better for her mother now, Sandy replies affirmatively, adding, "But it's still not better for me because she doesn't understand that it's still hurting me."

Neither Sandy nor her interviewer name what is hurting her, although both speak about her counselor and the need for her to be involved. "It" may allude to some form of abuse, and it may also refer to her mother's withdrawal of attention. Although she recognizes the reasons for her mother's changed relationship with her husband and thus with her, Sandy's empathy doesn't obscure her own feelings, which she continues to talk about. Sandy's openness in speaking about wanting her mother's attention and about being abandoned and hurt is striking. She frames their relationship in tenth grade in terms similar to those she used in the previous year, but her description takes on more significance, given what is happening in her life:

> We're really close. I think, I don't think anyone can have a mother and daughter relationship like we do. I mean because we, instead of mother and daughter, we act mostly like sisters or like best friends . . . I mean 'cause she acts like she's a teenager that's why . . . I mean a lot of mothers

act so strict and like, I don't know, you usually can't talk to your mother that much, really much. I mean, some, a lot of kids are afraid to tell problems to their mothers, especially certain problems, like really personal ones. But my mother, you can tell her almost anything. She wouldn't say nothing, she'd accept it, or she'll keep it a secret or she'll try to help me out of it. I know like there's certain things she would tell my stepfather, but not most of the things.

For Sandy and her mother to "act mostly like sisters or best friends" and for her mother to act "like she's a teenager" or, in other words, as Sandy's equal, suggest Sandy's realization that her mother is also powerless in her relationship with Sandy's stepfather and can't protect her. Her mother's pregnancy makes the reality of her stepfather's altered behavior and his "good job" crucial to the family's survival. Sandy's mother needs her husband to provide for herself, Sandy, her two sons, and the new baby she is expecting. She cannot risk that relationship by supporting Sandy in the arguments and other difficulties of family life.

When Sandy is asked if she has had to make a decision in confronting a problem, she speaks of a "kind of private" situation. As she has so frequently told her interviewer, she "needs more confidence" and doesn't talk to anyone when she's upset. Her attempts to speak about her feelings with her stepfather "get a lot of yelling . . . he tells me I am a baby, and stuff." One way for her to be in relationship is with her body and the "private situation" Sandy speaks of is this:

I haven't really told anybody. I might be pregnant and like I feel now that I do want the baby, but it's just I'm afraid to tell my parents about it. I mean, you know how I told you I haven't really been happy in my life? I mean, I'm really glad about this and I think having a baby would really make me a little happier because it would make me have something of mine, like, that loves another person. I mean, I don't know, at first when I thought I was, I wasn't really sure if I should or not, I think of it and just having a cute little baby, I know I'm young and everything, but I know I could take care of it because my mother had me when she was young. I was just about the same age when she got pregnant. And she did it okay, I'm here.

Sandy's poignant insights about her life and her reasons for wanting a baby have a particular logic related to her desires, her feelings, and her knowledge. In spite of her history of emotional (and perhaps other) abuse, Sandy is still open to relationship. This makes her vulnerable but it also makes her a political resister—she refuses to give up on her desire for connection. "Just having a cute little baby" can be understood as a reflection of Sandy's cognitive level and how unsuited she may be for motherhood at this time in her life.

As Sandy talks further about the situation it becomes more complicated: "I don't know, like I said, the only thing I'm afraid of, I mean, me being pregnant, they're going to be disappointed that there's only one thing, the baby is black, half black . . . I bet if it was white my parents wouldn't care as much as another race . . . I know my parents will be upset, but I don't really, if I love the baby, I don't think I would care what they would say. I would care, but if they don't want nothing to do with it, they don't have to have nothing to do with it. I mean, it's my baby, I can have it if I want to." The literature on adolescent pregnancy,[5] particularly that on motivation, provides some perspective on Sandy's pregnancy: she is undoubtedly going to receive additional attention from her family, and although we do not know the sequence of Sandy's mother's pregnancy and Sandy's own, the idea of competition between mother and daughter has been noted by psychologists and social workers who deal with adolescent mothers (see Nathanson, 1991; Musick, 1993). Her interviewer comments that Sandy must have thought about having a baby. "Yes, I did. But I think I'd be a lot happier if my parents go along with it." Sandy is scared to tell the father of the baby, not because he would mind, "I mean, he told me he doesn't mind having kids, but I don't know, it seems like he doesn't have very much money to support it, but I don't really care about that."

A short time after her third-year interview Sandy, who it turns out was not pregnant, left home and was living on the streets, although she still kept in touch with her school counselor. The following year, Sandy did have a baby, living at first in a shelter and then in public housing. She returned to school for a short period before deciding that it was not where she wanted to be at that time.

Culture, social class, and her particular family situation inform

Sandy's "logic" when she discusses her relationship with her mother and her reasons for wanting a baby. Sandy has "not been happy," she tells her interviewer, and her "mother had [her] when she was young . . . she did it okay, I'm here." Sandy's schooling, hampered by her lack of confidence and frequent absences, by teasing, and by her stepfather's undermining comments and attempts to silence her has not been able to provide her with an education that will lead to a high school diploma. Economically, her choice to have a baby is unwise, and the consequences for her and her baby without outside suppport may be dire; psychologically, it has a logic that is tied to her desire for relationship.

Over the three years of the study, the Hispanic and Portuguese girls seem to adopt the conventions of femininity and womanhood in both the dominant culture and their own, which act in synergy. At the same time, they also have a well-articulated critique of the double standard in their families—standards of sexual as well as gender role behavior. A number of girls say that boys have more freedom and less responsibility for household chores and activities, such as taking care of others, than girls. When girls speak about the difference they see, they identify the double bind that mothers are in—how to protect their daughters and at the same time give them more freedom.

Lilian, who is Latina, makes it clear that she is both aware of and angry about the double standard she perceives in her family when she reports what she can and cannot do compared to her brothers. Her interest in receiving fair treatment is clear in her description of the ideal mother, who also prepares her daughter for womanhood:

> She would treat us all equally, all fair, you know, not just like, treat my brothers different because they are older, and because they are boys, but to treat us all equally . . . She'd be strict, I mean, but also treat us fair, though. Strict as to make us all do the same things, not like I have to do more because I'm the lady of the house or they have to do less because they work. She favors my brothers, so then I don't, we don't talk and we begin to argue and then I won't talk to her and she won't talk to me . . . She says she treats us all the same. I don't agree though. I say that she lets them, I mean, well, they're older, of course, that's what everybody says, and they're males. But still, I think I should be able to go out with my friends until nine o'clock, at least on weekends . . . Because everybody always says

you know, men get to do whatever they want, you know. Well, that's it, what my brothers say. My brothers say oh, you're a girl, you can't do this, you can't do that. I think, I think she . . . protected me because I'm her only daughter . . . I think it should be equal.

Lilian then describes an incident when her divorced mother and father didn't want her to go out: "You know they don't want you to go, like, should I stay home, and that way they won't be mad, or should I go and then, you know, just have to, they ignore me all the time, not ignore me, but they'll be like, 'It's your decision,' you know, I guess that's it. And they always say like, 'Well, if you want to go, you go ahead,' you know, 'I'm not going to stop you, it's up to you.' It's like that's a decision, because you go, like, should I stay home, because that way I will be mad, or should I go, so that's a decision."

Lilian knew her mother didn't want her to go "just by the way she said it," and hers is a familiar dilemma of adolescent girls: she doesn't want to risk her mother's anger and disapproval but at the same time she doesn't want to give up her own desires.

Lilian claims that everything is fine but then sounds confused. Her confusion suggests both her resistance to acknowledging the more difficult aspects of her relationship with her mother and her loyalty in not doing what Lilian Comas-Diaz (1987) says is tantamount to an act of treason for Hispanic women—complaining about her mother to another person, an outsider. When asked what it is about her relationship with her mother that makes it important to her, she replies in a way that seems at first to conform to the ideal (numbers in parentheses are pauses in seconds): "Trust . . . Yeah, confidence, I can go to her and tell her anything." *What is it about it that makes you able [to tell your mother everything]?* "I don't know, just, I don't know. She just does, I don't know how to explain it." Her interviewer then asks, *Are you close to your mother?* "Yeah, sort of" (6). This assertion is belied by Lilian's giggle and her vagueness as she responds to the interviewer's next question: *Can you describe a time when you felt especially close?* (8). "Um (*giggles*) um (5), I can't think of anything. I mean, not that I haven't been close, I just, I don't know, I can't think of anything." *Was there a time when you felt really good about the relationship?* "Yeah, I guess (6). I don't know, I don't remember."

The contradictions in her interviews—reporting her negative feelings and claiming that everything is fine, then sounding confused—may be Lilian's resistance to her interviewer's questions or evidence of psychological distress. Other sections of her ninth-grade interview, and of her interviews in other years, reveal that Lilian's relationship with her oldest brother was a source of great distress to her. When she reflects back on this time from the perspective of tenth grade, Lilian says that her favorite words were "I don't care, I don't care, I don't care." In a context of possible abuse by her older brother and her questioning of her sexual orientation—which she raised in tenth-grade but was not heard—Lilian speaks of a despair that led her in ninth grade to consider suicide.

More Than the Images

Adolescent girls' sexuality has traditionally been viewed by the dominant culture as problematic and in need of regulation (Luker, 1984; Petchesky, 1984). This is particularly true for poor and working-class adolescents: images of irresponsible, promiscuous girls who do not think or care about themselves, about the future, about anything, often prevail.

But images are silent. When the girls in the Understanding Adolescence Study talk about what they are thinking and feeling, they have a great deal to say. Some of it is hard to listen to because some of it is about violation and possible abuse, which are not in any way confined to poor girls, but as Sandy attests, her friends and their parents are unable to help her, and outside intervention may mean separation from her mother, something she does not want. It is difficult to hear that, despite the openness about sexuality shown by Anita's and Ruby's mothers, both girls had babies and dropped out of school. Early motherhood and/or school dropout are harder to compensate for later in a context where there are few economic resources to fall back on and where there may no longer be networks of extended kin who are able to provide material and emotional support (Ladner, 1971; Stack, 1974). It is hard to hear when girls feel they need to silence their sexual interest and curiosity.

In the United States, ideals of mother-daughter relationships that are open, that allow for discussion of feelings around sexuality, are viewed with skepticism by most daughters, and many women who are mothers are ambivalent about their daughters' (and their own) sexuality and find it hard to speak about it. It is unusual, especially for poor and working-class daughters and those from religious and cultural backgrounds where virginity until marriage is stressed, to ask questions and to speak openly about what they are thinking and feeling in their bodies. The kinds of questions girls may have are not likely to be answered in health and sex education classes, which for the most part leave out the possibility of girls' desire and an understanding of how cultural values and beliefs around sexuality influence the decisions girls do—and do not—make. It is here that women can listen to girls and be responsive as girls speak freely of the often difficult realities of their lives and of the joy, pleasure, and vitality that can so easily be squelched or turned away from as girls become adolescents.

5

Developing Ties: Girls and Women

My aunt . . . she's the type that she's crazy . . . You know, she listens.

—Ana, Latina American, tenth grade

Ours is a culture replete with stories of mothers and motherhood, stories of what and how a mother should be. Motherhood has been institutionalized, escaping neither the scrutiny of psychological inquiry nor the exhaustive analyzing of literature and the media. This is not at all true, however, for relationships between girls and women other than their mothers: no myth, theory, or convention defines these relationships. Few stories are told, in psychology or in the dominant or popular culture, about relationships between women and girls, few names given to this connection.

While these relationships have not been written into the public sphere, they do exist and they are important to girls. The girls in the Understanding Adolescence Study told an abundance of stories of important and meaningful relationships with women other than their mothers. The women in the Women and Race retreats described connections with girls that had similarly powerful effects on them. These stories flow across lines of race, culture, and class.

To some extent, because they have not been elevated to myth, relationships between women and girls are free from the burdens of conventional dictates, free from the weight and inevitable distortion of idealization and unrealistic expectations. But while they have not been idealized or typecast, neither have they received the larger culture's notice or esteem, and by not being culturally valued, promoted, or even named—at least in the dominant culture—such relationships may be undervalued and underutilized by those who might benefit from them. Being kept out of social consciousness and public discourse, such relationships are robbed of their potential as a political force.

The *othermother* tradition in many black communities is one exception to this more general absence of naming and valuing relationships between girls and women, although women's roles as othermothers are not specific to girls. Patricia Hill Collins writes that "aunts, grandmothers, and others who had time to supervise children served as othermothers." The benefits of this relationship extend not only to the children and adolescents but to the women as well, for "the significant status women enjoyed in family networks and in the African American communities continued to be linked to their bloodmother and othermother activities" (1990, p. 122). For many women, the role of othermother includes teaching children strategies for survival in a racist environment and thus exemplifies the political force that can arise when these relationships are validated on a community level. According to Collins, the sense of accountability that othermothers feel provides "a foundation for Black women's political activism" (p. 129).

Important relationships between girls and women other than their mothers may be most prevalent among racial or ethnic groups where extended family groupings are the norm.[1] Many black families maintain "strong kinship bonds" within extended family networks that include both blood relatives and "fictive kin" (Collins, 1990; Giddings, 1984; Hines and Boyd-Franklin, 1982; McAdoo, 1987; Stack, 1974). Hispanic and Portuguese American families are also likely to be made up of extended kinship networks (Bernal, 1982; Falicov, 1982; García-Preto, 1982; García-Coll and Mattei, 1989; Moitoza, 1982; Vásquez-Nuttall and Romero-García, 1989). *Comadres* are the othermother equivalents in these cultures.

Although the girls in the Understanding Adolescence Study were not explicitly asked about relationships with women other than their mothers, stories of other women nevertheless emerged in the interview narratives. For some girls, the question *Can you tell me about another person [besides your mother] who is important to you?* provided a moment to speak of important relationships with other women—aunts, adult sisters, sisters-in-law, older friends, and neighbors. Other girls named women when asked who helped them think about their futures, or when describing to whom they would turn for advice in a difficult decision or from whom they would seek support in a troublesome situation. Amid the diversity of race and ethnicity in this study, these spontaneous narratives describe aspects of these relationships that remain insistent across differences, aspects that form an unambiguous and powerful template for meaningful relationships between women and girls.

Meetings at the Edge

Despite the obvious importance of their relationship with their mothers, many of the adolescent girls in the study described strains in this relationship at this point in their lives. Emerging sexual interests, wanting to spend more time with friends, and a desire for more freedom frequently came into conflict with their mothers' beliefs, values, or concern for their safety. At the same time, many girls spoke of a social world that had become a place of conflict as well, particularly in high school. Rumors and gossip—especially around real or presumed sexual activity—were endemic, creating a serious threat to sustained and honest relationships at school. For many girls at the edge of adolescence, taking themselves out of relationship with others at school, keeping to themselves, or not trusting others became ongoing strategies of self-protection. It was against this backdrop of actual or threatened loss of connection and trust that, for some girls, women other than their mothers were able to be dependable allies and important sources of support.

While most girls described predictable tensions in the process of renegotiating their relationship with their mothers, the development of a few girls was marked by increasing levels of disconnection in this relationship. For these girls in particular, connections with other women seemed especially valuable. This was true, for example, for fifteen-year-old Ana, who in tenth grade responds to questions about her relationship with her mother by describing the distance that has come between them: "We don't . . . talk so much," Ana says, "because I am hardly home." When asked how she feels about this, Ana replies, "I don't feel anything, I'm used to it." Ana now also seems to find little opportunity for connection at school: "When I leave this school I don't leave happy, I don't." Ana often refers to the pain she feels because of her fear of constant rumors and gossip: "I feel like I know that somebody must have talked about me today."

In this context, where Ana appears to be estranged from so many, she speaks about an aunt who provides a haven: "My aunt . . . she's the type that she's crazy. She's that type that I wish my mother could be . . . I usually go to her house and, you know, I start talking and she'll start asking me about boys and stuff like that, and school, and she'll start encouraging you for things . . . And we will end up talking about some things, and she's like, 'Yeah, in my time this and this happened,' so I feel like it's almost the same. So you know, she listens."

Ana is one of a number of girls who drew our attention to the importance of relationships between girls and adult women other than their mothers. Many girls—not only those who were experiencing difficulties in other relationships—described the positive difference that these women made in their lives, in the context of both sustained relationships and brief encounters. In at least one of their interviews, 85 percent (n = 22) of the girls in the study described an important relationship or encounter with women.[2] These women acted as advocates, served to validate the girls and their experience, and fostered girls' sense of self-respect and confidence. These relationships were often a source of great pleasure for the girls, a place for genuine connection and a safe escort into the adult world.

Ana names some key elements linking all the stories of positive relationships with women. In summarizing what makes her relationship with her aunt an important one, Ana names what is foremost among these elements: "She listens." Her description is as elegant in its simplicity as it is deceptive. The kind of listening that Ana and other girls describe as important to them is rare; as Alfred Tomatis—who has investigated the connection of speaking and listening to emotional and physical health—has observed, those "who truly know how to listen" are a "tiny and select group" (1991, p. 10). Even more uncommon may be those who truly know how to listen when girls speak about thoughts and feelings that fall outside the social bounds and cultural expectations of appropriate or acceptable behavior. Maureen Barbieri, a teacher at the Laurel School, was dismayed to discover that although "I thought I'd always listened," in fact, it was "only recently that I've been listening to the voices of my young female students" (1995, p. 3). This learning to listen came after she became aware of her alignment with norms that supported and rewarded conformity and "good girl" behavior and consequently kept her out of relationship with the girls in her class. For girls who are marginalized by the status accorded their racial, ethnic, or class location, assumptions about what girls know and do not know and the limited social value given their voices and experiences compound the obstacles to listening. As the writer and poet Sandra Cisneros remembers, "when I was eleven years old in Chicago, teachers thought if you were poor and Mexican you didn't have anything to say" (Lopez, 1993, p. 155).

In addition to listening to her niece, Ana's aunt shares her own experiences, helping Ana to feel that she is understood: "She's like, 'Yeah, in my time this and this happened,' so I feel like it's almost the same." For many of the girls in this study, being listened to and feeling understood by an adult is a rare and powerful experience. Taking girls seriously, especially girls who might be labeled at risk, often means validating what girls know and feel to be true, and so it is perhaps no accident that Ana also says of her aunt, "she's crazy." The label "crazy" that Ana affectionately ascribes to her aunt also reflects the cultural marginalization of unconventional women.

Ana also highlights some differences among girls related to race and ethnic background. Like many of the Latina and Portuguese girls, Ana experiences strict limits at home on speaking about boys, dating, or sexual matters. Often the women whom she and other girls named as important are the only adults with whom they are able to talk about these topics. With Ana's aunt, for example, the subject of "boys" comes up easily: "I start talking and she'll start asking me about boys and stuff like that."

Ana's relationship with her aunt seems to offset some of the stressful aspects of her dual cultural status, because her aunt has also had to develop strategies for coping with the disparities and sometimes competing conventions of two cultures. Ana finds that differences of culture and language make it difficult for her mother to understand the "pressures" and "temptations" she faces at school. Her aunt, however, has lived in the United States for a longer period of time than her mother; thus Ana's experience of differences in culture and language are attenuated: "She's so different. She'll listen to you. She knows how it is because, um, see, she knows more, even though she's from a foreign country, too, she knows more English, she understands more of the words that I'm trying to say. She married an Italian guy, so he, you know, she knows things, right . . . She came [here] when she was around seventeen or something and . . . she's, like, more used to here, she knows what things go on in school." Ana's aunt has an insider's knowledge; she is familiar with both spheres of Ana's life, home and school, and shares Ana's bicultural awareness and experience. She "knows how it is." For Ana this is an essential connection, one that may also aid her in maintaining the richness of cultural experience available to her.

Ana's cousins are similarly drawn to her aunt: "All my girl cousins . . . that are fourteen, fifteen, they all go to her . . . A lot of my cousins just find it so easy, . . . because sometimes their mothers don't understand it and they get a different wrong idea, like a wrong point of view of what you're trying to say. You know, they think you are saying one thing, they'll say, 'Oh, she must be telling me this, this, and this.' They understand it wrong. And so you're trying to clear it up and they won't, you know . . . all my cousins . . . go to her, and they say . . . their mothers would probably get mad . . . And so what the aunt will do, she won't tell your mother . . . She won't say 'No, don't do this.' She's just, 'You make the decision whether it's right or wrong.' " Having opportunities to talk through—and thereby think through—issues of importance to them without fear of judgment, betrayal, or misunderstanding and anger, Ana and her cousins may be better able to know and understand their own thoughts and feelings. This process in turn may help them cultivate their ability to make thoughtful and responsible decisions.

In speaking of an encounter with another adult woman, Ana demon-

strates that important connections with women do not necessarily require the sharing of confidences or of very personal thoughts and
feelings. When Ana applied for a job in tenth grade, the woman who
interviewed her talked to her "as if I was a regular person . . . I was
nervous because I had never done that, and . . . I talked to the lady, we
stood there for an hour talking, and she gave me an application and we
talked about the skills I had and all this stuff. And I felt like a person on
my own, I did, I felt like a person on my own . . . you know, like I was an
adult. That's how they talked to me, and I felt good because I was like,
'Oh boy, they're listening to me.' And we filled out the application and
we talked about something, the lady talked to me as if I was a regular
person." Feeling respected and taken seriously, and noting the woman's
interest in her skills and competencies, Ana responds to the meeting
with enthusiasm. The distressing element of this story, however, is that
it also conveys Ana's sense of the extraordinary nature of this encounter
and implies that most adults would not take time to talk with her, would
not make her feel like "a person on my own."

Lilian, who like Ana is Latina, also says in eighth grade that she cannot
talk to her mother about boys, "because she's strict about that." She
rarely sees her divorced father "because he works all night long and I
really don't get to see him until, like, Sundays, and when I do, he's either
out with friends or even doing more work." Lilian often feels bad at
home because of the constant fights she has with her older brother over
her greater household responsibilities. Lilian says she would go to her
twenty-year-old neighbor, Jean, to talk about a problem: "Yeah, I talk to
her. It's more easy to talk to her [than to my mother, because] my mother's strict and Jean really likes to hear what we think, kids our age and
our time, because she said she used to be that way when she was young,
just like me. It's good to talk to her."

Lilian's connection with Jean, someone "just like me" who listens to
her, is particularly important in light of her difficulties at home. Jean
helps her to think through how she might respond to her family by
asking Lilian questions and sharing her own experience: "She always
asks me, what do I want to be when I grow up. And how am I going to
live my life, am I going to make mistakes like with my family—like her

family, they don't like what she did. She ran away from home when she was sixteen . . . and she asked me if I was going to do the same thing, and I said no, I'd just work it out . . . She says, 'Don't make the same mistakes I did' . . . She just came to realize that running away, she wasn't as close to her father as she used to be, they got into big fights because she ran away and stuff. And she was sad because she always wanted to get along with her father, and her father never wanted to come down and visit her, he never wanted her up there, and it was pretty bad."

By sharing her experience, including her regrets and "mistakes," Jean gives Lilian the opportunity to consider how she might feel if she chooses running away from home as a solution to her family problems. Jean also shares with Lilian her sadness at not being able to be "as close to her father as she used to be," and in so doing may provide an opening for Lilian to speak of her feelings about her own father, whom she "really doesn't get to see" and who is not available to her even on his weekly day off, when he is "either out with friends or even doing more work."

Lilian does not name an important relationship with a woman in her ninth-grade interview. She does in tenth grade, however, when she speaks of a close relationship with her older cousin, a young woman in her early twenties. Again, the trust and identification with her cousin that Lilian feels create a context in which they "really can talk." Lilian draws a distinction between giving advice and delivering lectures: "We're able to talk about anything. I can tell her anything I want. You know, with mothers, you know, some daughters are close to their mothers, others are not. Well I'm not that, I can tell my mother stuff, but [my cousin] seems to understand more. My cousin understands because she's been through it. And maybe she's, in a way she's still going through it, you know, in a way. Like, she understands more and she can give me more advice, while my mother's just more, like, 'Oh, you shouldn't do that, and you shouldn't do this.' But yet you try to tell her, 'But Mom, that's what I'm asking you, for advice,' and then they don't understand, and with [my cousin] I can tell her anything and she'll understand. She gives me advice. I give her advice, you know. So this, we really can talk." The problem with her mother's advice is "it's not advice, it's more like, um, a lecture with my mother, you know."

The importance of relationships in which she feels understood and is "able to talk about anything" becomes dramatically highlighted in tenth grade, when Lilian reveals that she had considered suicide for a time during the previous year. She decided not to act on these thoughts only after she was able to speak to a youth counselor about what was troubling her. Although she does not share the details of this experience because "it's sort of personal," she says that she and a female friend "were going through the same problems," and hints that her distress was connected with her sexuality or sexual experience. And although we cannot know what the situation was that was causing her so much anguish, her responses to questions about going out and about sexual decision-making raised the possibility that she might have been involved in a lesbian relationship.[3] Whatever the cause of Lilian's pain, her attempts to protect herself by keeping her problem out of relationship put her at great risk, as it ultimately proved to be a secret she could not continue to live with.

The dimensions of sexuality—from the positive, to the problematic, to the traumatic—are areas about which girls are least likely to be able to speak with their parents or peers, and where relationships with adult women may in fact be of particular value. Girls may feel most comfortable speaking to a woman they can trust, especially if they cannot trust their peers with certain information and their mothers might, as Ana said, "understand it wrong," get "a wrong idea," or "get mad." In a climate where sexuality is either silenced or spoken of only in terms of its dangers—sexually transmitted diseases or teen pregnancy—girls have difficulty speaking about the excitement and pleasure of sexual curiosity and desire, and may therefore be at risk for losing a healthy sense of connection to their own bodies. By expressing her interest in Ana's thoughts and feelings "about boys and stuff like that," Ana's aunt may be helping her to minimize the psychological risk of sexual repression and to hold on to a healthy awareness and appreciation of her sexuality.

For adolescents whose sexuality does not fit culturally sanctioned behavior or interest, not being able to talk about their sexual orientation places them at considerable risk for psychological isolation. For lesbian adolescents—and Lilian may be among them—the risk of suicide is three times that of heterosexual adolescents (Gibson, 1989; Women's Action Coalition, 1993). Being able to voice concerns, questions, or interests that may be unacceptable elsewhere may well be lifesaving. Lilian described her mother as "very strict, she doesn't like to hear things about, about violence, or about drugs . . . because she says that's bad stuff. She always thinks good stuff." Thus, when she reflects back on the problems she was experiencing in ninth grade, Lilian explains that "I didn't really want to talk about it to my mother. I wanted to keep it out of the family." She also felt she needed to take great care in deciding whom she would finally talk to: "There are some things you don't want anybody else to know . . . Some things . . . you only want to share it with one particular person . . . and you want to be able to trust the person, and also ask this person for advice, you know. But you're not going to go to just anybody and say, 'I have this problem, can you help me?' That person can, you know, turn around and make a fool out of you."

The possibility that relationships with women can allow girls to speak the unspeakable is especially relevant in relation to sexual abuse. Experiences of sexual abuse in childhood or adolescence often lie at the root of symptoms of extreme psychological distress, such as depression, eating disorders, suicide, and self-mutilation. Judith Herman describes how "self-injury . . . purging and vomiting, compulsive sexual behavior, compulsive risk taking . . . and the use of psychoactive drugs become vehicles by which abused children attempt to regulate their emotional states. These self-destructive symptoms . . . become much more prominent in the adolescent years" (1992, pp. 109–110). Healthy relationships play a key, if not central, role in recovery from abuse. Herman reports that many of the abused women "who had escaped without permanent harm remembered particular people who had helped them to integrate and overcome their sexual trauma. Most frequently cited were supportive friends and family members, who assured these women that they were not at fault" (Tsai, 1979, reported in Herman, 1981, p. 33).

Girls who are identified as at risk for early pregnancy may in fact be more likely than other girls to have been sexually abused. One investigation involving girls who became pregnant as teenagers found that two-thirds of the girls in the study reported having had one or more unwanted sexual experiences, including molestation and rape (Boyer and Fine, 1992). A girl who is considered to be at risk and who has also experienced some form of sexual abuse is likely to have a complicated relationship with her mother as well as distant, if not conflicted, relationships with her teachers; she thus might be in particular need of a safe and supportive relationship with a woman (Sullivan, 1993).

This may be true for Sandy, who dropped out of school in tenth grade to have a baby. In eighth grade she speaks of the pain she experiences in school, where "a lot of people in the class, they are always teasing me . . . They call me retarded and all that." Sandy describes ongoing problems with an abusive stepfather, who "doesn't treat [my mother] very well either and she says that she wants to divorce him." Sandy wants to leave the house "because he's bothering me a lot," but she does not want to leave her mother.

Sandy's important relationships are with women who can offer her some protection from her stepfather. In ninth grade, she finds support and sanctuary with a neighbor: "My downstairs neighbor, she is like a mother to me, too. And when I have problems, she helps me out, and she doesn't really like my [step]father that much so she's always on my side." Sandy and her neighbor share something in common: "She went through a lot of things like that, related to that. Her boyfriend . . . used to do this stuff to her." Although she does not describe in detail what "this stuff" is, incidents with her stepfather are bad enough and frequent enough that Sandy routinely goes to her neighbor's apartment to call the police each time there is a crisis.

In tenth grade Sandy recalls that her grandmother was important to her and had once been a source of protection: "She passed away a year ago . . . She was just so nice and everything. I always wish that she's still alive and I could talk to her and I know she wouldn't let my stepfather treat me the way he does. I know she wouldn't. It's just that she had ways. I think she had, like, powers or something to just take people over and just boss them around . . . Yeah, she could. My stepfather wouldn't ever try to get wise with her and talk back to her because he knows better, I know." Sandy's wish is for a relationship with a woman who, like her grandmother, has "powers" to do something on her behalf. Yet she seems to have no one to turn to in tenth grade. Her interviewer was able to fill that role temporarily by making arrangements for her to speak to someone and get help.

In addition to the women who filled needs unmet by their mothers, some girls mentioned relationships with women that added to or complemented their relationship with their mothers. Carla, an Italian American girl, does not experience the kind of tension at home and school that Lilian and Ana do. She says she feels close to her mother, enjoys spending time with her family, and likes school. In ninth grade Carla says her mother's friend Kathy is important to her, because "she's funny and we get along." Carla felt especially close to her when Kathy responded with surprise and delight to her request to be her sponsor for the Roman Catholic rite of confirmation: "She was like, 'Me? Me?' " Carla is one of the few girls to describe or recognize the pleasure the adult woman derives from the relationship. Her relationship with Kathy is "almost like a mother-daughter thing," and having her mother's friend as her sponsor is important because "she really likes that, because then we get closer and all this stuff." This relationship continues for Carla in tenth grade: "She's like my second mother. She's looking out for me. She's looking out for, like, what I'm doing, and also she cares. It's a happy feeling . . . It's like she helps me, she's, like, my godmother like at confirmation, so we got closer there, and like she comes by my house and she sometimes just talks to me."

Unlike Carla, most of the girls in the study did not speak about, and perhaps were not aware of, the positive effect they had on women. Filling in this gap, the women in the Women and Race retreats described their relationships with girls with enthusiasm. Katie Cannon spoke of how, in the group, "it's the story about a girl that gets us going . . . when you start talking about Lisa [one of the women's goddaughters], there's a different energy in the conversation . . . because we did connect something about the story . . . and it's important when you . . . even say her name." Joyce Grant noted that when girls' voices were brought into the conversation "the energy is different," and connecting with this energy led to her feeling "very impatient and very emotionally involved with issues around children." Judy Dorney responded equally strongly to girls' presence in the group's conversations: "We've brought the girls with us here today, you know, and, in our minds and hearts, and they, they're with us! They're in our psyches and in our bodies in a way, and that gives us some strength and some knowledge and some power."

A Practice of Relationship

Important dimensions of relationships between girls and women were also evident in the process of our inquiry—the interview itself—in which the practice of psychology is framed as a practice of relationship. The interviews demonstrate that when women approach girls as authorities on their own experience and listen to them intently and with respect, girls can speak openly about their thoughts and feelings, at times sharing information they have never shared with anyone else. This is true for Sandy, for example, when she confides in her interviewer that she suspects she is pregnant and fears that if her stepfather finds out, he will force her to leave home. Beset with problems of trusting girls and women in the tenth grade, Pilar tells her interviewer that she has been able to speak freely because "you were, like, into my conversation . . . it seemed like you were interested in it," rather than "someone cold; if they're just here asking me questions and they don't care about what I'm saying, they're just doing it because it's an assignment." Although Pilar spoke often of secrets she kept from others, she was nonetheless able to tell her interviewer the very things she kept back from her family and friends: "That's how comfortable you made me feel, I just kept telling you everything."

The interview process also demonstrated one of the most important benefits of speaking with and listening to girls in this way: it can help girls to develop, to hold on to, or to recover knowledge about themselves, their feelings, and their desires. Taking girls seriously encourages them to take their own thoughts, feelings, and experience seriously, to maintain this knowledge, and even to uncover knowledge that has become lost to them. Ana, for example, says in tenth grade that she has learned things about herself in the interview: "[Speaking] helps me by just realizing, because when I answer these questions, I realize things that I did not even picture. I am like, 'Oh boy,' you know? The way I see it, it feels like I have gone through a lot and it's really taught me a lot."

Ana also uses her ninth-grade interview to sort out her feelings about a school counselor's unavailability. Early in the interview she says that her parents find it hard to understand problems at school because they are new to this country, and that her school counselor is always too busy to talk with her. At the start of the interview she feels there is nothing she can do, but by the end, she says talking about this problem may have helped her decide to take action on her own behalf: "Well, [the interview] could have an effect on me, like the fact about my counselor. I am going to go and talk to him." Thus Ana did not need to be told what to do in order to take appropriate action, she needed only to clarify and confirm what she already knew.

Ruby also felt that speaking about her feelings helped her to understand herself better. She says of her interview in tenth grade that "it lets you know a lot about yourself and how you feel about things. I mean, I leave out the door and I'm like, 'Wow, I didn't think I thought that,' you know. Like I leave out the door and I might say something like, 'Oh, I didn't know I really felt that way.' But since the question came up, it let me know how I felt. I think that's good. I can do this forever, you know . . . keep on going. I'll bring a lot up with just easy questions that you would ask anybody, you know. It lets you know about yourself." Ruby expresses enjoyment at the interviews and interest in how her interviews have changed over the three years. The psychological isolation that she feels at school and at home is not evident in her relationship with her interviewer. She is eager to connect with a woman who is interested in her and to learn about herself and her own development.

Speaking with her interviewer also brings Ruby to a new understanding of the direction her future is taking. While in her earlier transcripts she speaks of career plans that include pursuing social work, and of living alone, in tenth grade we hear Ruby's realization that she may, in fact, be on a very different path: "Unfortunately, because I really don't want to, but, I don't know, I think I'm going to get married and have two kids and all this kind of stuff. I don't know why. At first, I used to picture myself as, I don't know, money, and coming home with my briefcase, and I don't think that's going to happen . . . I picture myself getting married and having kids and god (*laughs*), being home and taking care of them, although I wouldn't want that to happen. I'd rather do that later on in life, you know. Maybe get a job after I get out of school, a good paying job, hopefully (*laughs*) and maybe take a couple of courses at something, you know, just enjoy life before I do that, and it just seems like I'm always going to just go directly doing that." *How come?* "I don't know, it just seems like the thing to do I guess. My family, everything, it just seems like that's what's going to happen. I don't intend to let it happen, right. Wow."

"Wow" says Ruby, as she becomes aware of how her future has changed shape without her notice. Ruby's sudden realization of the forces that are silently directing her life comes as a surprise to her. She was born when her mother was sixteen years old and offers some indication that this was not a deliberate choice on her mother's part. Describing her mother's life as "not great," Ruby says that she does not intend to follow in her footsteps, but she has just discovered the pull in that direction—"it just seems like the thing to do I guess." Perhaps with the continued presence of other women who, like her interviewer, could listen and thereby help her sustain the knowledge of her circumstances, Ruby might have had a greater chance of achieving the kind of future she wanted for herself.

Freedom to Listen

The narratives of the girls in this study not only speak to their need for relationship and to the ways in which women can join them by listening, sharing their experience, and building an environment of trust. They also tell about who the women are that are able to be present with them, to listen and "really talk" without, as Lilian says, giving "a lecture." Listening to girls and helping them stay with what they know may be easier for some women than for others. Ana's aunt, for example, has no children of her own; this may free her to listen to her adolescent nieces without feeling compelled to tell them what they should do or needing to report to their mothers. Perhaps she does not feel the pressure to enforce cultural norms and is therefore able simply to be present for Ana and her cousins. Ana's aunt is unconventional in a number of ways—she listens to girls, she encourages them to speak about topics that are off limits in their families, and she has married outside her culture. Ana's aunt stands just enough apart to be able to join with girls—to speak what otherwise remains unspoken, to understand their experience, to "know what goes on"—and all of Ana's cousins recognize this.

Women like Lilian's neighbor and cousin, Sandy's neighbor and grandmother, and the interviewers may also have been in an advantageous position to listen to these girls without needing to change them, to make it possible for them to share their experiences and express their feelings in a climate of trust. These women, because they were "not their mothers, teachers, or therapists," had "the advantage of standing outside of what are sometimes painfully complex and difficult relationships for girls at this time in their lives" (Rogers, 1989, pp. 13–14; see also Rogers, 1993).

Patricia Hill Collins remarks on this connection in black communities: "Othermothers often help to defuse the emotional intensity of relationships between bloodmothers and their daughters. In recounting how she dealt with the intensity of her relationship with her mother, [one writer] describes the women teachers, neighbors, friends, and othermothers she turned to—women who, she observes, 'did not have the onus of providing for me, and so had the luxury of talking to me' " (1990, p. 128). The participants in the Women and Race Retreats may have shared this luxury as well; although a number of the women were mothers, none at the time was the mother of girls.

Intercepting Messages

Because we did not interview the women these girls spoke of, we do not know their perspectives, the rewards these relationships held for them, or what their particular concerns or hopes for the girls might have been. Women's perspectives on their relationships with girls, however, were readily apparent among the participants in the retreats, who spent considerable time reflecting on their experience of these relationships. To facilitate this exploration, each woman's task prior to the first retreat was to compose a letter to herself as an adolescent or to an adolescent girl in her family, social, or work life. In these letters women expressed a unanimous desire to pass on their experience and knowledge to girls at a time when girls were traversing a difficult passage. In part, sharing their experience included preparing girls for, and protecting them from, the injuries of racism and sexism—both the overt acts of discrimination and violence as well as the more subtle dismissals and silencing they might encounter. Another concern of these letters was to intercept and interrupt the harmful and misleading messages girls risk internalizing, including cultural messages that define acceptable standards of beauty and behavior.

Writing to her nine-year-old niece, Lyn Brown wonders how much she should say about playing by the rules in a system fraught with injustice. She worries about what messages Jennifer has already absorbed about how she should look and behave. Jennifer, like Lyn, is white and lives in a rural area of Maine, where her father works in a mill. Lyn writes: "In my mind I carry a picture of you—you are standing alone, your weight shifted to one foot, your right hand on your hip, a basketball in the crook of your left arm, wearing your light blue team T-shirt and dirty white high tops. You have a look on your face—self-conscious, impertinent." Lyn recalls the day she took Jennifer to basketball practice: "You were the only girl to show up although there are three of you on the team. I watched you warm up from the balcony of the community center gym with some frustration and anger as two boys colluded to keep the ball from you. You looked at me and shrugged, and I motioned to you. We met on the stairs. 'Don't let them do that to you,' I said. 'Go after it, be aggressive.' 'He pulled my finger back,' you said, showing me where it was sore. 'Then pull his back,' I replied angrily. I remember the way you looked at me—surprised—then you said, 'It's against the rules, Mr. O'Brien wouldn't like that.' I wanted to say to you then that almost nobody plays by the rules really, but especially the people who make them."

But breaking the rules can be costly, and Lyn does not follow her impulse to voice these thoughts. Witnessing with increasing concern some of the other ways her niece is being coached, Lyn also realizes that she has made similar decisions not to speak: "Since then I have *not* said other things to you—like how crazy it makes me when grandma says, 'Don't (and you fill in the blank—be rude, run, eat too quickly, speak too loud) it's not ladylike.' And why I think it is scary that at nine years old you are concerned about your weight, that you have a perm, that you mousse and spray your hair before basketball practice. Being near you this summer has made me wonder about a lot of things—mostly wonder what people are telling you. What messages are you taking in?"

Prompted by Lyn's letter, Judy Dorney asks what messages she might be sending to girls through her attitude toward her own body: "What do I do as a woman to help girls feel good about their bodies, as they are? And so then I have to think, well, what do I feel about my body? And how do I show that? . . . What do I think about, you know, in trying to think about . . . do I color my hair? . . . [It's a] superficial little example but, that's an issue for me. Do I give in to that ageist mentality, and then what am I doing for girls by being another woman who doesn't show her age in that way, and therefore what messages am I perpetuating about aging as a woman?"

Katie Cannon writes to her fifteen-year-old niece Beth of the "double whammy" of racism and sexism that black women experience: "high social visibility, derogatory ascribed attributes, and institutionalized, systemic rationalization of inferior status." She warns Beth of messages that she will receive "as a black woman-child," saying that "there are few areas of life in which injustice is more blatant and failure more painful than in the area of physical beauty." For black girls and women, who have been "deeply affected by the discrimination against the shade of our skin and the texture of our hair," the standards of beauty held forth by white society pose a powerful threat to self-image and self-love, and are an "assault on the personhood of the black woman" (Washington, 1975, quoted by Cannon in her letter). Hoping to arm her against what Cornel West has identified as "the widespread, modern, European denial of the intelligence, ability, beauty and character of people of color" (1993, p. 25), Katie offers her niece concepts "related to Black women and physical beauty that I want you to read and ponder, to turn over again and again in your mind, to wrestle with, to not read silently but to rap aloud until clarity comes." She prods Beth to speak and rehearse the words she offers, to allow the lessons of resistance to permeate her psyche. In her letter, Katie speaks to her niece not only in her own words but also through the testimony of other black women—Abbey Lincoln, Toni Morrison, Alice Walker, Deborah McDowell, Mary Helen Washington, Maya Angelou, Pearl Cleage—whose words and experience reinforce the importance and urgency of heeding the dangers she names.

Toni Morrison has written of the devastation of white images of beauty in her novel *The Bluest Eye,* in which Pecola, a young black girl, comes to believe that if only she is given blue eyes she will become beautiful and will be freed from the terrible abuse and isolation of her life. The younger narrator, Claudia, was able to resist the destructive effects of these impossible standards, having "not yet arrived at the turning point" in her development that would "allow [her] to love" the Shirley Temple images her sister and Pecola so lovingly gaze at. The need to support girls' resistance to such standards of beauty persisted in stories shared by the women in the retreats.

Christine Robinson spoke of her eight-year-old goddaughter, who is black, and for whom "this whole [racial] issue is particularly difficult . . . because . . . she had been a foster child in a white family, and she really wants to have blue eyes and blond hair because all of the children in her school, which is a school for the deaf, are white." Christine may have been one of the few black woman in her goddaughter's life at that time who could "talk to her about the beauty of black people." But Christine was also well aware that, against the amplified messages of white standards of beauty surrounding her at home and at school, "getting her to understand that is also going to be a challenge." Like Katie, who wanted her niece to memorize the lessons of her own worth and beauty, Christine found a way to provide a similarly constant reminder to her goddaughter; she "went out and bought this print of two little black girls lying on the grass talking to each other so we can put this over her bed, so at least she can get the visual image."

In a society that has had such enormous difficulty in dealing adequately and respectfully with race and difference, the conflict and ambivalence become even more complicated when the differences reside in the bodies of our children. Speaking of the increasing number of children of mixed race, for whom messages of beauty, value, and identity have become exceedingly complex, one of the black women described the situation of her niece, who is of mixed race: "I just had dinner with her mother this weekend . . . My niece is going to turn six in a couple of months . . . On her last birthday we bought her a black Barbie doll and although . . . she was very polite, and played with the black Barbie, she definitely loves the white Barbie . . . This year, at only *six years old,* she just lights up and she says, 'Mom, I want the white one.' Mommy, who's a black woman, is like, you know, 'What do I do? . . . I have a black child who is half white but, I am raising this child as a black woman, and how do I deal with this?' And so, you know, she said, 'Well, what will you do if I buy you the black one?' And so she's very quiet and she said, 'Well, I guess I'll play with them, but I really want the white one.' So, I guess I'm thinking . . . about where the messages come from so early, and how to counteract, how to help children to resist—especially little girls to resist—that self-denial."

Yet the decision to bring up a biracial daughter "as a black woman"—since the world would most certainly see and respond to her as a black woman—is not a solution that is without consequences. Another black woman described the dilemma: "To some degree it sort of, it feels like you're killing off, . . . because, the preparation that you undertake in getting a black child ready for racism . . . necessarily kind of paints the enemy as white. Okay, now what do you do with Daddy? You know? What do you do with Mommy? Or some interracial families go the other way where they sort of annihilate race, and go the route of, 'We're all the same and, we're all humankind and . . . let's just pretend that race doesn't exist.' And you tell that to the child, and sure enough, as adolescents then they run into all sorts of difficulties, because everybody else in the world believes that races exist . . . So I think that it is really complicated and I think that it's going to be an increasingly important issue in this country, because there are more and more biracial children, the mixture is both, you know, black and white and Hispanic."

Another woman illustrated these difficulties with the experience of a friend from college, who is "light skinned, straight hair, who is very proud of the way that she looks . . . But she always makes the point that, when she has a child, she's going to marry, she's going to have a child with the blackest man she can . . . Because she does not want for this child what she has been through . . . Which always seemed to be such a contradiction because, . . . I mean, she always has a date, and, you know, she was really cute and highly desirable, but there was a very high price that she paid for it that she would not acknowledge out loud to other black folks. But the way that she was going to acknowledge it was through her body, and the next generation."

The women in the Women and Race retreats thus began to delineate the complexities of women's and girls' relationships across generation, race, ethnicity, and class, and pointed to the necessity of continuing to find ways to connect with girls across these differences. Among the girls in the Understanding Adolescence Study, it seemed for the most part that the women they identified as important to them were of the same or similar cultural background, not teachers or youth workers but aunts, grandmothers, older sisters-in-law, mothers' friends, and neighbors. But the girls spoken of by the women in the retreats were not only those in their families or social networks who shared their culture or class: they were also goddaughters and students who were of mixed race or of different race or social class. Girls may feel they can speak in the presence of women who are similar to them in race, ethnicity, and class without the burden of shame or the fear of betrayal or misunderstanding, and these women may indeed be those best able to understand girls' experience. Women who share girls' cultural or class background may also be best qualified to pass on effective survival strategies or to point out strategies that may not be serving girls well. And if women who are different from girls in culture and class can connect across these differences, the relationships that are formed may open the possibility to the hopes Katie raised—that there might be "a generation of girls who are not racist, a generation of girls who will not internalize racism." For women to join with girls across these differences, however, requires that they do the work of becoming aware of and responsible for their own power, which often includes race and class privilege. Building these connections also requires women to actively educate themselves and learn about cultures and class experiences different from their own through research and literature and, perhaps most important, by listening to girls. Such relationships, entered into with awareness and an openness to learning, may help increase girls' and women's understanding of each other across race, ethnicity, and class, and may interrupt the cycle of disconnections that continues in a society so highly stratified by these dimensions.

The question of how women can join with girls is inevitably linked with how women connect—or fail to connect—with other women. As Carol said during one retreat in answer to the question "Could I join black girls?," she is compelled to "really clarify my relationship with black women, and black women's relationship with me." What Joyce said she learned during the retreats—"that white women have as much pain as I have"—is similarly important if she is to respond effectively and appropriately to white girls. Joyce also pointed to the need to find ways to connect personally across race when she said that learning about white women's pain was "not new, but . . . to hear it is different than kind of intellectually understanding it." The question of how to connect with girls calls women to undertake the often difficult and painful work of addressing and bridging differences so that they might have a better chance, for example, of preparing black girls or girls of mixed race for racism without having to "paint the enemy as white." It calls women to be activists in establishing alliances across race and ethnicity. Patricia Hill Collins describes how, within black communities, the role of othermother "stimulates a more generalized ethic of caring and personal accountability among African American women, who often feel accountable to all the Black community's children." In an increasingly diverse society, where that diversity is often represented within one family, and perhaps within one child, there is a correspondingly greater need for women and men to cultivate a deeply felt sense of accountability to all society's children.

Relationships with girls also call on women as individuals to be aware of their day-to-day choices, as Joyce pointed out in her response to Lyn's letter: "Here we sit struggling with how, not only how we can work better with girls, but how we can work better in our own lives. And what we can bring to girls is our own honesty, is a sense of our own integrity and our own struggle. I mean, it is not situational, it is not, to me it is not that you should jump up and be involved in this basketball situation alone. It is you as a person relating to this young woman, and that you may be the only person in her life who will share these kinds of things. It calls us . . . to continually decide whether we're committed to the people we choose to be, or want to be."

Joyce described the ongoing choices she faces: "I mean, I'm very aware of that . . . in my own life, of sometimes the joy of accepting that, yes, I'm going to be this kind of person and I'm going to take on these kinds of issues. And there are other times when I sit at meetings or I'm a part of a group that I just dread the fact that I'm again being challenged as to whether or not I am going to be the person who has to raise this ugly issue. So . . . you can represent a person in this youngster's life with certain values and commitments and the courage to say certain things, to shape the world very differently . . . You may be the only one, but that to me is a tremendous commitment, and if you look, as I look back in my life, my own life, those people stand out. Those people who dared to say those kinds of things, be those kinds of people, and I admired them for it. And I'm proud of myself when I have the courage of my own convictions, and I'm ashamed of myself when I don't, even though no one else may know."

But as Lyn acknowledged in her letter, whether or not to advocate breaking the rules or to speak publicly about controversial issues is a difficult decision, for such decisions are rarely without consequences— whether they be staying on a team, staying in school, or keeping a job. Women must also consider what girls are ready to hear. The girls spoken about by the women in the retreats, who range in age from six to fifteen, are each at a different stage of cognitive and emotional development. The painful truths Katie tells her fifteen-year-old niece, for example, may not be helpful or understandable to a much younger girl.

To Joyce's comment that "you may be the only person in her life who will share these kinds of things," Carol added that sometimes one other person is all that may be needed: "I think it goes back . . . to the extent to which . . . in crucial moments . . . people feel all alone. And then confusion comes in as to whether what you think happened happened, or whether what you feel is about something or nothing, or whether what you think makes sense does make sense. And it seems to me that one of the ways in which silence is perpetuated . . . is that people are convinced . . . that what they are feeling is about nothing, what has happened hasn't really happened or doesn't really make a difference . . . That's frankly what we have seen with girls.

"I think it often takes one person, one other person who says, 'You know, you're not alone . . . What you are feeling is your feeling about something that really happened. You're not crazy, you're not making trouble about nothing, you're not disturbing things for no reason' . . . For white girls . . . the accommodation is . . . so easy and so rewarded, and it's confused with being 'nice' . . . 'kind' . . . 'empathic' . . . 'responsive to other people' . . . And the mechanism of this [accommodation] is . . . dissociation." You can disconnect from the knowledge you hold in your body, Carol explained, "by breathing shallowly, by having your voice cut off from your breath . . . After a while . . . you don't even know yourself anymore," that is, how you feel, what you think, what you know. "So the power of women, the one woman who says, 'This really happens, I can say . . . I felt this, too' . . . is enormous . . . What we're talking about is perpetuating or breaking silences."

Connections of Promise

"Being taken seriously," writes the activist and theologian Ada Maria Isasi-Diaz, "is so important to me. If I sit down with someone to talk and I feel that I'm being taken seriously, I go away with a real deep sense of experiencing the divine. I believe that in the taking of each other seriously we go beyond ourselves."[4]

Whereas girls' relationships with their mothers are likely to bear the distinctive stamp of culture, the character of important relationships with other women remains remarkably constant. Across race and ethnicity, the portraits that emerge from the girls' narratives depict a woman who takes them seriously, who is interested in their thoughts and feelings: she "likes to hear what we think, kids our age and our time." The relationship need not be an intimate or confiding relationship, although these are the ones that are mentioned most frequently. What is essential

is mutual interest and respect, in which the woman is "into my conversation . . . interested in it," and in which girls feel respected and acknowledged, like "a person on my own." The woman may be "like a
mother to me" or "the type I wish my mother could be." She does not tell
girls what to do but describes her own experience and asks them questions to help them make their own decisions: "She won't say 'No, don't
do this,'" but rather "'You make the decision whether it's right or
wrong.'" A woman who is important to girls may be unconventional:
"She's so different. She'll listen to you." The relationship is equally important to her: "she cares," "she comes by my house and she sometimes
just talks to me." She can learn from girls: "she gives me advice, I give her
advice." She is also able to use her power to protect girls when need be:
"she's looking out for me," she has "ways" or "powers" and "wouldn't let
[others] treat me [in a bad] way."

Girls value relationships with women who "understand more," who
"know how it is," and "know what things go on in school." This knowledge comes from having had experiences similar to those of the girls, perhaps shared cultural experience: she "used to be that way when she was
young," has "been through it," "went through a lot of things like that." She
speaks of her experience with girls, telling them "in my time this and this
happened" so that they "feel like it's almost the same." She can be trusted
because "she won't tell your mother" so they are "able to talk about anything." Such a relationship is a source of great pleasure, and girls describe
learning more about themselves: "I can do this forever, you know . . . keep
on going . . . it lets you know about yourself," "I realize things that I did
not even picture . . . The way I see it, it feels like I have gone through a lot
and it's really taught me a lot." It is important to remember that these are
the women who may be labeled "crazy."

For women, "it's the story about a girl that gets us going," creating "a
different energy in the conversation" that can generate a sense of urgency
and of being "very impatient and very emotionally involved with issues
around children." Letting connections with girls into their "psyches and
bodies . . . gives [women] some strength and some knowledge and some
power." Relationships with girls become political, raising questions for
women to ask the girls and themselves: "What messages are you taking

in?" "What do I do as a woman to help girls feel good about [themselves]?" "What messages am I perpetuating as a woman?" Relationships with girls require the courage to be the "one person who says, 'You know, you're not alone,' " "the one woman who says, 'This really happens, I can say . . . I felt this, too.' "

Connecting with girls in a meaningful way means meeting with girls at the edge of their knowing, being willing to stay with their questions and knowledge about race, culture, class, bodies, sexuality, pleasure, and danger, and joining with them to develop and sustain their critical perspective toward conventions and their own survival strategies. This joining constitutes a taking of one another seriously that not only enables women and girls, as Isasi-Diaz suggests, to go beyond themselves, but to come back to themselves—to their strengths, experience, questions, and knowledge.

6

Disappearance, Disappointment, and Betrayal

Carol: "Why do women betray girls?"
Wendy: "Why do women betray themselves?"
Carol: "That's exactly the same question. Turn it around more positively. Would it be possible, for the moment, for us as women, not to betray ourselves, not to betray girls? The challenge of this is to . . . really cross all the lines that have been made within the society."

—Women and Race Retreat, January 1991

The girls in the Understanding Adolescence Study tell many stories of beneficial relationships with women other than their mothers. They also tell stories of disappointment and loss, of feeling belittled or betrayed and unsupported or unnoticed by women. Some girls tell stories of important connections with women in the eighth grade but not in subsequent interviews; a few make no mention at all of women other than their mothers.

Although the Women and Race retreats were organized around the hope and the promise of bringing girls and women together, the conversation often turned to another side of these relationships—how women betray girls and each other, and how numerous and daunting the obstacles to women's joining with girls and with each other can be. Some of the disconnections and obstacles described, in words and in actions, by the girls in the study and the women in the retreats were unavoidable outcomes of the complex, imperfect, and unpredictable nature of human relationships. Other instances of betrayal or abandonment appeared avoidable, however, such as those brought about by structural inequities of gender, race, or class; it was the divisions caused by these

142

inequities that the retreats sought most directly to address and act on. A first step in making connections across the lines of social difference that create disconnections and distortions in relationships is to investigate the differences between and among women and girls. But these differences can be difficult and painful to explore.

"Too often," writes Audre Lorde, "we pour the energy needed for recognizing and exploring difference into pretending those differences are insurmountable barriers, or that they do not exist at all. This results in a voluntary isolation, or false and treacherous connections. Either way, we do not develop tools for using human difference as a springboard for creative change within our lives" (1984a, p. 115). In the process of finding ways to recognize and explore these differences, the retreats illustrated some of the difficulties and defining themes of this venture. The girls' stories about separation from women in and out of the school system and their narratives about "treacherous" or missing connections underscore the pressing need for health-sustaining relationships and the capacity of negative relationships to do harm.

Unnecessary Losses

Girls reported only a few instances in which women were openly or consistently hurtful to them, when women increased their sense of distrust toward others and diminished their confidence in themselves. More common were times when women failed to support girls or missed opportunities for connection. In a few cases, women were notable for their absence or disappearance over time. Since we did not directly ask girls about negative relationships with women, what we heard about this dimension arose spontaneously and thus may not be representative of the full range of girls' experiences. Nevertheless, their narratives offer repeated evidence that what women say and do—or fail to say and do— makes a difference to girls.

Oliva is a Latina girl who might be characterized as among the most emotionally expressive of the girls with whom we spoke. She describes herself as a poet, and speaks often of her own feelings of love and hatred, of experiences of power and vulnerability, of relational conflicts and betrayals, and of her desire to "change the world" by helping the home-less and fighting drug abuse. Oliva is also among those girls who de-scribe difficult relationships with their mothers that grew more distant over time. By tenth grade, Oliva says of her mother, "I don't really have a relationship with her." Oliva also finds herself pained by the social and emotional costs exacted by rumors and gossip at school. Trust—or the lack of it—is a predominant theme running throughout Oliva's inter-views and a repeated concern in all her relationships. "Real, real friends," says Oliva, "like friends that you can confide in, I don't have many. I really don't have many. Because you really can't trust anybody."

Like Ana, who described a diminishing sense of trust and connection with her mother and friends, Oliva also speaks of repeated betrayals by family, girlfriends, and boyfriends. But Ana found safety and support in her relationship with her aunt, whereas Oliva's contact with an aunt only reinforces her sense of mistrust. In eighth grade she says that her aunt told her mother she saw Oliva out with a boy when Oliva said she had in fact been home. "And my mother knew I was home, because she called me, but she still believes [I was] at the movies and stuff. She . . . distrusts me." Whether or not Oliva was actually somewhere she was not sup-posed to be, however, seems secondary to the informant role she per-ceives her aunt to be playing.

Unlike Ana's aunt, who has no children of her own, Oliva's aunt has a daughter, and the problems between mother and daughter spill over to Oliva as well. In tenth grade Oliva says that she dislikes her aunt because "she says bad things" about her daughter. Oliva's response combines loyalty to her cousin and feelings of personal affront: "It hurts me be-cause me and. [my cousin], we're like, we think the same. We act the same . . . We'll know exactly what each other's thinking. That's how we know each other so well. It's like if someone talks about her, it hurts a lot to me. And the same if someone ever talked about me it would hurt her. I know it would. So I get mad."

Oliva thus finds herself in something of a dilemma about how to be-have when she is with her aunt. Clear about her sentiments toward her, Oliva says, "I don't expect my aunt to talk to me. I don't want her to talk to me." Yet she feels she is expected to act otherwise. Oliva is "polite" to her aunt, albeit reluctantly so, and consequently says she feels like a "hypocrite": "I don't like her very much. But I have to say 'hi' to her, because she's my aunt. So I feel bad about that sometimes. Like, why do I have to say 'hi' to her when I don't like her? . . . I do it for my mother." While being civil to her aunt may not be an unreasonable request, the politeness Oliva feels is required of her does not allow her to address or resolve what she experiences as an ongoing and painful injustice. Oliva's relationship with her aunt reinforces her perception of being in a world where authenticity and genuine relationships do not exist. This experience may be adding to what she has already learned about being a woman from her peers, who work at "making everyone else happy but themselves," and from her mother, whom she sees sacrificing her own needs for those of others—even as those others then fail her by not responding when she needs help in return.

Oliva plays out this pattern of trust and mistrust in the interview process itself, which in the tenth grade was conducted in two sessions. In their first meeting, Oliva and Carol, her interviewer, engage in an energized conversation, and Oliva talks freely about her thoughts and feelings, her experiences and concerns. Speaking enthusiastically about her poetry, she gives Carol some of her poems to read. When they meet a second time, however, Oliva looks like a different person. She is disengaged, seems depressed, and barely makes eye contact; her hair, previously pulled back into a ponytail, now falls forward, partially shielding her eyes and her face. In the second interview Oliva talks mainly of experiences of betrayal on the part of other girls at school, conflicts over boyfriends, and problems with her mother. Her former enthusiasm about school and her poetry are absent.

In the second interview, Oliva says that she knows the rules for getting along in adolescence: "If you make it . . . worse, you know, bad for you, like make problems for yourself, of course it's going to be bad. But if you just . . . you know, be nice, and calm, everything will be fine. It will be fine." Having recently been sent out of the country to stay with relatives in Central America for several months in order, she says, to protect her reputation, Oliva knows from experience that the stakes are high if she fails to be "nice and calm." The difficulty is that Oliva also knows from experience that "being nice" can mean fraudulence and self-betrayal, and that her intense desire for connection often involves conflict. She may be in the process of losing her former resistance to disconnection by using this new strategy to ensure that "everything will be fine."

Oliva left school during her junior year to have a baby. Her pregnancy may, in part, be an outcome of seeking connection, rebellion against attempts to control her behavior, or her acceptance of the messages these suspicions inadvertently conveyed. Whatever the causes of her actions, and whatever the relationship or lack of relationship in which she conceived the child, Oliva's disconnection and mistrust, and the concomitant lack of support she experiences from her family and friends, endanger her future well-being and that of her child.

Donna, who is Italian American, tells of a similarly undermining relationship with an aunt, who seems to diminish her sense of her own abilities. Donna has definite career plans; she wants to go to a two-year college and learn business management. She says in tenth grade that the most important thing that someone could do to help her in the future is to have "confidence in me," speaking as if this knowledge comes as a surprise to her: "Um, have confidence, I don't know, confidence, is that the word? . . . Yeah, confidence in me . . . To tell them that, you know, I don't even know. I don't know. How did that word come out of my mouth? I don't even know how to describe it. I don't know . . . They feel good about you." Despite Donna's apparent surprise at her spontaneous response and her partial undoing of that knowledge with repeated "I don't knows," the truth of the need she names is evident when she begins to describe the messages she receives from her aunt, who expresses doubt that she will go to college. Donna describes how that makes her feel, and this time the words come without hesitation: "Like I'm nothing. Like she doesn't have any confidence in me." For any adolescent seeking to find her way in the world, low expectations from adults can be devastating; for adolescents who face greater academic risks than most, such expectations may present the even greater threat of becoming self-fulfilling prophecies.

Other girls speak of women who are important to them in their eighth- and sometimes ninth-grade interviews, but they do not mention them again in subsequent interviews. Along with other losses of relationship and signs of psychological or academic distress, the disappearance of these women from girls' lives is additional cause for concern. Ruby, for example, says in eighth grade that her aunt understands her in some ways her mother cannot. When she speaks of the burdens, as well as the advantages, of being the oldest in a large family, she also says that she would go to her aunt for advice on a problem: "She's the oldest, too, so she sort of understands me better. She says if I need to come over there on weekends to talk about things, that I can come over and tell her." In ninth grade, however, Ruby's aunt receives only brief mention as someone who relays information about what her mother wants for her: "[My mother] talks to my aunt and my aunt talks to me and she's like, 'Ruby, your mother . . . wants this for you and she wants that for you, and you don't see this.' "

By tenth grade, women drop out of the stories Ruby tells about her life. She speaks more frequently of keeping to herself, and about how it has become increasingly difficult to find people she can trust. If her relationship with her aunt has in fact diminished in significance, then she has lost an important resource, someone who might have been able to support her through a critical time of increasing academic, social, and family strain. Like Oliva, Ruby dropped out in her junior year to have a baby, despite her plans to do otherwise.

Women also disappear from the narratives of Isabel, a Portuguese girl, who over time becomes less engaged in her interviews and speaks in more conventional language. In tenth grade she sounds depressed and complains of being bored in school. In her eighth- and ninth-grade interviews, however, Isabel says she expends a lot of energy trying to get around her family's strict rules, reporting in ninth grade that "I've got my own sneaky ways." Isabel may have learned how to get her own way despite her family's restrictions, but she also seems increasingly distrustful, learning a multitude of ways to hide herself.

In eighth and ninth grades, Isabel has an advocate in her older sister-in-law. She says in eighth grade, for example, that her parents won't let her wear makeup. When the interviewer remarks that she is wearing a little makeup in the interview, Isabel explains, "Yeah, my sister-in-law bribed my mother and father and she bought me the makeup and she told my father I would be wearing it every day . . . In a way he disagrees, but what could he do?" Her sister-in-law plays a prominent role in fighting for her and protecting her; Isabel seems to feel safe and heard and cared for in this relationship. When Isabel was upset over a boy in ninth grade, her sister-in-law "was there for me, she even slept over and stuff . . . I don't know, like she would, even though she was tired, she would still stay up with me and talk to me."

In her tenth-grade interview Isabel does not mention her sister-in-law; neither does she discuss her strategies to do what she wants despite her family's strict rules. In general the interview text is sparse and Isabel sounds disengaged. Her voice seems to be disappearing under conventions, phrases that have the "correct" form but sound empty. Isabel says, for example, that she felt "good" about the interview because "it's always good to be helpful." It may be, of course, that she has opted to stop participating in the study but feels obligated to show up for her interview to "be helpful." The Latin American cultural value of *simpatía,* which encourages harmonious social interactions and maintenance of a certain level of conformity and cooperation, may also be influencing her to comply outwardly with her interviewer without actually sharing any personal information (Marin and Marin, 1991). Or she may be withholding information in speaking to an interviewer whose ethnic background differs from her own out of loyalty to her family. While we hold this interpretation open as a possibility, her earlier openness with the same interviewer, added to evidence of depression and detachment in tenth grade, suggests that she is not simply providing socially acceptable answers.

Whether these girls are moving away from women—or it is women who are not sufficiently available to girls—these appear to be unnecessary losses that may be setting girls up to repeat a cycle of loss and separation with their own children and with others in the next generation of girls. Oliva and Ruby were well into a pattern of separation and disconnection from others before they became pregnant with their own children, and Isabel, although she does not drop out of school or become pregnant, seems to be following a similar path in her relationships.

Women are virtually absent from Joan's stories. Over the three years of the study, Joan, who is white, mentions no women who are important to her and consistently names her father and boyfriend as the only people she trusts. Her interviews undergo dramatic change over the three years. In eighth grade, Joan is open and engaged in her interview. In responding to a question about a time she felt good in school, for example, Joan speaks about her thoughts and feelings when she got a good grade: "I didn't think that I was going to get a good grade because I didn't think that I had studied enough for it . . . I was in shock. My face just lit up. I just kept saying to myself, are you sure this is the right grade?" This response stands in sharp contrast to her angry reply to a question about school in tenth grade: "You don't want to know about my life at school and I'm not going to tell you about my life at school. Only my father and certain people that I know, know about my life in school, and I know that I can trust those certain people."

Although she also talks with the same interviewer each year, which for some other girls seemed to establish a sense of connection and trust, by tenth grade Joan is openly hostile. She expresses anger about being asked "personal questions," and ridicules or refuses to answer most of the questions posed to her. Jill, who interviews her, reacts with rather pained amusement to Joan's reply when she is asked to describe herself: "I don't get mad, it's not very easy to get me mad. I'm almost always in a good mood. I am an easy person to get along with. I am an easy person to talk to." Jill records in her interview notes feeling "a real sense of loss" that year, "not only in [what is] missing in the interview, but also in the connection that I felt, and that she may have felt, too."

Joan says several times in tenth grade that "I don't know who to trust." Like Oliva, she has found from past experience that when "I have taken people's word for it before . . . it usually comes out to be bad." Joan appears completely disconnected from women. Earlier, in eighth grade, although she had said that she and her mother "don't have much of a relationship" (adding that they were close when she was younger), she still expressed a desire for connection with her: "I wish that I could sit down and have some kind of talk with her." By tenth grade, however, Joan no longer speaks of wanting or hoping for more of a relationship with her mother. In addition, Joan seems to find no support among her peers at school, and she mentions each year that she feels bad about being teased at school. While Joan does not offer details, the teasing may have something to do with the fact that she is older than her classmates by several years. She says that the teasing makes her feel "like nobody. Just that nobody cares what I want to say or what I want to do, and that upsets me."

Although Joan says that she does trust her father, she also describes frequent arguments with him and "so much confusion at home." While having room in a relationship for disagreements and anger is a strength, Joan describes a relationship in which there is frequent fighting but no apparent room for disagreement, no room for her opinions: "When I get into arguments with my father about school, and how I am, he claims to think that he is always right. I'm trying to tell him that he is not right and I just get into an argument and I just cry because he makes me upset because he thinks I'm always wrong."

Joan says their conflicts get "solved" by her saying that she is sorry: "Sometimes if I am really, really, really mad, I just go in my room and slam my door and just yell all these things back at him and he doesn't like it and he gets mad at me. And then I come out and usually at suppertime I talk to him about it. Sometimes he doesn't want to listen and sometimes he does. And sometimes I say 'sorry' because he wants me to say 'sorry,' because he knows that I was wrong in doing what I did." Being told that her knowledge about her experience of school and about "how I am" is "always wrong," and experiencing the additional injury of having to apologize for her anger about this invalidation, Joan struggles to maintain the authority of her own voice and knowledge.

Joan then mentions that her father hit her for eating cookies when she hadn't eaten her supper, noting this episode casually and without further comment. She says, too, that "my father has taught me that people take advantage of you if you care about them too much." Seeming so much out of relationship this year, Joan may have heeded his advice and tried to stop herself from caring.

Among the girls who seemed most disconnected from their own inner world, stories of others who were important in their lives were virtually absent, and the women who interviewed them reported experiencing little or no sense of connection with them. The girls also tended to speak in highly conventional language that often appeared disconnected from their feelings or seemed in opposition to their actual behavior. They often told stories in a vague or general fashion, and they seemed to be experiencing an absence of relationship in their lives. Although we do not infer the absence of women from their lives (or from their narratives) as the cause of their psychological distress or disconnection, their stories suggest that their level of risk will continue to escalate without meaningful connection and sustained interest from others.

Tanya, for example, who is African American, makes minimal reference to other girls or women who are important to her. Tanya's responses include many long pauses, and she does not answer many of the questions. When she does respond, she tends to speak in generalities and rarely names a specific person or incident. The following excerpts are her ninth-grade responses to questions about feeling good about herself in and out of school (numbers in parentheses indicate pause length in seconds): Her interviewer, a white woman, asks, *Can you tell me a time when you felt good about yourself or happy in school?* (8) "I don't know." (4) *What comes to mind, a time you felt good about yourself, or happy about yourself in school?* (15) *Is it easier to think about something that makes you feel bad . . . in school?* "Uh uh. I don't know, I can't think of anything." (5) And later, *Can you tell me about a time when you felt really good or happy about yourself outside of school?* (20) "I can't think of anything either." *Um, something sometime when you felt good or happy, and it wasn't in school?* (8) *It doesn't have to be a big thing . . . what comes to mind when I ask you that?* (5) "I don't know." *Do you think there are times when you feel good when you're not in school?* "Yeah." *Do you have any thought about what you might be doing when you feel good?* (10) *What do you like doing outside of school?* "Watching TV."

In tenth grade, now with Amy as her interviewer, Tanya comments on her difficulty in answering the interview questions of the previous year, attributing it to a lack of experience in relationships: "[It was hard to understand the questions] because they were new to me and I never actually, nobody actually, like, sat down and asked me questions like that." Tanya tells Amy that she liked her tenth-grade interview because

"[I liked] sitting down and talking face-to-face because I don't really actually do that, like, I'm always around a lot of people and so actually, like, just sitting down and talking to one person . . . I'm never talking to one person." Psychologically lost in a crowd, Tanya also conveys a sense of being lost when she speaks of having difficulty getting up in the morning to get to school and trouble finishing her homework, and imagines her future, for the most part, alone.

Tanya describes the problems she has with her school work: "In the middle of the, um, of the year, I would just give up and put all the work aside and forget about it because it was hard to concentrate, and once I start something, I couldn't finish it, and I would have all this stuff that I began but couldn't finish." Tanya suggests in both ninth and tenth grade that having a tutor would help her, someone to "monitor me and just say sit there and encourage me to finish. So I wouldn't just stop and put it aside." In her tenth-grade interview she describes an afterschool program in which she seems to have experienced the benefits of being attended to in this way, saying "it seems like at [the program] I do my work more . . . They would always push you, it's like, they wouldn't just give you the work and expect you to do it."

At the end of her interview, Tanya gives additional evidence of how being connected with someone who is interested in her might help her connect with her work. When asked if the interview had any effect on her, Tanya says that "Maybe I feel like I have gotten some stuff out and maybe I'll feel better, like I can go and do what I said I could do." The absence or scarcity of others who are interested in her and her future, and to whom she can express her thoughts and feelings and get "some stuff out," put her social, emotional, and cognitive development at risk. Despite her interest in going on to college, without sustained connection to interested others, particularly adults, Tanya is at risk to continue drifting through—and perhaps out of—school.

Tiffany is similarly quiet and somewhat inaccessible in her interviews. She dropped out of school in the ninth grade to have a baby, and has since had a second child. The texts of Tiffany's interviews are made up of extremely short, seemingly superficial and conventional responses, and most of her answers are followed by giggles. She makes no mention of women in these texts, and of her mother, Tiffany says, "I don't talk to [her] that much." Tiffany was not interviewed in ninth grade; numerous appointments were set up to meet with her that year, but she did not keep any of them. It seemed to her interviewer that Tiffany gave the appearance of being very cooperative and compliant in the interview when she was actually not engaged at all.

Tiffany also seems to be out of connection with others and with her own thoughts and feelings. She does not feel listened to; in tenth grade she says that she felt good about helping a friend because "someone listened to me for once . . . No one ever listens to me." When Tiffany became pregnant the first time, she spoke about it only to her boyfriend. Even in the interview she sounds disengaged from the process: "I didn't know whether to terminate it or just keep on going . . . I didn't know (laughs). I don't know, I just didn't do it . . . He was the only one I talked to . . . he wanted me to keep it." In her narrative we hear Tiffany's disconnection from her own knowing as well as the logic of her decision to have a child. In the vacuum Tiffany describes, where "no one ever listens," she tells of someone talking to her, listening to her, and wanting her to do something. With this glimmer of relationship in a landscape of no relationships, it is no wonder that Tiffany makes the choice she does.

As we worked in our interpretive community with interviews of the girls who seemed most disconnected from themselves and others, we found ourselves disconnected from them, having difficulty staying with or experiencing our own responses to what these particular girls were saying because they themselves were glossing over or dismissing the emotional impact of serious events in their lives. There were just one or two girls in each group who showed such dissociation (one Portuguese, one Latina, one white, and two African American girls). The voice-centered, relational method highlighted this pattern, particularly the first and fourth listenings, in which we documented our responses to girls' narratives and then listened specifically for evidence of dissociation in the interview and in the interpreter's response.

One of the girls, for example, mentioned that her mother had recently been released from the hospital after having had major surgery for a life-threatening condition. The operation itself had profoundly life-changing results, permanently limiting her mother's physical activity and ability to work. We were astonished to discover that none of us had recorded any response to this event in our first listening to her narrative. Recognition of our own disconnection, of our lack of empathy for the significance of this event and the immensity of this change for mother and daughter, came only after the fourth listening for dissociation, which called attention to how the girl, and in turn we ourselves, had glossed over this event. Because of the sparseness of interviews such as this, in the absence of multiple listenings for voice and attunement to psychological dissociation, we could readily have set them aside as not particularly informative. Putting these interviews aside, however, would only have confirmed the girls' suspicions that no one really listened to them.

In the absence of relationships, or in the presence of what Jean Baker Miller (1988) calls "disconnections and violations" in relationships, girls' sense of well-being, their ability to trust themselves and others, even the likelihood of their staying in school were clearly at risk (see Belenky et al., 1986). In the context of failed or absent or abusive relationships, girls may find that they "don't know who to trust," may be made to feel "like [they are] nothing" or "nobody," may learn that "you really can't trust anybody" and that "people take advantage of you if you care about them too much." They may also be at risk for muting their own voice and their sense of self if they learn too well that it is better to stay "nice and calm" or that it is "always good to be helpful," no matter what they are feeling. If it is girls' experience that "no one ever listens," that "nobody cares" about what they say or do, that they are "never talking to one person," the potential for healthy social, emotional, and intellectual development is severely compromised. What develops instead is an enveloping sense of isolation and powerlessness, a loss of faith that others will come through for them. For many girls, the desire for relationship and attention is most evident in their eighth-grade interview and, for some, in their ninth-grade interview. By tenth grade, many appear to have been initiated into a cycle of disconnection from their own desires and from other people.

Obstacles to Relationship

Without specific information that might suggest reasons for the absence, disappearance, or hurtful behavior of the women mentioned by the girls in the Understanding Adolescence Study, we can only consider possible obstacles to sustained and positive connection. For women to join with the girls means connecting with Oliva's creativity and sexuality, with Joan's anger and rage, with Tanya's passivity and isolation. For women to join with girls means connecting with passion—a word whose Latin root means suffering—the desire, love, hope, anger, and pain that both girls and women feel. And these feelings, strong and closely held, are sometimes the very feelings women do not want to risk with each other or fully experience themselves.

Relationships with girls may be impeded by women's experience of loss in their own adolescence and of the pain of feeling helpless and powerless in the face of that loss. In the Women and Race Retreats, bringing girls' voices to the meetings and speaking about their work and their relationships with girls revived the women's own girlhood experiences. As Christine observed: "I think that we always bring the girls that we were—that we still are—with us." This was true around the experience of conflict. Wendy described the incident at the Wellfleet retreat as "one of girls on a playground, . . . but the minute it starts to get fractious, the minute we start, at least in my mind, to really get at something, then . . . we've been so well trained to know that that is dangerous, that we pull back from it." Joyce mentioned a similar response when tension arose at another time: "It was a moment where . . . you know, my eyes sort of went, 'Oh oh, what is going to happen' *(laughter)* . . . And I remember, it felt like, again I mean I always have these playground images, it felt like all of a sudden, the circle got real big, and everybody kind of stepped back, and it was a very dramatic, at least for me it was." Wendy said that "the group . . . for me has meant . . . reliving as a girl again. You know, the fights we would all have with our friends and the ability to get together or not get back together, or take a long time to forgive or remember it for always, or all the other memories that came up . . . There is a lot of not being in touch with the girl-child that, for me in my life, I had moved on to being an adult woman without having finished up with a lot of the girl-child experiences . . . Those doors kind of got opened in the group."

What these conversations also opened up in the group, and what connections with girls may evoke, particularly when girls' knowledge and feelings lead women to know and feel more clearly, are not only remembrances of pain in adolescence but also women's reconnection with similar struggles they face as adults. This was particularly true for the women in the retreats in reflecting on efforts to break the silences surrounding controversial, difficult, or previously taboo topics. Carol spoke of her weariness of this process: "You may be the one at a meeting to raise the ugly issue, whatever it is. No one else around the table will join you—until you leave the meeting . . . I am so tired of that . . . I can't tell you." Joyce was similarly well acquainted with this experience: "I'm so full of anger about that. And it happens all the time . . . You know what's troubling about this is that the issue [of breaking silences] is so large it permeates everything . . . And you're going to do it alone!"

Carol went on to comment that what girls have demonstrated as true for them is true for women as well: "To speak and not be heard is so devastating. And it takes so much energy to work out whether you're crazy, whether it's just your issue, whether you're making trouble." Girls and women learn that it may be "worse to speak, unless you know that there's some chance . . . to be heard." Despite the false comfort of the notion that adulthood brings with it a resolution of the conflicts and uncertainties of adolescence, the experience of the women in the retreats made it clear that staying with and voicing thoughts and feelings that contradict what is socially constructed as "reality" get no easier with time. As Joyce said: "It's really funny, you don't get thick-skinned over it. I find myself, the older I get, the more vulnerable, more sad. More hurt."

The stakes may also increase over time when the consequences of being unsupported in raising difficult issues on the job include putting a career in jeopardy. Joyce continued: "For some, they will continue to diminish you in their eyes, they will compartmentalize you and say, 'You should not be [in this leadership position] because you do not get along, you keep provoking' . . . I tell you, it, I feel alone. I was going to say, 'you feel alone.' I feel alone."

To the list of obstacles Christine added the difficulty of speaking with girls about issues women themselves deny or are deeply ambivalent or uncomfortable about. Noting that "a lot of women are uncomfortable talking about sexism, relationships, racism," and that "there is a whole lot of . . . baggage that we haven't worked through," she stressed the importance of working out "some of [our] own issues" with other adults before speaking with girls about them. Christine, whose work often requires her to speak openly with adolescents and adults about adolescent sexuality and sexual behavior, added that "people don't feel comfortable talking to kids about a number of these issues, most of which . . . they as adults have been silent about. A lot of it's because nobody ever explained it to us very clearly. And also because some of them are the things that are the most painful in our lives that we have never resolved ourselves . . . So we don't have that within us to give to other people. How can I talk to you about a healthy intimate relationship if I've never had one? I mean, how can I talk to you about what . . . a supportive relationship between a man and a woman is . . . if my life is turmoil? . . . There has to be some structure for adults to get through and resolve some of those kinds of issues . . . before they go to the kids . . . Because it's not appropriate to just stand up and confess [your personal problems]."

But neither is it helpful to girls if women portray themselves as having resolved all areas of pain and struggle. Women encounter obstacles to relationship with girls if they attempt to deny reality, for in so doing they can perpetuate traditions in the culture that place girls at risk: "[Women] may discover that they have succumbed to the temptation . . . to be perfect role-models for girls and thus have taken themselves out of relationship with girls—in part to hide their imperfection, but also perhaps to keep girls from feeling their sadness and their anger. Women . . . , however, also may discover that they are harboring, within themselves, a girl who lives in her body, who is insistent on speaking, who intensely desires relationships and knowledge, and who, perhaps at the time of adolescence, went underground or was overwhelmed. It may be that adolescent girls are looking for this girl in women" (Gilligan, 1990a, p. 531).

Katie recognized this call from girls for truth-telling, saying that when "girls reach adolescence, they're ready to talk, they want . . . honesty . . . But then the question is, why aren't women ready to talk?" Carol, referring to work she had carried out with colleagues Annie Rogers and Normi Noel, pointed out that this insistence on women's honesty was perhaps most readily apparent among girls in early adolescence. "In one [elementary] school that we worked with, girls made observations about their mothers' sadness and their mothers' anger . . . The girls wanted to be able to talk about what they were hearing in women in the most ordinary . . . sense, living in this society . . . So it's not even . . . necessarily about [more serious issues like] incest and alcoholism . . . it's girls' seeing unhappiness in women and girls' seeing women's inability to speak about it . . . There's this desire on the part of girls to talk about what they know and of women to connect with girls in some genuine way that rings true."

Women's and girls' ability to "talk about what they know" with each other, however, depends on trust. Concerns about trust were prominent among the girls in the study and, as Christine observed, "the whole issue of trust and safety kept on coming up" during the retreats as well. Some of the interactions at the retreats, Wendy said, reminded her of all the skirting around angry feelings she experienced as an adolescent, of girls learning to conceal certain feelings: "the girl part of me was more accessible to me in this group, because in fact, this is the first time in my life that I've been with 'all girls' as an adult . . . So it accessed for me all of the things around being a girl . . . All of the different behaviors that have gone on in this group, I mean, I remember girls saying to one another in high school, 'You're mad at me,' 'Oh no I'm not.' 'Well then how come you haven't spoken to me for the last couple of days?' 'I didn't see you' . . . And we, you know, around the fight, . . . at Wellfleet . . . it felt very much to me that we did go through, at least I did go through, all of the stages of . . . 'Oh you weren't there and . . . you won't believe what happened when we were in Wellfleet,' you know . . . I felt that. Coming back to it . . . The issue is, back to the issues of, you know, trust."

Concerns about trust were manifest in the retreats when the women spoke about and enacted difficulties in revealing strong feelings and being seen as vulnerable. Of a similarly mixed race women's group formed as part of an anti-racism conference, Papusa Molina writes: "It was rough . . . El conijo miedo [fear] of exploring, of exposing ourselves, of daring to be vulnerable and risk looking at each other in our totality without masks and false postures, rose up. The struggle between the intellectual and the touchy-feely approach erupted from the first moment" (1990, p. 328). This struggle "between the intellectual and the touchy-feely," however, presents a false choice, for coming into relationship across significant differences requires both intellect and feeling. Deriding a group's attempts at emotional engagement may be intended as healthy skepticism about or vigilance against premature or false intimacy, but it can just as easily serve as a defense against genuine intimacy and an obstacle to authentic relationship.

Issues of trust and intimacy, central to any process of group formation, immediately become more complicated and layered in the presence of different cultural norms about the extent to which it is appropriate or safe to express strong feelings and share personal information. Some of the women in the retreats spoke of the limits they wanted in the group: some did not want to appear "vulnerable," to be seen crying, or to "talk personally"; some echoed the concern mentioned by Molina when they said they did not want it to be a "therapy group." But differences, especially cultural differences, inevitably evoke strong feelings and personal histories; it may be essential to express and address these if the silences around separation by race, class, and ethnicity are to be broken. To reveal personal history may also entail revealing one's survival strategies, however, and this requires enormous trust. As one of the black women remarked, once revealed, survival strategies are no longer effective. Consequently, in the retreats, the desire to break silences and connect across difference continued to vie with the pull to remain cautious, to draw back, to defend against the repetition of past hurts.

Disconnection and mistrust along lines of difference are so charged in part because they are deeply rooted in childhood. In an exercise during the retreats exploring "dangerous memories," women shared powerful experiences from their girlhoods, some of which included "terror" of the physical harm that could come of speaking or of being in the wrong place. One of the black women remembered her mother telling her not to go to a Civil Rights speech, warning her, "You're going to get yourself killed or you're going to get other people killed." Christine's first dangerous memory went back to 1960, when "my parents bought a house in suburban Cleveland, Ohio, before the Civil Rights legislation was passed. We were the first black family to live in the neighborhood, and we had twenty-four-hour police protection . . . There were fire bomb threats, and I remember riding my tricycle around the corner, I was three or four years old, you know. The policeman was there and my parents made it very clear that, . . . [they said] everything was going to be fine, I was going to be fine. But you knew, at that time as a very young child . . . that something was very wrong."

Carol, "growing up a Jewish child during the Holocaust," also learned early about the dangers of being in the wrong place. Although she and her immediate family resided in New York City and thus did not live in daily fear for their lives, the loss of other family members and friends, and the steady stream of survivors, of "refugees from Europe, always in my house," became constant and potent reminders that life and death could depend on where you were and on being aware of who was, and who was not, Jewish.

Judy said, "I think I was maybe thirteen and I was in Virginia, my mother had died, and I was . . . with my cousins for the summer because my father worked and I had to go someplace where I would be taken care of. And we were driving to Florida, and we stopped at a gas station . . . maybe in Georgia and . . . we had used the rest rooms and . . . I remember a car pulling in, a black family wanting to use the rest room, and not being allowed to use the rest room. And [I remember] being very disturbed by that and not understanding at all why, just not getting that. Just not getting that and, I don't know . . . I'm not even sure why I think of it as a dangerous memory except that it felt like I was learning something that I . . . maybe wasn't supposed to know, or something but . . . it just felt wrong to me."

In the letter she wrote to her niece, Lyn recalled "confusing memories" of what she learned growing up in a white working-class area of rural Maine. She remembered stories and rhymes recited by adults and sung with her friends while playing jump rope that included racially demeaning words and stereotypes which brought her pain as an adult: "I took in words and ideas at your age and earlier that I have not sorted through yet, . . . confusing memories because they were messages given to me in times of real pleasure—with them I remember my father's voice, his deep breathing, the warmth of his body, his smell. I remember the joy of friendship, the agile movement, feelings of being included . . . And these words . . . the stereotypes, meant nothing to me . . . That is what I used to think—that is what I told myself as I came to know the meanings of what I had taken in: they meant nothing to me; I was absolved. I will simply begin again, I will know this time. I'm writing to you to say that these words and rhymes and stories carry with them a legacy of pain and violence—they haunt me now . . . Cruel things, horrible things have been said by people I have loved and trusted most—what did they know? How am I to respond?"

These dangerous memories and their emotional imprint—the fear and rage that attended the experience or anticipation of racial crimes and injustice as well as the guilt, shame, and confusion of witnessing or inadvertently perpetuating racist language, attitudes, or behavior—were part of the personal histories of the women in the retreats. In being voiced, these memories became part of the group's collective history, and in laying bare the radical separations underlying these experiences, this voicing deepened understanding and opened the possibility of a different future.

Related to issues of trust were difficulties in coming to terms with the existence and the effects of differences in power. Jill observed during one of the retreats that "the less powerful in the group are very interested in having a conversation about power, but it has not always been so for everybody in the group . . . [which is why] it's got lost so often." The educator Lisa Delpit has noted this connection, writing that "those with power are frequently least aware of—or least willing to acknowledge—its existence. Those with less power are often most aware of its existence. For many who consider themselves members of liberal or radical camps, acknowledging personal power and admitting participation in the culture of power is distinctly uncomfortable. On the other hand, those who are less powerful in any situation are most likely to recognize the power variable most acutely" (1993, p. 123). The issue of power differences in the retreats was in fact raised by those who felt they had less power in the group—women who had been Carol's or Katie's students, women who had fewer financial resources, women who held comparatively less powerful positions in their work lives.

Judy, who had been a student of both Carol's and Katie's, expressed frustration at the last retreat "because I feel like we have not taken on the power. I think what it came down to for me is a sense that . . . [issues] of class and gender and race, et cetera, are really issues of power . . . And I felt like we got to sort of a brief shining moment on the last retreat when, in the afternoon I think, we made a list . . . of what are the power differences among us, or what are some of the risks that we might take in speaking honestly in this group, at different times, about different things. And we made a list, and I thought that was a very honest, courageous . . . statement, and that is one of the stories that I tell people when I talk about the work that we've done. And when I have mentioned that list, people are sort of in awe of that, and they're, like, 'You really said those things?' . . . And I guess my frustration is that I wish we could have really . . . just walked right into them."

The list generated by the group touched on power issues but more centrally addressed the fears about speaking openly: of "being perceived as racist" or "ignorant," of "feeling vulnerable" or "expressing feelings," of "strong people asking for help," "showing scars," of "being chastised, abandoned," of "going out of bounds." Discussions of the power differences Judy pointed to—which underlay the dynamics of who attended or missed meetings, who spoke or remained silent, whose words were given more or less weight—were more difficult to sustain.

Christine felt similarly frustrated "around the whole power discussion that came up, for example, around money and who in the group could afford to pay their own way and who couldn't . . . Those kinds of conversations happened a lot on the side, where we hear people saying that, but they wouldn't say it in the larger group. And I got the sense that . . .

if we can't iron out some of those kinds of things here, then it's not very hopeful that we can really iron out the larger issues." As Janie said, it is crucial to identify ways in which "we silenced ourselves, or allowed ourselves to be silenced. I think that there's a tremendous amount of value to identifying this, . . . because I think that these are the kinds of issues that certainly do break groups up and get in the way of people with obvious and not so obvious differences coming together."

Structuring Separation

Obstacles to relationships among women and between women and girls are built into institutions, including schools. The experience of girls in the Understanding Adolescence Study and the teachers, counselors, and administrators in the Women Teaching Girls, Girls Teaching Women (WTG-GTW) retreats draw a portrait of schools, particularly at the secondary level, that are not structured to support relationships. Contrary to the stereotypes of the at-risk label, the girls in this study care about their education and about relationships with their teachers at school. Unfortunately, once they enter high school, there is little evidence that they experience meaningful or sustained connection with teachers.

For the teachers who participated in the retreats led by Judy Dorney (the series of retreats that paralleled the Women and Race retreats), a sense of connection with colleagues was similarly lacking, or in constant jeopardy, because of the school system's policy of moving teachers at will. These teachers spoke with the passion of long-held frustration about overextended workloads and a system that discouraged such relationships through unexpected lay-offs and random placement in different schools each year. One teacher, for example, told of how she had long felt unable to act on her strong desire to teach illiterate girls to read because she was always anticipating a move. It would be irresponsible, and perhaps do more harm than good, she felt, to begin something she knew she would not be able to finish. From the very first meeting the teachers spoke of how rare it was for them to have an opportunity to meet with their colleagues and reflect on their work, either with girls or with each other, and how time together in the retreats helped to heal their feelings of isolation and build connections with the girls they were teaching.

Among the girls in the study, relationships with women teachers seemed virtually absent when they reached high school. Asked about her response to the interview in ninth grade, Valerie says that "being listened to" was what she "especially liked," adding, "you just feel like there is someone out there that's really paying attention to me." Asked if there are people who "really pay attention" in school, Valerie says there are not, highlighting one of the major obstacles the teachers in the retreats said kept them apart from their colleagues—a sense of being overwhelmed by the extent of the need and by their limited ability to respond effectively: "There are a lot of other kids, . . . so, I don't really think a teacher has enough time to pay attention to one student, because there are an awful lot of others."

In listening to girls' accounts of disappointment or loss in relationships with teachers, it is important to emphasize that we did not ask girls explicitly about these relationships and thus do not either infer that the absence of positive relationships with high school teachers in their narratives means that teachers are not important to them, or place the responsibility for maintaining relationships solely on the teachers. It may be that girls' relationships with teachers are strained because of their behaviors of symptomatic risk, such as frequently being late for or skipping class, which some of the girls in the study mentioned. Relationships may also be affected by teachers' low expectations, which girls are sure to recognize. Both girls and teachers are responsible for developing and maintaining connections with each other, but they cannot do so in a system that is, in effect, structured to restrict or discourage relationships.

In response to the question about an important relationship with someone other than their mother, only one girl, on one occasion, named a woman teacher. In fact, she was the only one who mentioned that a teacher was important to her during the high school years. When the girls were in eighth grade—still in elementary school—two of them mentioned men teachers as important to them and to whom they could talk about problems.

The girls we interviewed expressed a desire for relationships with teachers in all three years of interviews, but for many girls, the transition from elementary to high school brought disappointment and a sense of loss in the wake of disconnections or inattention from teachers. When the girls reached high school, those who spoke of teachers were more likely to do so in the context of episodes of disappointment or perceived injustice. Discussions of relationships with teachers were most frequently elicited by a question about a painful experience: *Can you tell me about a time you felt bad about yourself, or unhappy, in school?* Although a girl's declining school attendance and performance might well be associated with an increase in difficult encounters with teachers and other school authorities, there is evidence that the longer contact girls have with teachers in elementary school may also be related to the greater number of positive stories of relationships with teachers in eighth grade. As Carol noted in one of the Women and Race retreats, the saying "primary school teachers teach children and secondary school teachers teach subjects" was true for the students in this study.

Faith, a Portuguese adolescent, speaks of the importance of the long-term relationships she had with her teachers in elementary school, but in ninth grade she reflects on the loss of these relationships: "[I felt bad] having to leave elementary, because you have been there a lot and with all those teachers, you knew them all through the years, they have been there, and now I won't be seeing them. I would just see them around, but they wouldn't be with me in high school." What made that hard, she said, was that "I knew they wouldn't be there for me."

In addition to the systemic hindrances to relationships they noted in the WTG-GTW retreats, there are individual reasons for teachers to maintain a distance from their students. In her tenth-grade interview, Barbara offers an analysis of some of the psychological dimensions involved when teachers keep themselves out of relationship with students. She speaks of her hurt when a teacher gave his attention—and a higher grade—to a boy Barbara suspected had cheated: "I was mad . . . I felt hurt, you know, disappointed, because you know, I looked up to my teacher because, like, he helped me with my work and stuff. But all of a sudden he just turned his attention to another kid. I felt jealous . . .

[Teachers do that sometimes] so that they don't get hurt themselves . . . They don't get involved really. I notice that teachers don't get truly involved with the students because they're afraid of getting hurt by the student . . . Because teachers have feelings, you know, that they try to pull back a little."

But the need to "pull back a little" and "not get truly involved" can also be an appropriate and reasonable response. If schools, mirroring the larger society, are not structured to support relationships, those few teachers who do open themselves up to students are likely to be overwhelmed by the multitude of the unmet needs they encounter. Heightened concern about charges of sexual abuse, while of critical importance for students' protection, may also cause teachers to be more hesitant about their involvement with students. Abusive relationships are, in fact, more likely to occur in conditions of isolation. The retreats with the teachers offered one way to address this dilemma, enabling them to begin to talk to each other about their work and their relationships with students, providing collegial support for sharing their successes and failures in the classroom, and initiating a push for change at the institutional level to create a more supportive environment.

Because girls were out of relationship with teachers, many felt they lacked a voice in the system. Even those who appeared outspoken in their interviews revealed little evidence to suggest that they had been—or would be—heard or have any say in disagreements with teachers or the administration. Diana voices a relatively common complaint: "[I feel bad] when teachers try to blame you for something when you know yourself that you didn't do it and they're not quite sure if you did it or somebody else did it, and they put the blame on you with another story. That makes me mad . . . Because some teachers think, sometimes people think that teachers always have to be right, and I don't think that's true because they're not always right. And sometimes the kids are right and they don't listen to their side of the story. And I don't think that is very fair . . . because they're adults and they get first say and last say, and that's not fair." What would be fair, says Diana, is "if teachers and parents or whatever, staff members, would listen to both sides of the story and get the facts straight, and don't just take the teacher's side because they're the teacher, just listen to both sides of the story and then decide who's right and who's wrong."

Oliva voices a similar protest in eighth grade. She says she feels embarrassed when teachers yell at her in front of other students, especially for something she says she did not do. By tenth grade, however, she has learned that "There's nothing I can do." "She's a teacher, and she has the authority . . . I tried to talk to my principal. And she said there's nothing we can do, or something. So it's like she said, there's nothing that can be done." Her feeling of being unsupported and unheard by a series of women at home and at school reinforces her sense of powerlessness.

Ana learns the same lesson in ninth grade, when she tells about feeling bad when a teacher wrongly accused her of cheating. Ana went to a woman in authority at the school, who apparently came to believe her side of the story but who also confirmed her belief that "you cannot argue" with those in authority: "I couldn't say anything because you can't argue with a teacher, they'll call your mother or whatever, you know, so I was, like, forget it then. And I got a zero for it . . . I felt so bad . . . [The administrator] . . . called me and [asked], 'Why did you do this?' And I explained it to her, and she was like, 'Yeah, because that teacher is a man that you cannot argue with,' he'll just, like, ugh! I told her I didn't have no intentions of cheating or anything . . . but you can't argue with the person, you know."

Ana receives a double message: she is believed but she will not be heard, nor will she be supported if she tries to argue her case. Her teacher, Ana says, is a man who "wouldn't let you prove your point . . . wouldn't even let you talk." Ana may be learning a parallel lesson of powerlessness at home, where her father "doesn't let you prove your point." Ana also speaks in ninth grade of how her mother favors her brothers by believing them before she believes Ana and by paying more attention to them: "she's real close with the boys." Ana speaks of her frustration when her brothers are permitted more freedom, but her concern is dismissed: "they are, like, you know, 'You're a girl.' "

Not surprisingly, Ana is one of the girls whose ninth-grade interview transcript contained a larger number of "I don't know" responses than her eighth-grade interview, from less than one for every four pages to an average of more than two per page—close to a ninefold increase. Despite evidence of Ana's capacity to be articulate and insightful, the repeated messages to relinquish her own authority and voice, and the apparent lack of anyone to stand up or speak out for her, put her healthy development, and her sense of value and power as a woman, increasingly at risk.

A different story unfolds for Donna. In tenth grade she speaks of almost being sent to a nonacademic program as a time when she felt good about herself in school: "When, like, I was failing, I was failing real bad second term, first and second term of this year, and um, my house master, you know, she wanted to put me over into the [alternative program] . . . And um, you know, my father, I asked my father to come up and fight it and I promised that I was going to do better and I did. And my grade point average went up fifteen points and she gave me, um, a certificate of achievement. And that made me feel good . . . That made me feel real good."

Donna's sense of her own capabilities, her persistence, and her ability to ask for—and receive—help from her father, all contributed not only to getting "one more chance" from her teacher, but to motivating her to "[turn] it all around": "I just put my mind to it and I said well I've got to do it, because I know if I don't, she will send . . . me over there anyways, even if my father did come up, and I just promised her, asked her to give me one more chance, and she said, 'This is it.' So I turned it all around and I just started, like I was, like I just started school and I did good." *Do you think she was surprised that you did that?* "No, because she knew I could do it because last year I did it. Last year I was a good student, and she knew, you know, she knows my parents, you know, and she knew my brothers and sister. And she said, 'I know, Donna, you're not stupid, I know you can do it.' You know, and she said but we can't keep, she told me that she cannot keep me there because I'm not doing anything. And I'm just wasting people's time, you know, and that's when my father came up and talked to her. I told my father, I said, 'If I get sent over there, I know what's going to happen . . . I'll probably drop out of school' . . . But my father said, 'Well, Miss Ellis feels that you should be there, because you're not showing her anything.' So I said, 'Well, that's true,' but somehow she just gave me another chance, so."

The responsiveness of these adults enabled Donna to gain a "hearing" at school and to marshal her own forces to regain lost academic ground. Donna's teacher is straightforward with her and remains willing to discuss her decision and, ultimately, to reconsider it. She demonstrates respect and care for Donna by encouraging her to be responsible and accountable for her schoolwork, by listening to her, by expecting the best from her, and by giving her a fair chance to remain in the academic program. What made the difference for Donna was not only her persistence and her father's advocacy, but also the teacher's history of connection with Donna and her family; the teacher knew Donna's siblings, her previous work, and her parents. Donna says of her parents, in fact, that "they both keep in touch with the school." Thus it seems that Donna, who "probably would have dropped out of school" if she had been sent to the alternative program, had a safety net made up of the network of connections among her family, her teacher, and herself. Unlike Ana, Donna learned that she could succeed if she spoke up, that she would find support if she asked for it. And contrary to or perhaps defying the predictions of her aunt, who made her "feel like I'm nothing" by saying she would not make it to college, Donna successfully graduated from high school and was accepted at a local two-year college.

The contrast between these divergent stories underscores the importance of connections between teachers and students and between teachers and families. Ana's siblings do not attend this high school, and she seems to have no links to authorities at the school. She sought support from one school authority without apparent success and felt she had no other adults to back her up. In examining the different outcomes to these two stories, we also note the cultural differences between these girls. Donna comes from a white, working-class family, whereas Ana's family, while also working class, is Latin American, and her parents speak little English. In addition to the barrier of language, as other research with Latin American families has shown, Ana's family may be reluctant to get involved in school matters because of a culturally supported belief that school authorities "know what is best for their children" (Vásquez-Nuttall, Avila-Vavas, and Morales-Barreto, 1984). In the absence of school outreach across this cultural divide, girls like Ana are likely to be left to fend for themselves when they encounter problems at school.

A review of research commissioned by the American Association of University Women (AAUW, 1992) reports that girls often do not receive enough attention in school (see also Galbo, 1989; Sadker and Sadker, 1994). By virtue of their academic status, girls who are "at risk" may be even less likely than other girls to receive positive attention. The Understanding Adolescence Study also offers consistent evidence that these girls feel they lack a voice in the system and that they benefit—both academically and psychologically—from having an advocate in school.

Stories told in the WTG-GTW retreats illustrate how creating space and time to build community among teachers and between teachers and girls can have immediate and positive effects on girls. One teacher, who participated in the retreats along with her principal, described how the experience helped both of them be more responsive to the girls in their school. A group of her female students had approached her expressing frustration about the activities offered in the gym class they took with the boys in their class. Each week the predictable activity was a game of basketball, a routine that pleased the boys but left the girls increasingly discouraged. Their efforts to register their dissatisfaction and to suggest other activities to their male gym teacher, however, did not result in change. Their female teacher, taking their concerns seriously, encouraged them to take a more active stance. They subsequently wrote a group letter to the gym teacher and to the principal outlining their concerns and wishes. The teacher and her students then met with the principal, the gym teacher, and a few of the parents. Because of these actions, more varied activities were incorporated into their gym classes, enabling the girls to participate more fully.

By listening to her female students and taking their objections seriously, this teacher was able to work with them to find ways to take their voices into a more public forum and bring about effective change. The principal agreed that her own participation in the retreat process also enabled her to respond to the girls. Instead of teaching them what Oliva and Ana learned, that "there's nothing that can be done" or that they "couldn't say anything" or "you can't argue," the teacher and principal taught girls that their concerns were of interest and value, that their voices had power. They collaborated with the girls to develop specific strategies for getting their voices heard and achieving change in their environment.

Other teachers and administrators also found that, as a result of their time with colleagues in the retreats, they began to take advantage of or create opportunities to connect with girls both in and out of the class-room. A high school principal in the WTG-GTW retreats formed a girls' group that gathered for weekly breakfast meetings, giving some of the girls who were having difficulty in school a special place where they could have a voice in the school and join with other girls in a way that would not be likely in the normal course of school life. A middle school teacher found herself aligning with girls in a new way when, during a half-hour lesson on women's history, the boys in her class grew restless and began to question the importance of the topic. In the past, she would have responded to the boys' impatience and moved on to another lesson. This time, aware of the unintended message this would send to both boys and girls, she instead stayed with the lesson (see also Barbieri, 1995).

Risking Relationship

Looking to a different future for her daughters, African American writer Kesho Yvonne Scott describes the at once disruptive and transforming power of connections between women and girls:

> The complex web of oppression my mother and I shared still has the potential to capture my daughters. Unlike me, however, they seem to know that this need not be. At the least, they seem to know that they have the right to ask me 'how not to get caught!' . . . There it was: the question that neither my mother nor I had ever asked ourselves. Once I realized the full significance of the question, I could not dismiss it. I had to face it, and facing it meant facing pain: the pain of consciously recognizing my own habits of survival through my children's eyes, the pain of seeing them dance a new dance . . . But the other side of the pain is hope.
>
> The question blows my mind. Over and over I ask it again to myself. It makes me feel tense, upside down . . . The power of my daughters' ques-

tion is [a] clue to its answer. That they can ask means that we can answer. The strategy for winning is in that recognition, and in the teaching, of ourselves, to risk dialogue. I opened up to dialogue between myself and my girls. In order to do that, I had to dialogue with my own sisters . . . with my mother and my grandmother . . . There are no guarantees that this strategy . . . will succeed. But the lack of change so far suggests that opportunities have been missed in each generation . . . It suggests that we should at least try a new pathway. To do otherwise—to think that we do one another favors by not reminding each other of how difficult it has been . . . is to opt for mere survival over liberation. (1991, pp. 188–189)

If girls feel that "no one ever listens," perhaps it is because they are saying what no one wants to hear. Girls' questions raise the possibility of a future that can be different from the past; they urge women—as has Audre Lorde—to "examine their position,"[1] to hold up to scrutiny their strategies for survival, their practice of teaching, their daily decisions to speak or remain silent. Girls' questions require women to face pain, to expand their capacity for joy and hope and pleasure. They call upon women to allow themselves to become vulnerable and to risk relationships with girls and with each other across differences and across separations.

The girls in the study and the women in the retreats describe the enormous risks they feel in permitting themselves to be vulnerable—of being the subject of rumors and the gossip of their peers, of being rejected by colleagues or dismissed by authorities at work or school, of regenerating past hurts, of being overwhelmed by the needs of others, of feeling that they have betrayed members of their family or culture or class. In the absence of relationship, when "no one listens," acknowledging vulnerability to self and others may well pose too great a risk. But the ability to be vulnerable is also a relational strength, creating openings for building trust and power in relationship (Miller, 1982). As the psychotherapist John Welwood writes, "acknowledging our basic human vulnerability—our openness to reality—is a source of real power" (1990, p. 83).

By risking relationship with each other and by examining difference, the Women and Race retreats sought to interrupt cycles of disconnection and betrayal and to find, as Scott suggests, "new pathways" for women and girls across culture and class and generation. What was true of the women in the retreats is true of girls and of our research as well: Learning about difference is not about epistemology, not simply about whether, or to what extent, we can know another human being or another culture. Exploring difference is about relationship. It is about bringing ourselves, again and again, to the edge of our not knowing, to the edge of our silences, to the edge of subjects that feel, and sometimes are, dangerous. Each time, we play out the drama of difference: when we reach that edge, when we come up to a moment of pain or confusion or impasse, what do we do? Do we stay or do we leave, do we continue to speak in the presence of these feelings or do we close down around them and retreat to the world we know? To hold difference and sustain hope requires us, moment by moment, to hold steady, to stay with ourselves and each other, to continue to learn how to speak in the presence of profound silences.

7

The Risk of Development

Whenever I'm ready to give up, to like push me, like say, "Go
on, you can do it," if I'm ready to give up or something. Because I need somebody to like catch me and pick me back up.

                                    —Mary, Irish American, ninth grade

If you tell somebody your ideas, they might be like, "Oh,
that's stupid," put you down. And then you'd be like, "Oh, I
don't want to do this anymore."

                                    —Bettina, Portuguese American, tenth grade

[Teachers could help if they would] teach you how to fight
back in the world, because there are going to be a lot of sharks
out there.

                                    —Barbara, Irish American, tenth grade

When girls speak about their hopes for the future, relationships are central—as both help and hindrance. Those they name as important potential sources of help support their goals, encourage them when their
courage falters, and teach them strategies for dealing with adversity in
the world. Yet relationships can also be an equally powerful hindrance if
they become the source of discouragement or ridicule. The potential
obstacles to future plans that loom largest, however, are responsibilities
for future spouses and children, relationships which, girls anticipate,
will consume all their time and energy.

Girls' hopes for the future and for the course of their lives shortly after
high school challenge and confirm expectations of risk. In high school,
most girls' educational aspirations are high. Some girls defy expectations
and complete and continue their postsecondary education. For others
the reality falls far short of their hopes, and they continue to struggle in
complicated or painful circumstances. The girls who seem best able to
sustain their vitality and confidence during the early high school years

174

and to achieve some measure of their plans after high school are those who maintain a healthy critical perspective, and whose relationships sustain and cultivate this perspective and their hopes for themselves. Some of the girls whose lives take a different direction anticipate their disappointment while they are still in school and speak of the loss they are about to experience. Twenty of the twenty-six girls in the Understanding Adolescence Study graduated from high school. Of the six girls who did not graduate, four had one child and one had two. None of those who completed high school had a child.

Dreaming the Future

At the end of their interviews each year we asked girls about the future, and our questions elicited some of the same hopes described by middle-class girls: college, a well-paying job, a nice place to live, and later, for some, a family. Like many middle-class girls, some of the girls in the study describe a life quite different from that of their mothers. Yet this familiar version of the American Dream—supported by the ideals of hard work and equal opportunity—may be out of reach to them long before they even get to high school. The opportunities afforded to middle-class and affluent girls vary substantially from those afforded to poor and working-class girls.

When the Understanding Adolescence Study was over, the girls were still in high school. While we were writing the final report to the Boston Foundation, we visited the school several times and ran into some of them in the hallways or, when the weather was sunny, outside the building. The smell of newly mown grass mixed with the haze of cigarette smoke, and the atmosphere, as in high schools everywhere, was charged with energy and noise. Some girls greeted us warmly, others were shy, and a few seemed not to recognize us, or perhaps chose not to acknowledge us. These chance meetings were filled with information: "How is this year going?" solicited a fair share of "Okay," "Good," or a groan, but, especially when girls became seniors, there was more: "I can't *believe* I'm graduating," "I got into college," "I'm in my sister's wedding, I *have* to get thin."

The girls' hopes and plans—spoken about by some with the optimism of adolescence—often contradict society's general assumptions about how "at-risk" adolescent girls think about the future. These assumptions are rife with stereotypes that go something like this: these girls have little motivation or desire for achievement; rather than making plans for the future, they are present oriented; they may even be expecting a future in which public assistance plays a role. They have an external locus of control and are easy prey to negative influences from peers.

The future the adolescent girls in the study envision for themselves differs from these stereotypes. Across racial and ethnic groups, with few exceptions, they express a strong preference for establishing themselves in a job or a career before making commitments to relationships with spouses, partners, or children. Fifteen of the twenty-six girls said that they "will probably go" on to college. Among those who mentioned a specific career choice, the beauty/fashion field, becoming a lawyer, and secretarial work are the most frequently named. A few girls express an interest in social work, accounting, and owning a business.

As we were completing this book several years after most of the girls' high school graduation, we began again to investigate what they were currently doing. Some had kept in touch with their high school counselors and were easy to locate; others seemed to have dropped out of sight. The six young women who had not completed high school were hardest to find; telephone calls ended in disembodied messages or unlisted numbers. Of the fifteen girls who had planned to go to college, seven enrolled after high school, but two, Pauline and Rochelle,[1] were unable to continue for financial reasons and are now working locally. Of the five who remain in school, Diana, Julia, and Carla are enrolled in four-year colleges, Maria is taking college courses part-time, and Donna is enrolled in a two-year community college program. One of Lilian's friends thought that she might also be taking college courses, but we were unable to contact her directly to confirm this. Oliva, Ruby, Anita, Sandy, and Tiffany all dropped out of high school when they became pregnant. Mary, who dropped out, returned to school, and then left without graduating, is working. Fourteen of the young women from this study are employed full-time, some as office workers in secretarial or clerical jobs, others in retail or convenience stores. Four of those working full-time, Barbara, Dahlia, Bettina, and Faith, also completed year-long secretarial training programs.

Over the three years of the study, girls' responses to our first question about the future—*When you think about the future, how do you imagine your life?*—were nearly uniform across different racial and ethnic groups. Overwhelmingly, they describe job or career goals first and mention marriage, family, or other significant relationships second, or not at all. Responses to our second question—*What might get in the way?*—reveal that many girls see "relationships" as an impediment to what they want in the future. The specific relationships they refer to are those with a spouse or male partner and with children. While a few girls cite "money" or "grades" as potential problems, the most common answers to the question of what might get in the way are "kids," "a boy," "getting married too soon," or simply "getting married." Obstacles to future career plans include not only the obvious one of teen pregnancy but also relationships formed too soon after high school, before careers and jobs are well under way.

These responses are nearly identical to those of adolescent girls in the Emma Willard School Study (Gilligan, Lyons, and Hanmer, 1990), who also planned to become "successful" first, before marriage and family. The Emma Willard girls see careers "as having ongoing importance," while "marriage is portrayed as problematic, often transient" (Mendelsohn, 1990). Although the ideals of the girls in the Emma Willard School and the Understanding Adolescence Study overlap, their prospects for the future differ considerably, as research on social class differences points out (Anyon, 1982; Steinitz and Solomon, 1986; Rubin, 1992; Brantlinger, 1993). The girls in the Understanding Adolescence Study are far less likely to have access to the social and financial supports needed to plan and negotiate entry into higher education and make career connections. They may also be the first in their family to have plans that involve "moving up and out" in terms of school and work, and are thus likely to face this as an additional obstacle. Moving beyond their mothers is psychologically difficult for many girls, filled with the ambivalence of wanting and not wanting a different life for themselves, of feeling guilty, and at the same time, of recognizing that their mothers may likewise want and not want a different life for their daughters (Gardner, 1993; hooks, 1993b).

Although the girls in the study all share plans to settle into jobs or careers before becoming involved in long-term relationships, they differ somewhat in their views of these relationships as potential obstacles. The Latina and Portuguese girls' concerns center on prescribed duties and roles for women in marriage, which might interfere with their plans. Some are quite explicit about the problems they might encounter with a husband who expects them to be a "housemaid" or full-time "housewife." Christina says, "Say I am married, they might want you to stay home and do all the cooking and everything, not to have your own career." Isabel also cites as an obstacle "getting married early . . . You know, you have to clean your house, you have to do the food and sometimes it's hard. And probably you would have to go to work and stuff and it is going to get mixed in your schedule." The black girls focus primarily on how being responsible for children could keep them from other pursuits. The white girls do not emphasize marriage or children as obstacles but also want to be settled in a job or career first.

These concerns about marriage or children are grounded in the reality of the lives of other girls they know or of the women in their families. For example, Ana, a Latina girl, and Maria and Isabel, both Portuguese, report similar worries. Ana tells how her observations of how life has gone for a friend have shaped her own desire to be settled first in her career. "If I wanted to have a kid, it'd be when I know that I already have my business settled, okay, my career and everything, then I might say that I want a child, you know. I would know that that probably wouldn't mess me up right there . . . See, I want a child, but I don't want it now, I want to be prepared for it and stuff because I see now how girls have babies and they don't even, they can't even take good care of it . . . The girl couldn't do anything now, you know. Now she probably has to live on welfare or something . . . I observe things when I see it." Ana observes, too, that the father has abandoned both mother and children. Like the other girls in the study who speak about pregnancy in adolescence, she harbors no romantic notions about living happily ever after, nor does she expect the father of the child to be available to support mother and child physically, financially, or emotionally.

Maria shares Ana's ability to "observe things when I see it" and thus fears that early marriage might "wreck my future." Maria's future plans echo both Ana's intended strategy and her rationale: "I want to finish high school and I want to go to college and I want to finish my education and then get settled and then I could find, you know, somebody will come along and if he's the right one, I'll marry him and we'll have a family . . . I don't want to get settled with anyone yet, because I know a lot of friends that did and they ended up either quitting school or they didn't care about college because they wanted to get married so I'll just keep it at this for now." Asked what might get in the way of her future, Maria says, "the right guy might come along, you know . . . But I'll try my best not to let it get in my way . . . 'Cause I really don't want to wreck my future." Two years after high school, Maria has met "the right guy" and is married and working full-time, although she is also taking college courses on a part-time basis.

Research on college attendance and persistence corroborates Maria's concerns, finding that delays in marriage and childbearing are important in whether women are likely to enroll and remain in college (Cardoza, 1991; Sohlberg et al., 1993). "Domestic labor," Desdemona Cardoza writes, had a "sharp negative impact on degree completion." Cultural unease that a wife's level of education might surpass her husband's may also diminish the likelihood that married women will continue their education. Although Cardoza's study focuses on Hispanic women, the Portuguese girls in the Understanding Adolescence Study describe expectations about women's domestic role that are very similar to those mentioned by Latina girls.

Isabel tells her interviewer that she, too, has observed that "kids" have gotten in the way for other girls. When asked what might get in the way of her future, she sounds disappointed in, and for, her sister, who is "just a housewife": "Kids. If I get married at a young age. Because my sister got married when she was young." *And is she not doing what she wants to do?* "She's just a housewife, I mean she could have done something better . . . I think she would be happier if she wasn't married."

Alongside the surety of girls' hopes for the future, many reveal a growing awareness that their plans may be out of reach. In ninth grade, for example, Isabel is certain about her plans to go to college. By tenth grade, however, her words carry a ring of impending disappointment when she speaks of her desire to attend community college: "I want to. I want to, but I don't know. It's not, I *do* want to go. I really do want to go. But I don't know, I think something is going to get in the way, because when I put my mind set on something, and then something just ends up breaking it. So." The interviewer asks Isabel what kinds of things she thinks might get in the way, but Isabel at this point replies that she does not really know.

For Isabel, this certainty and this clear articulation of what she knows and what she desires for the future stand in sharp contrast to her almost equally certain knowledge that the future might more closely resemble the kind of life she does not want. Isabel's aspirations have parted company with her expectations, a change highlighted in the following excerpts from her interview responses: "I want . . . I want . . . I don't know . . . It's not . . . I do . . . I really do . . . I don't know . . . something . . . something just ends up breaking it . . . I don't really know." Isabel's narrative moves from an active "I," who knows what she wants, to an unnamed, undefined "thing" that "just ends up breaking it." This shift from "I" to "it" signifies a loss—of voice, of control, and of connection to her knowing—and may reflect the helplessness she feels about changing what seems inevitable. It may also reflect her recognition that something outside of herself—in this case, perhaps, social class—may shape her future. In tenth grade Isabel expresses a concern about money and criticizes the system of financial aid: "Everybody has a right to have their education. And if, if they don't give it to me, [it will be] like someone invading me. Putting me down, because they do give money out to people that don't need it and then they just leave other people behind that need money." As she predicted, Isabel did not go on to college after high school. We do not know, however, if lack of funding was the determining factor.

A similar shift from certainty about what she wants to doubt that her hopes will materialize is evident in Elena's words. Elena, who is Portuguese, speaks in tenth grade of the contrast between what she wants and what her mother, and eventually Elena herself, believes will happen. Elena says it is "scary":

> I kind of like kids, so sometimes in a way I want to, like, do something that has to do with kids, but I don't want any of my own for a while *(laughs)*. I mean it's cute, I love kids and to be with them, and teach them things and all this, but then in a way, I mean when they're not yours, you can always give them back to their owners and not have all the responsibility of these kids, so I kind of like that, so I say kids are very bleak in my future, I very much doubt I'll have them, but my mother says I'll be the first one to have them in my family, and have a lot of them, that's what my mother says, and it usually comes up, usually the opposite happens of what you want basically she says, sometimes, not all the time, I should say, not usually. *What do you think about that?* I don't know, it's scary. When you say you don't want to have kids and all of a sudden you have them. It's not that I don't want them, it's just that I want them later on in life, like in my late twenties or early thirties is when I want them. I'll probably have them when I'm twenty-one. *(laughs)* My mother's right.

We notice Elena's use of the word "bleak" in this passage. It is "bleak"—and "scary"—to trace the loss of her own voice as she speaks: "I want . . . I love . . . I mean . . . I say . . . I doubt . . . my mother says . . . my mother says . . . the opposite happens . . . I don't know . . . it's scary . . . you say . . . you don't want . . . all of a sudden you have them . . . [she's] right." Elena's emphasis moves from what she knows— "I want"—to a place outside her knowledge or control—"I don't know," "you don't want," "my mother says," "the opposite happens." In doing so, she seems to accept the eventual reality of a future that is at odds with her plans and preferences. Elena learns from her mother that "usually the opposite happens of what you want basically," and although Elena temporarily takes back this pronouncement—"sometimes, not all the time, I should say, not usually"—she ultimately returns to her mother's beliefs: "my mother's right." At twenty-one, Elena has not fulfilled her mother's predictions; she is not married and does not have children.

We were able to track down most, but not all, of the Latina and Portuguese girls—now young women—in the study. Faith, Bettina, and Dahlia all completed a year-long secretarial course and are now working full-time and living at home. Christina, Elena, Isabel, Ana, and Maria (who is also taking classes) are also working full-time, and Julia, and possibly Lilian are in college. Oliva (who had a baby and dropped out of high school) and Pilar have moved, possibly out of the country.

Whereas all the girls say that they want at least to delay marriage or starting a family, some were adamant that they would never marry or have children. This was particularly true for the group of African American girls in the study, three-fourths of whom (six out of eight) specifically state at least once in their three interviews that they do *not* want any children. More than the other groups of girls in this study, the black girls also frequently report having responsibility for childcare, of siblings, nieces, or nephews, and many link this experience with their reasons for not wanting children.

Anita, for example, is resolute about not having children. Each year she says that she wants to be a lawyer, and each year she gives the same response to what might get in her way. In eighth grade: "Kids, kids, kids. Who wants them, who needs them." Asked why this would be a conflict for her, Anita is more specific: "Because you have to sit down and you have to feed them, breast feed them and you can't get out and you can't work. The kids are too little to go out . . . and I won't be able to work and you put your child on welfare. I wouldn't want a child on welfare, no way."

In ninth grade Anita is still firm about her future plans: "I ain't going to let nothing get in the way. The only thing that could probably happen is a baby . . . Yeah, I don't want no kids. I don't want no kids, no, uh uh." In tenth grade her response to what might get in the way is succinct: "If I ever got pregnant." In the same interview, Anita tells her interviewer that she is not using any form of contraception. A year after the study is completed Anita has a child and despite her insistence that she "wouldn't want a child on welfare, no way," she is on public assistance. Although she successfully negotiated transportation difficulties and childcare, which allowed her to attend school during the term, Anita dropped out at the end of eleventh grade. Her hopes of becoming a lawyer—she has taken an elective for students interested in law—or of high school graduation may in fact have been rendered impossible long before she became an adolescent mother: when Anita has her baby and joins a special program, educational tests reveal learning disabilities that were not diagnosed previously.

Tiffany, in eighth grade, makes a similar declaration: "I know I'm not going to have any kids." *No kids. How come?* "I hate little kids . . . They're brats." This is a strong statement for Tiffany, who otherwise provides her interviewer with polite, relatively unrevealing responses. Tiffany has one child in ninth grade and another in eleventh, by which time she has dropped out of school. In 1995, she has married the father of her children and moved to the state where her husband's family lives.

Ruby, while less adamant about it, cites her mother's experience and advice, as well as her own responsibilities for her siblings, as reasons why she does not want children: "Kids [would get in the way]. That's what my mother thinks." Asked later, *Do you think your mother is happy with her life?* Ruby says, "Maybe, but I think she could be happier, because she said she didn't want to have so many kids, because she was young." *How old was she when she had you?* "Sixteen." In ninth grade Ruby repeats the same idea: "I don't want kids. I have too many brothers and sisters. I will have all those nieces and nephews." Ruby describes her mother's life as "not great," and, listening to her speak of how her mother "didn't want" "so many kids" when she was "young," we remember that Ruby is the oldest, and thus the child "she said she didn't want" who presumably prevented her mother from being "happier." It is perhaps no surprise that Ruby wants no children—just like her mother.

For some girls, this inexorable move toward a future they say they do not want occurs in the context of an impossible choice: either to become a wife and/or mother overburdened with responsibility and lacking the time, money, assistance, or opportunity for other pursuits—what girls termed "no future"—or to be "successful" and have a career and probably be alone. Ruby reflects this choice when she speaks about society's images of the ideal woman. When asked in ninth grade, *What do you suppose are society's ideas of what an ideal woman is like?* Ruby observes: "I think a housewife. I don't know, two kids, three kids. Husband working, you staying home and cleaning and cooking, you can do that. That's how I think they think it. Unless you want to be a sophisticated lady . . . you know, the briefcase, comes in the house, puts her stuff down." Asked what *her* idea of the ideal woman is, Ruby responds, "Probably the sophisticated type, living on her own, nobody depending on her . . . Yeah, an independent woman," which means, Ruby says, "Doing everything for herself, working. Putting things in the house, buying her own food and stuff, and be a person like that."

Ruby recognizes two ideals of womanhood held by the dominant culture—one the traditional "housewife," the other a more recent construction, the "sophisticated" woman. The latter was described by many of the girls in the Emma Willard Study, 40 percent of whom responded to the "ideal woman" question with an uncritical description of the "Super Woman" (Steiner-Adair, 1990). The Emma Willard girls not only mentioned the new cultural ideal of the "independent and autonomously successful Super Woman"—complete with briefcase—they identified with this image as *their* ideal. As Catherine Steiner-Adair notes, "the primary quality that makes the Super Woman superior is her total independence from people" (p. 171). The Super Woman is, in effect, a woman without relationships, much like the woman Ruby describes.

The idealized images that Ruby speaks about present her with an impossible choice. If she wants close relationships, she may fall into the "housewife" option. Ruby has observed that her mother, whom she describes as a housewife, has a life that is "not great," and Ruby wants something different for herself: "Yeah . . . I don't know, I think her life's not great. I mean, put it this way, right now, I don't think she ended up, well, she always wanted me to be different than her anyways, so she doesn't know I want to be different though." The interviewer asks why her mother does not know that Ruby wants to be different, adding, *because you don't talk about it?* Aware of the potential for hurt, Ruby responds, "No, I am not going to tell her, 'I want to be different. I hate the way you live.' No."

Yet for Ruby to choose the "sophisticated type," she must imagine herself to be "living on her own" and "doing everything for herself." Not only does Ruby's performance in school reduce her chances of having a career and supporting herself, but the Super Woman vision of success—which means no relationships—does not fit with other evidence of what she seems to want. As Steiner-Adair found, the predominantly white, middle- and upper-middle-class girls from Emma Willard who took on the ideal of the Super Woman were those who scored in the eating-disordered or anorexic-like range on diagnostic measures, whereas those who rejected or critiqued this ideal did not. Steiner-Adair referred to this as the "body politic"—a way of "tell[ing] their story with their bodies" (p. 176). The story is one of facing an impossible ideal, one that requires disconnection from self and others. Perhaps from a different vantage point, Ruby is telling her story with her body: pregnancy may, in part, be the story of her own rejection of the "ideal" and of her desire for relationship.

In her study of black teenage mothers living in Boston, Constance Williams proposes, as have many researchers working with adolescent mothers, that "becoming a mother as an adolescent represents the repetition of a familiar cultural pattern" (1991, p. 58). Williams explains that "these daughters are not socialized in the sense that their mothers explicitly told them to get pregnant or not to marry, but if one considers the socialization process as occurring through implicit as well as explicit messages—or do as I do, not as I say—these teens are indeed socialized to motherhood" (p. 127). The adolescent mothers in Williams's study, speaking from within their social identity of mother, use their experience in looking after younger siblings, nieces, and nephews as preparation for motherhood, proof of their suitability for their new role.

Tanya, like Ruby, is the oldest in a large family and speaks of having to care for her younger siblings. Tanya makes a direct tie between this experience and her resolve in tenth grade to remain "single": "When it comes to kids, I've had my fill with my sister and my two brothers and that's enough kids to last me for my life, you know." Although she graduates from high school and does not have a child, in ninth grade she nonetheless voices a vague foreboding:

> It's not just one thing that I imagine, it's like a whole bunch of different things. And I don't know which one to pick . . . If you just like are thinking about what's going to happen in your future, in your life and then all these things are going through your head . . . and if there's one bad thing and the rest are good, you just stop on the bad thing. And you think about it and

> you try to push it out of your mind and then like you just go back to it and think that because you pushed it away, that will happen in your life . . . It's like when I grow up, do I want to get married, or do I want to have kids, because I don't want to have any children. I mean I have enough like brothers and sisters to worry about now and I don't plan on having any kids or anything, like thinking about getting married . . . I imagine myself like, I don't know, like I imagine myself like with a good job and single but then being married with children just comes into my head and just takes over, and erases being single with a job.

Tanya is aware that her life may not turn out as she hopes and that "it" will happen despite her wishes to the contrary. Like Ruby, Tanya describes an either/or situation: either relationships or "being single with a job." That poor and working-class girls see a dichotomy between work and family should come as no surprise, given the lack of childcare, transportation, and emotional support for poor women who work and are either solely or partially responsible for raising a family (see Children's Defense Fund, 1994; Gordon, 1990; Polakow, 1993).

In eighth grade Valerie says she wants to go to college and major in business; she also plans on "no kids, no husband." In tenth grade she hopes "that I'll be successful in whatever I decide to do" and that, "in today's world, success means making a lot of money." She still wants to go to college but her worry that she will not have the money leads her to be less sure that this will happen. Valerie has not thus far continued her education after high school and works full-time with children in a school. Pauline and Rochelle, whose plans also included college, withdrew during their first year because of financial difficulties. Diana, who worked for a year before enrolling, is now in college. We were unable to locate Tanya after her high school graduation.

Like girls from the other racial and ethnic groups in the Understanding Adolescence Study, the white girls speak about work first, then marriage and family. Sounding like the white working-class girls Lois Weis describes in Working Class without Work (1990), they also reject the "domestic code" in favor of paid labor. Yet four of the six white girls voice a consistent desire to have a family, and none states explicitly that she does not want children. Only Carla says that marriage might get in the way if it preceded her attempt to start up a business, but she voices this concern only in ninth grade: "I might get married before I have done this . . . [the conflict would be] that I wanted to make something of my life and then I didn't." Carla, whose strategy for resisting pressure to make decisions about sexual activity was to delay going out, also described a close relationship with her mother and a good relationship with another woman that is "almost like a mother-daughter thing." She is now a student at a four-year college. Donna is attending a two-year college, and like the majority of college students in the nation, both are working part-time. Mary, who "made this pact—eighteen years old, I graduate from high school, and I'm moving out of my house," has not returned to school or a GED (high school equivalency) program. She is working in a retail store and living, not at home, but with a younger relative who has a baby. Barbara, who thought it "would be fun, to argue a case and win" as a lawyer, is working as a secretary after completing a year-long course. Joan is working locally. Sandy lives in an apartment near her parents' house. Her desire for a baby, "something of mine, like, that loves another person," was not enough to help her know how to take care of her child, who failed to thrive and for a time was under the care of social services. Her word, "something," perhaps signaled that she did not realize the relational needs of a baby. Subsequently reunited with her child, she is living with her boyfriend and working for a human services organization.

Power and Pleasure: Resisting Stereotypes

When describing their possible futures, a small number of adolescent girls in the study voice a desire for a sense of power and pleasure in their work. Julia, who is Portuguese, responds with enthusiasm and confidence when asked in tenth grade what she imagines for her future. Her plans reflect a healthy critical perspective of stereotypes that would limit her choice of career goals: "I want something like adventurous, like something out of, really psychic, something I really like, like travel and stuff where I get to go to all those nice places. I think it's so cool, you know. I imagine myself flying on TWA." Asked what might get in her way, Julia says, "It's people, they say girls, they don't fly, you know. They're so, huh, like you shouldn't, girls don't join the air force, you know. It's like, they kind of think guys are more than girls. I don't think that. I go against that 100 percent, I think I can be anyone I want. And no one is stopping me. I just go off for what I dream for and if I really try hard, maybe I'll do it." Julia says the "they" to whom she refers include "the boys, they are construction workers, [they say] you get your hands dirty, I'm like so, just because you like it, because I know this girl, she became a construction worker, and she likes it. And the guys are like, 'Oh my god, she's a construction worker,' and she's like, 'Is there a problem with you?' And she tells them off really bad and she, but she loves her work because it's so much fun . . . She's really strong and stuff . . . They say girls are stuck being a teacher or being a secretary. I don't think that. It's so boring. I want to become like something really cool."

Julia, resisting stereotypes "100 percent" and envisioning unconventional possibilities for herself, is supported in her resistance and her knowledge by the presence of a woman who has successfully followed a nontraditional path, a woman who "loves her work" and who is physically and personally "really strong." Three years after her high school graduation, Julia continues to challenge convention and is pursuing a science degree at a women's college.

Several other girls also speak about wanting power, a desire that women in general are not encouraged to voice and one that poor or working-class girls are not expected to achieve. Bettina and Barbara, for example, who have both completed secretarial school and now work full-time, talk about achieving success and power in their work. What Bettina imagines for her future is "progress. Power. Yeah, I think so, because I want to be very successful . . . Success, I want to make, I want to make a good living. I want to earn enough money for my family, for me. I want to develop in a company, something like that, if I am a secretary or something like that, keep on going up, higher rank. Some day to be president of that company or something." Like Julia, Bettina's wish is also for work that brings her pleasure, hoping that "I would enjoy it and look forward to it every day." Barbara responds to being asked to imagine her future in a single word: "Successful." She antici-

pates her enjoyment of feelings of power and success—of "winning"—
when she describes why she wants to be a lawyer: "You can prove your
point to people, you know, put them on the spot. You know, like get
them to say something like real important and you can win the case or
something. I don't know. You know, like winning a case is fun, you
know. It's good."

Julia, Bettina, and Barbara have translated their hopes for success into
acquiring the education and training to pursue potentially fulfilling careers or to obtain jobs that offer the possibility of advancement. Although
they may not become pilots, company presidents, or lawyers, their resistance to limiting images and expectations nevertheless seems to have
served them well. But the belief, as Julia declared, that "I can be anyone
I want" can also be a dangerous one if it is not informed by a realistic
appraisal of academic history, preparation, and ability, as well as an
awareness of opportunities in the job market and obstacles that may be
specific to class, race, or gender. Girls' high aspirations and resistance to
stereotypes must be rooted in reality if they are not to set themselves up
for disappointment and failure. For some of the girls in this study, the
dream of a professional job, graduate education, and financial success
they share with girls from more privileged educational or social backgrounds is especially disheartening because of the realities of their high
school struggles and their lack of social, economic, and educational support. And although most girls in the study express justified concern
about the obstacles family responsibilities might present, we hear little
evidence, except among the few who are concerned about grades or
money for college, of an awareness of the kinds of funds, connections,
information, and preparation that are required to adequately plan for
their future.

Women Teaching Girls, Girls Teaching Women

The Women and Race retreats and the Women Teaching Girls, Girls
Teaching Women retreats initiated explorations of how women could
join with girls and with each other, especially of how to do so across
significant social differences such as race, ethnicity, and class. Because

they are a beginning, the retreats are best discussed in terms of process rather than outcomes; however, a number of actions and important insights did result from these meetings.

When asked about relationships that were important to them, the girls in the Understanding Adolescence Study did not mention teachers in high school yet they persisted in voicing a desire for connection with teachers. The teachers in the Women Teaching Girls, Girls Teaching Women retreats expressed a similar desire for more sustained and meaningful connections with girls. They were also frustrated at what seemed a pervasive sense of isolation—the difficulty of maintaining close, collegial relationships with other teachers in a public school system that seemed to move teachers around capriciously, and also a sense of distance from the girls who were their students. For the teachers, connections with women colleagues felt essential if they were to listen and respond effectively to girls—if they were to invest themselves in teaching girls. Continuing a conversation that began in the Women and Race retreats, the women in the Women Teaching Girls, Girls Teaching Women retreats found that in asking themselves and each other how they could make or strengthen connections with girls, they confirmed the necessity of strengthening their connections with themselves—their own convictions about what it was important for girls to learn and know—as well as with each other. For some, their practice began to change.

As they became more attuned to girls' voices and presence, and to the diverse strengths and needs of the girls with whom they worked, the women began to invent ways of strengthening their connections with girls in order to teach them and learn from them. One principal formed a weekly breakfast group for girls who were struggling academically. A social studies teacher stopped herself from cutting short a lesson on women's history in response to the restlessness and criticism of the boys in the class. Another teacher helped her students organize and change the activities in their gym class, thus teaching what, in tenth grade, Barbara said she wanted to learn: "how to fight back in the world" constructively and effectively. One of the counselors started an ongoing girls' group. Listening to girls who, as one girl in the study said, want teachers to "teach things that are real meaningful," the teachers often found that what was meaningful to their students was meaningful to them. To respond to the girls, they often had to undo dissociative processes in themselves that had led them to dismiss their own interests and knowledge as trivial or parenthetical or irrelevant. Here, the retreat process provided an essential context for the kind of self-reflection and relationships that would support women in becoming more present and more alive in their teaching—the qualities that adolescents most respond to and value. The process women began here—of becoming more connected with one another and more reflective about their own practice in teaching girls; and more curious about girls, more attentive to their voices and questions, better able to listen to and hear the range of their voices, more open to learning from girls and gaining courage through relationships with them—continued after the weekend meetings had ended.

Framing and Formulating Policy

An immediate danger in articulating policy implications is the ease in which a subtle but deeply undermining shift can occur when the focus turns to creating policies and programs that benefit girls. If considerations of policy focus on girls but lose connection with girls' voices, or if policy discussions define problems only in terms of "girls' needs" and neglect girls' strengths or the need for change on the part of adults and the educational or social system, then we arrive again at new ways to "help" girls, new ways to reinforce dissociation and disconnection, new ways to reimpose, consciously or unconsciously, old labels of "victim."

The process of our research suggests some ways to counter this shift. Foremost is the inclusion of the voices of girls in the development of programs intended for their benefit. Too often girls are talked about and talked at, but rarely are they spoken to or listened to: as one of the girls in the study said, "[people] just don't ask what we think." If girls' voices do not centrally inform the direction of policy and programs, their needs are likely to be misconstrued and their strength and resilience ignored or lost. Another significant factor is an awareness of the consequences girls have encountered in telling what they know: what gets them into trouble is "my big mouth." Those attempting to find out from girls "what we think," therefore, must pay particular attention to "who is listening" and how they are listening, so that girls have a resonant and safe space in which they can speak and be heard. From a practical standpoint, including girls in planning and implementation can ensure that programs and policies are feasible and relevant for girls from diverse racial and ethnic backgrounds and from working-class or poor backgrounds. Such programs are also more likely to be effective: being a part of creating policy or programs is very different from being the "beneficiary" or "recipient" of one. The latter are designations girls are sure to recognize and likely to resist.

To include girls' voices requires learning to listen to them, but it also requires recognizing adult resistance to doing so. Some difficulties in listening are a result of limited understanding of different cultural and class experiences and of the meaning of class and culture in girls' relationships, education, family life, and future opportunities. Resistance can also arise when girls ask questions that challenge adults' own beliefs and survival strategies: as Kesho Yvonne Scott says of her daughters' question about the possibility of a different future (1991, p. 189), "[It] blows my mind . . . makes me feel tense, upside down." Listening is difficult when girls say what adults do not want to hear or believe. Listening to Diana, for example, requires hearing a soft-spoken but tough-minded critique: "Some of the teachers . . . are just standing up saying things and . . . the class doesn't really understand them . . . They are not really saying anything that means anything." Connecting students' engagement—or lack of it—with that of their teachers, she adds, "If the teachers slack off, the students slack off." Diana's comments are difficult to dismiss when set alongside research on textbooks, for example—still the staple of many teachers' classroom time and reading and homework assignments—which finds that they are for the most part "bland, inaccurate, and unlikely to help students learn to think," written not to offend, but not to educate either (Webb, 1995, p. 1). The sociologist James Loewen also backs up Diana's complaint, citing research findings that "92 percent of teachers are unwilling to initiate discussion of controversial issues." " 'Among the topics that teachers felt children were interested in but that most teachers believed should not be discussed in the classroom,' " Loewen says, " 'were politics, race relations . . . and family problems such as divorce' " (Webb, p. 2). If teaching that "means anything" includes controversial topics, then Diana's critique is likely to meet considerable resistance.

Girls whose voices are socially marginalized because of their class, race, ethnic background, or sexual orientation may also be more difficult to listen to than other girls because they are often more willing and able to speak painful or difficult truths. Whereas most girls in the Laurel School Study felt reluctant to portray themselves, their school, or their families as less than the ideal or other than they "should" be, many of the girls in the Understanding Adolescence Study evidence little hesitation in acknowledging the presence, in these areas of their lives, of anger, betrayal, sexual desire, unfairness, wanting power—all the thoughts, feelings, and experiences that girls are expected to cover over or deny. In the Understanding Adolescence Study, for example, Barbara says that although she is aware that the "ideal mother" is "the 'Leave It to Beaver' " mother who is "all perky and all that . . . happy when anything is wrong and she always has the answer for everything," she also knows that "That's not true, though. That's on a show." She describes her relationship with her own mother as close, and this includes fighting as well as "getting along good."

Likewise, the girls in the Understanding Adolescence Study do not speak of experiencing the same social pressure or obligation to cover over painful realities at school as do students at the Laurel School. Mary, like many other girls in the study, makes no pretense about the existence of rumors, gossip, and racial tension among students. After describing a particularly distressing incident, she says, "There's tons of that stuff going on in school," adding that students often treat each other "unfair. Very unfair." This differs from Laurel girls' understatements of what seem to be very similar social experiences: thirteen-year-old Niti, for example, gives a nod to the existence of rumors and gossip but conforms to her rule "I have to be nice" when saying so: "Nobody's mean from where I stand, but there are people who have hurt feelings." Brown and Gilligan write that, "in this world of perfectly nice girls which [Niti] aspires to fit into, everyone—as she knows, including herself—'is talking behind people's backs' " (1992, p. 201). The girls in the Laurel School Study may have been more at risk for covering over these realities because, in Audre Lorde's words, it may be easier for them "to believe the dangerous fantasy that if you are good enough . . . quiet enough . . . then you will be allowed to co-exist with patriarchy in relative peace" (1984a p. 119). No such promises are likely to be made to the girls in the Understanding Adolescence Study.

From our research process we find that there are ways of learning to listen. These are specified in the Listening Guide, which, with an interpretive community, offers a method for developing the practice of listening. For example, the first listening to a girl's narrative and the listener's response highlight the content of what the girl is saying, whom she is talking about, where it is happening, and what the listener might expect to be said that is not. It includes other aspects of the listener's response to the narrative—her sense of connection and disconnection, similarities and dissimilarities in experience, and how broad social factors, such as race, ethnicity, class, sexuality, and gender, may shape her understanding of the narrative and her reaction to what she is hearing. The second listening closely follows the voice of the narrator and how she represents herself in relation to what she is saying, where she is actively present and where she is absent, where she enters the conversation and where she disappears from it, and her own commentary on the story she is telling. Attending to the girl's narrative and her listener's response and listening closely to the girl's experience of herself in relation to what she is voicing make room for difference and maintain the importance of girls' experience in their own words. These listenings also attend to what is spoken or remains unspoken, whether this changes over time, and how the interaction between the listener and speaker may affect what is voiced and what remains unvoiced.

The third and fourth listenings allow for a deeper and more complex understanding, so that, for example, the sense of self-confidence Ruby projects does not drown out evidence of her increasing sense of isolation. Her tenth-grade description of herself as "self-confident . . . I seem like I know what I want" might otherwise obscure important information about her distress and impending school failure: "I'm worried about it. [The teachers] don't know that, though," and "I know I could do better. For some reason . . . I just give up altogether . . . I have no choice really, I'm going down." Listening for distress and loss also underscores the need for continuity in order to hear, for example, Ruby's shift from eighth grade, when it feels good to "know you're wanted" and can go to "lots of people" with problems, to tenth grade, when "I just try to stay to myself," "I really don't talk to nobody," and "I don't care."

Bettina's hopes for a future of "progress . . . power . . . success" can be recognized as healthy resistance to conventions that define desiring or achieving power or success as inappropriate for or forbidden to women. This healthy resistance can be supported and reinforced by a responsive listener; it can also be diminished if, as Bettina says, "you tell somebody your ideas, [and they are] like, 'Oh, that's stupid,' put you down. And then you'd be like, 'Oh, I don't want to do this anymore.' "

Finally, connection with other women—in our research, the interpretive community—can widen women's understanding of the diversity of girls' experience. As the retreats showed, this is not a simple process; women must be prepared for resistance to speaking and listening and know that relationship and understanding are not achieved in a few weekends, but are part of a long-term, ongoing practice. In the Women and Race retreats the participants discussed how "it often takes just one person" to make a difference to girls, a woman who is willing to listen and let girls know that they are not alone in what they feel or think or do. In a larger sense, however, it takes many others, women and men, to connect with girls at different points along the way, to provide a sense of continuity and public support, to offer girls opportunities to learn from multiple perspectives, and to create the necessary critical mass to address what girls voice as crucial needs and issues. When asked what might help her in the future, Isabel says simply, "Just be behind me at every step, you know. Just be there with me, I think it would help a lot." Valerie's wish while she is in high school is to "just feel like there is someone out there that's really paying attention to me." For girls to feel that adults are "there with them" and "really paying attention" requires the involvement of many adults, in the educational system and in the larger community.[2] As the Understanding Adolescence Study has shown, political resistance cannot be sustained alone without great psychological and social cost—and this is as true for women as it is for girls.

Implications for policy, then, all point to ways of strengthening or creating connections: between girls and women; among women, among teachers, between girls' present goals and realistic future opportunities. Although specific policy formulations must remain in the hands of those responsible for their implementation, whose understanding of their community or school system make them most appropriate for this task, we can point to a few key areas for intervention and prevention. We stress in particular the response of adult women, not because we think women are solely responsible but because so often they are the adults girls speak about. At the same time, men can and do play a positive role and share the responsibilities and benefits of supporting girls' education and healthy development.

Eighth grade may be an optimal point for intervention and prevention because it is a time when girls' strengths are clearly in evidence. In eighth grade, in the sentence completion task, for example, Ana writes that being with other people "makes me feel alive. I do not feel left out or alone." Many girls at this time may feel their own resilience and vitality while not having yet experienced the need to conceal their strengths or desire for relationship, to disappear in relationships, or to become strong by being independent. Joining and encouraging eighth-grade (as well as younger) girls—their relational strengths, their sense of connection with school, and their hopeful outlook for the future—may make it more likely that girls will enter high school with sufficient inner resources to carry them through the changes ahead. In eighth grade some girls also mention men teachers to whom they feel they can turn, and this may be a particularly important time for men to play a positive role.

It is during the early high school years when many of the girls in our study begin to silence themselves, when they experience frequent losses or betrayals in relationships, when they begin to experience their voice as "my big mouth." For many girls the move into high school is often attended by a move into psychological isolation: they become disconnected on some important levels from their own feelings and desires and from relationships with others, and they find ways to protect themselves by "staying to myself," "not talking to anybody," "keeping my feelings bottled up," and "not caring." Whether this move is a response to repeated betrayals by peers or adults, or whether it is what they understand maturity or good womanhood to be, the result is the same. Girls can maintain a public silence or remain outspoken; either way, if they feel that "no one listens" or that "you really can't trust anybody," they are likely to find that they are disconnected from themselves and from others and "not really tell anybody anything." During this time critical questions begin to arise: about whether or not to stay in school, which Mary defines as "making a life" or "having no future"; about sexuality and sexual activity, possible pregnancy and future relationships; about how to manage school and afterschool jobs or family responsibilities.

During the transition from elementary school to high school, girls also describe a sense of being unmoored, lost in the shuffle from one classroom to the next and missing the teachers whom they knew and who knew them "all through the years." In ninth grade, Valerie notes that "When you are in grammar school, you've got, the teacher is always watching you. And you feel like a little kid. And then just when you come up here you feel so, I don't know, unwanted." A move from childhood to adolescence that is accompanied by a shift from constant supervision to feeling "unwanted" only makes sense in a world where maturity or adulthood means being completely on one's own. It does not make sense to the girls in the study. Girls also speak of not having a voice in the school, of learning that "you cannot argue" with teachers or others in authority, and of not expecting already overburdened teachers and counselors to "have enough time to pay attention to one student, because there are an awful lot of others."

Policies and programs can respond to these experiences of isolation and disconnection in a number of ways—at the level of school structure, in individual classrooms, and through activities and organizations both in and out of school. Whatever their specific form, attempts to prevent or attenuate these losses in high school should begin in the ninth grade and continue throughout the high school years. Continuity with adults—what girls said they experienced in elementary school and missed in high school—seems to be key and includes the involvement of teachers, counselors, and school administrators as well as other adults from the community. Adults should not hold out promises of relationship to girls, however, if they will be unable to keep them. When girls have already had so much experience of feeling disappointed, abandoned, or betrayed, such pledges hold more promise of harm than good. Because many girls have learned to distrust others, adults should also be prepared for and be willing to weather their initial resistance to attempts to make connections. And women who decide to join with girls at this time need to be aware of the implications of doing so, and be prepared to face along with girls some of the more difficult and disheartening realities of their lives.

Educators can also find ways for students to be able to bring themselves—their thoughts, feelings, and experiences—more fully into their classrooms and classwork. Mary, who "used to be a good writer," says she lost her connection with her writing after she dropped out of school for a time. She returned with a new resolve to conform to school rules but also with new fears. "[My stories] don't feel the same," she says in tenth grade. "I look at a piece of paper, it's like this: Blank . . . I think of nothing." She could still write good stories, Mary says, if she were given the opportunity to write about her feelings instead of trying to fulfill the teacher's assignments. But she also says that, unlike the previous year, "if people reading [my stories] didn't like them, I think I'd die." Mary shared her fears with her teacher, but she "didn't comment. She didn't tell me what she thought." For educators to support Mary's writing—or Oliva's poetry, or any of the other girls' nascent or flourishing creativity and connection to their feelings—requires the awareness that an intense vulnerability often accompanies the desire for self-expression. Girls may be better able to sustain the tension and ambivalence generated by these feelings if teachers themselves can accept and respond to their own feelings of vulnerability.

Girls' hopes for their future suggest that relationship is as important for their career development and future plans as it is for their healthy social, emotional, sexual, and intellectual development. This is hardly surprising, for "networking" has long been a catchword in educational and career opportunity and advancement. What is troubling in this study is the discrepancy, for many girls, between their plans for the future and the probable reality ahead. Like the girl from the Emma Willard School who told Carol that she planned first to become a "big success" and later—at twenty-six—to marry and have children (Gilligan, Lyons, and Hanmer, 1990), many girls in this study describe plans that are probably unreachable. Unrealistic plans may be among the hallmarks of adolescence and in themselves present little cause for alarm. But unlike the girls in the Emma Willard School, the girls in the Understanding Adolescence Study are, by virtue of their academic status and "social location," already at the margins in school or in the larger world. They have little room for error and few resources to help them make up for inadequate planning. These girls do not need greater aspirations; what they need are more opportunities, more connections, and more information to allow them to explore their interests and plan ahead.

The kind of intervention this suggests is not simply more career counseling or more career days at school, however beneficial these may be. It also suggests ongoing opportunities for connection with women who work in many different industries, in jobs that do not require a college education as well as those that do. Learning from the experience of women with working-class and poor backgrounds, including those who have continued their education beyond high school or have entered professions dominated by the middle class, would also be invaluable. A number of girls in the study also mentioned their desire for moral support, for someone who would say to them, " 'Go on, you can do it,' if I'm ready to give up." Given the likelihood that many adults have already given up on them because of their "at-risk" status, this kind of positive support could have a tremendous impact. In addition, girls need adults who can help them make realistic assessments of their existing level of preparation and ability. For some, this may mean confronting difficult realities; for others, it may mean uncovering previously overlooked or neglected talent. Either way, such ongoing efforts offer the best possibilities for girls to achieve a worklife that brings them a sense of both power and pleasure.

When girls talk about their futures, they also say that early marriage and children might "mess me up" or "wreck my future." The fathers of the babies born to adolescent mothers are often several years older than the mothers, and many do not assume the financial and emotional responsibilities associated with parenthood. Continuing to advocate for health and sexuality education is critical, but it is also vitally important to recognize that more information in classroom settings will not reach young men who are not in school. Different ways of speaking about sexuality—of answering girls' questions, of including pleasure as well as the realities of sexually transmitted diseases, AIDS, pregnancy, sexual abuse and exploitation, and of acknowledging racial and ethnic beliefs and values—are needed. To this end, adult women who can be responsive, resonant listeners willing to speak with girls in a straightforward, honest way may be girls' most important resources.

Girls' realistic assessment that "kids might get in the way" has to be heard in the context of the serious discrepancies that exist between the number of daycare slots available and those that are needed. Reports confirm what most people know: poor children are most likely to end up in poor daycare. Head Start is obviously an exception, but this program is not available to all families who meet the criteria for participation.

Important for all girls are relationships in which they can safely ask questions and express their interests and concerns about sexuality. Being able to speak about the realities of sexual pleasure and danger may better enable girls to make thoughtful decisions about their sexual activity, provide opportunities for healing from experiences of trauma, and reduce the isolation that makes it possible for abusive behavior to occur or continue. Reports confirming sexual abuse in the lives of many girls who become mothers in their early and middle teens underscore the need for adolescent girls to be able to speak safely about their experiences.

Finally, it is important to note the girls in this study who, although said to be at risk, continue to do well several years after graduating from high school. Their experience suggests essential resources: strong connections with others, including mothers, other family members, or friends, in which they can speak about the range of their experience and feelings and trust that they will be heard; relationships with women other than their mothers in which they not only feel valued and understood but also that they make a difference to women; a healthy critical perspective toward expectations or stereotypes, one that is supported and encouraged by others, again, often other women. These strengths and their persistence in some girls suggest that they need not be lost or diminished in so many others.

Talking (and Not Talking) about Sexuality: Where Are the Men?

Five of the twenty-six girls in the Understanding Adolescence Study became mothers as adolescents and dropped out of high school. Because they became pregnant after the study was over, we know little about the circumstances. To our knowledge, none of the girls who had a child returned to high school or obtained a GED. Tiffany, who had two children when she was of high school age, married the father. The fathers of the babies born to at least two of the girls, Oliva and Ruby, were older than the girls by several years or more. Sandy, we suspect, experienced physical and perhaps sexual abuse.

To talk only about "teenage pregnancy" and "teen motherhood" is often a way of not talking about sexuality. This language, which has dominated public discourse, perpetuates girls' "high visibility but almost total lack of voice" (Wallace, 1990, p. 5), because their voice reveals the participation of men and boys and to an alarming extent girls' experience of exploitation and abuse. "Teen pregnancy" and "teen motherhood" can readily become euphemisms for statutory rape and the sexual abuse of adolescent girls by adult men.

A California survey in which teenage girls were interviewed found that, of 47,000 births to teenage mothers in 1993, "two-thirds of the babies were fathered by men who were of post-high-school age." Listening to girls reveals the high rate of involvement of adult men in teenage pregnancy: "With high school girls, fathers tended to be an average of 4.2 years older than their partners, and with mothers in junior high school, they were on average 6.7 years older." The term "teenage pregnancy" masks the substantial difference in power that characterizes these relationships: "Among California mothers ages 11 to 15, only 9 percent of their partners were other junior high school boys. Forty percent of the fathers were high school boys, and 51 percent were adults" (Steinhauer,

1995). Finally, the term "teenage pregnancy" carries no intimation of what is becoming increasingly evident to experts in family planning and sexual abuse: namely, that "in many cases of teen-age pregnancy, the girl had been sexually assaulted either by the father of her child or by someone else previously." More specifically, "in Chicago, the An Ounce of Prevention Program, a social-services agency, found that 61 percent of 445 young mothers interviewed in 1986 said they had been sexually abused, beginning at an average age of 11. Similarly, the Washington Alliance Concerned with School Age Parents, a pregnancy-prevention program based in Seattle, found in a statewide survey of 535 mothers ages 12 to 17 that the average age of the father was 24 and that 68 percent of those girls said they had been sexually abused at one point." Commenting on these findings, Charlie Langdon, the executive director of the Washington organization said: "When an adult male gets a girl pregnant, it's like an immaculate conception" (Steinhauer, 1995). Rather than listening to girls who become pregnant, taking them seriously, and responding to difficult truths about teenage pregnancy, which include sexual assault and statutory rape, and rather than facing other factors associated with girls' becoming mothers—diminishing opportunities for meaningful work that provides a living wage, the failure of commitment to the education of all girls—it may be easier to continue to allow girls alone to bear the responsibility and blame for their situation and to use the "at-risk" label to diminish or discredit the importance of what they are saying.

*   *   *

Girls in the study live in a territory between voice and silence: If they continue to speak from their experience they may find that their voice is out of relationship, too loud, off key. If they remain silent they are in immediate danger of disappearing.

In the end, what we came to understand was that, although these girls *are* at risk—for dropping out, for becoming pregnant, for getting into trouble by speaking out, or for falling silent—there is also risk in girls' continued healthy development. That risk is the risk of change. To listen to girls whose voices are ordinarily met with silence in the larger world is to invite disruption, disturbance, or dissolution of the status quo. To support the strengths, intelligence, resilience, and knowledge of girls whose culture or class is marginalized by society is to support political, social, educational, and economic change. It may be easier to sacrifice girls than to support their development, and when girls sense this, it may be hard for them, with the best of intentions, not to give up on themselves and sacrifice their own hopes.

Epilogue

In Fumiko Enchi's novel *The Waiting Years,* Tomo, a woman born into a low-ranking samurai family, has married early and had no chance to acquire "either a proper education or the usual social accomplishments of the well-bred young woman." Tomo's husband, Yukitomo, an important figure, asks her to help him by going to Tokyo and finding him a young girl. The girl must be "aged somewhere between fifteen and, say, seventeen or eighteen. From a respectable family, if possible . . . but she must be good-looking" (p. 13). People come to expect this, he explains.

Tomo sets out to find a girl who is young and beautiful and innocent. When she finds fifteen-year-old Suga, she is torn in her response to this girl who "was in fact still half a child." She wondered "in what way this immature girl would be broken in, how she would be transformed, once they took her to their home and delivered her into the practised hands of [Yukitomo]," and at the same time "unconsciously she closed her eyes and held her breath, only to see a vision of her husband and Suga with limbs intertwined that brought the blood rushing to her head and made her open her eyes wide again as though to dispel a nightmare." The girl she had chosen, the girl whose innocence and beauty had so moved her, would become the woman who would replace her.

At the end of the novel, Tomo, now old and ill, tries to raise her head from the pillow, intending to sit up and speak to her husband. Watching him steadily, she looks at him for the first time with "a direct and unwavering gaze. The approach of death had set Tomo free." One

205

night in February when the end is near, her daughter-in-law and niece keep watch at her bedside. Tomo turns to them and showing "naked feeling" almost for the first time, "spoke without a break": she wants them to tell Yukitomo, her husband, that when she dies, she wants no funeral: " 'Tell him that all he need do is to take my body out to sea at Shinagawa and dump it into the water . . .' Her eyes were alive and shining with excitement. Their gaze brimmed with feeling of such intensity that they were scarcely recognizable as the placid, leaden-hued eyes that normally looked out from under the heavily drooping lids" (p. 201). Urgently then, she repeats her message to the young women: " 'Tell him to dump my body in the sea.. Dump it————' " Encouraged by the sound of the word "dump," "she seemed to utter it with a kind of pleasure" (p. 202).

The younger women step out into the corridor. "In the glance they exchanged as they stood facing each other lay the unspoken feminine complicity of the two women who had been married and suffered themselves." One asks, "What do you think? Should we tell him?" The other replies, "I think we should, seeing how badly she wants us to." Both "felt a vague dread at the idea of having to shut away inside themselves the accumulation of emotion that Tomo had kept pent up in herself for so long."

When Toyoko, Tomo's niece, delivers the message to Yukitomo, "she had meant to present it as the delirious nonsense of a sick woman, but when she spoke her voice came out serious and shrill, as though Tomo's spirit had taken possession of her."

> The veil cleared instantly from Yukitomo's eyes. The old man's mouth opened as though to say something, then his expression went blank. In the newly bathed, watery eyes, fear stirred as though he had seen a ghost. The next moment, the unnatural effort of the muscles to restore a natural expression wrought havoc with the regular features of his face.
>
> "I could never permit anything so foolish. She will be buried in proper style from this residence. Tell her that, please."
>
> He spoke rapidly in a reproving tone, then turned aside and blew his nose vigorously. His body had suffered the full force of the emotions that his wife had struggled to repress for forty years past. The shock was enough to split his arrogant ego in two. (p. 203)

The greater valuing of silence in Asian culture and among the indigenous peoples in the Americas places a clear cultural frame around our discussion of voice. Tomo's break into voice is a cultural transgression. Her saying that she wants no funeral—no cultural ritual when she dies—reveals a complicated intersection between voice and silence, gender and culture. Appreciation of the value of silence comes into cultural tension with the realization that some silences between women and girls, between younger and older women, and between women and men are part of the internal architecture of patriarchy.

The Understanding Adolescence Study and the Women and Race retreats took place in the midst of growing tension and silences between women across race and class in the United States. In combining a psychological study of girls' development with a series of retreats on race and relationship, our hope was that the connection with girls would turn women's attention from the past to the future, and by doing so highlight the possibility of change in the face of past suffering and betrayal. At the bottom of this effort lay the old question: *Cui bono?* Whose good have the divisions among women served? It was our belief that these divisions did not serve the interests of girls.

In the name of girls, then, we went out to listen to girls whose voices have not informed psychologists' theories of human development, believing that their experience was essential for understanding the human world. We then asked women to come together to explore relationship in the face of differences that are psychologically and politically significant. The interests of patriarchy are clearly served by intensifying divisions among women; might women act in concert on behalf of girls to bring an end to a patriarchal society and culture?

It is repeatedly observed that women living within a patriarchal civilization are in a position to act as a vanguard in the process of societal and cultural transformation, because women are at once inside and outside the class system, because women are increasingly inside as well as outside of the various societal institutions that preserve and transmit culture across generations, because women have such a direct hand in raising and educating the next generation. Jean Baker Miller (1976) observed that women may hold a key to understanding the psychological order, because women are at once subordinated by men and at the same time intricately involved with men in the intimate sexual and familial relationships that form the crucible in which the human psyche develops.

Listening to girls who are more on the edges of a dominant patriarchal society by virtue of race, class, and cultural difference, we found their voices deeply informative; essential to composing a psychology of women and girls that is not imprisoned by the invisible racial blinder of whiteness, or by economic and political advantage, or by sexual and familial access to powerful men. Listening to girls of color, girls from different cultures, girls from families that are economically pressed, we heard relationships between girls and women, and also relationships among girls and women, described from different angles and reflecting different psychological and political realities. Listening to these girls as they came of age in a society and culture still struggling actively with its racism, we articulated the connections between the psychology of resistance and the politics of gender, class, and culture.

In the Women and Race retreats, the concept of resistance took on different meanings. As the retreats, with their focus on girls, generated the hope that the future could be different from the past, they also generated fear: What would it mean to let go of the past, even for a moment? What would it mean for women to suspend the old terms of identity and move beyond the race, class, and gender divisions that cordon women off from one another in familiar ways: women of color/women of no color; women with and without privilege of class, ethnicity, or sexuality? What would lead women to link arms across these categorizations? The political answer is a common vision for economic and political and societal changes. It is here that the engagement with difference becomes essential.

Resistance to the process of change, however, is psychological as well as political, and this resistance can take the form of repetition: reimposing the old in the face of the new. Returning to the past to repeat and remember what happened, however, also leads to the edge of working it through. In bringing the voices of black, white, Latina, and Portuguese girls into our conversations, we encouraged a process of racial and cultural exploration among the black, white, and Latina women who came to the retreats. Following the psychological logic of the retreat process, conceived by Judith Dorney as steps in a dance, we set out to move from silence into remembering, from remembering into mourning, from mourning into artistry, and from artistry into birthing—the creation and bringing forth of the new. In the actuality of the retreat process, we came through remembering to the edge of mourning—and then we stopped.

Perhaps this is as much as could be hoped for in the six weekend retreats we held over a two-year period, with long intervals in between and women living in different cities. But stopping at the edge of mourning also invites psychological analysis. Do white women need to hear and take in the depths of black women's grief and anger? And can black women show their sadness to white women, without feeling further enraged and betrayed, without white women entering into the difficult process of confronting their whiteness, their privilege, and its costs to women and girls of color? Can white women give up their privilege—their separation from women of color—without fearing that they will lose their identity (Thomas, 1995) and become, simply, women of no color? How can white women take off the mantle of privilege and power in the presence of women of color and expose and explore their often puzzling and intimate connections with a white, privileged, patriarchal social order?

To break a cycle of repetition, it becomes necessary at some point to go past the edge of the familiar and enter a place that is truly unknown. To open oneself to change, to feel the hope that such an opening brings, means also to become vulnerable to the reenactment of past hurts and betrayals. To feel the hope that change is possible creates the most intense psychological vulnerability. But in the absence of the willingness to risk relationship—the experience of really hearing and taking the other's voice into oneself—the talking just goes on and on, because in the absence of relationship, change is impossible. Betrayal then readily becomes the reason for giving up hope.

The subject of betrayal hung over the Women and Race retreats, just as it hangs over relationships between women and girls. What would it mean for women not to betray girls? we would ask ourselves and one another. What would it mean for women to stay with one another, to link hands across the usual fences of difference, to resist the old divisions, to become a politically effective majority, to act in concert to bring about change?

The incident at Wellfleet was a turning point, like the time of adolescence in girls' development. In retrospect, it seems predictable that we would come to this edge together, that we would feel the specter of past dangers and betrayals, that the girls would continue to encourage our hope, that we would struggle with feelings of helplessness and powerlessness. All of this had become familiar to the researchers in the Harvard Project in the course of working with girls. But we had not imagined so fully the difficulty in joining women across class and race and cultural and sexual differences—especially as this joining brought us to the precipice of new relationship—and we experienced directly, at this difficult edge, the power of not listening, of not hearing, of assuming that one knows, of turning away.

The still powerful divisions among North American women along lines of race, class, culture, and sexual difference also provide protective barriers against the hurts that women have inflicted on women, sapping the courage to go forward with one another in the presence of this painful history. As we approached the edge of the new, we saw what girls often see at adolescence: that you cannot have voice without relationship, that you cannot have relationship without voice. We had come to see the central psychological problem of a patriarchal and imperial social order: what would it take, we asked one another, to keep right on going through the places where black and white and Latina women often leave one another, whether overtly or by talking a talk "that was itself a silence"? (hooks, 1984, p. 7).

Talking around something, the habit of academics, generally builds fear about going in. Talking about something can be a substitute for getting into it. Getting into racism and into privilege, however, means leaving frameworks that in various ways have defined our lives and ourselves. The designing of the retreats around women's relationship with girls was so hopeful. Girls are half the population in every generation; the opportunity for change arises again and again. Perhaps it was this hope that made it feel so essential at times to reimpose the old order: women of color/women of no color, the naming of one group as the negation of the other.

It may be necessary at this point in history for white women to be in the minority in women's groups. Otherwise, it may not be possible for white women to hear the complex silences of women of color. "I was never taught absolute silence," bell hooks explains. "Taught to speak and beware of the betrayal of too much heard speech, I experienced intense confusion and deep anxiety in my efforts to speak and write" (p. 7).

As we made connections across lines of historically painful divisions among women, we also became more aware of our differences; as we began to speak more freely, we became more attuned to our silences. The acute sense of hope in the retreats made disappointments inevitable. Like girls at adolescence, women at this time are beset by changing realities. And given the many positive changes in the lives of the women who participated in the retreats over the two-year period—six moving to new cities and more powerful positions, one having a baby—it is possible that the retreats and the connection with girls energized women, strengthening their voices and their courage to act in the world.

In this book, then, we offer a partial record of a journey taken by eleven black and white and Latina women—a record written by three white women at a time of racial strife. We wanted to show the relationship between what we came to understand about girls' development from the Understanding Adolescence Study and what we came to know through experience with the women in the Women and Race retreats. We wanted to expose the paradox: that girls and women give up relationship with one another for the sake of relationships in which they often live in depression, in poverty, and with little or no voice. We wanted to ask: What would it take for women to act in concert to break this cycle? Could women do this on behalf of girls?

The repetition compulsion is the compulsion to repeat the past, to turn its familiar corners once again in an effort to discover whether this time it might come out differently—like laying out cards in a game of solitaire, like women living in the structures of patriarchy. Like Tomo, in Fumiko Enchi's novel, many women have lacked the proper education, have not had the requisite social accomplishments, have ended up doing what men have wanted, have taken away a young girl's innocence, have themselves been replaced by other women, have felt that they had to maintain existing arrangements. The choice to free oneself, to leave the structure, is a choice to look directly, with unwavering gaze, to show naked feeling, to speak without hesitation. The images and the sounds of this choice are carried in the faces and the voices of girls.

In eight-year-old Lily's book about friendship, conflicts or fights are a normal part of relationships, but conflict among women of different races and cultures and classes is difficult to work through. To Lily, who has just come from Afghanistan, the racism of U.S. society is obvious. In the final chapter of her book, "My Opinion," Lily writes: "Good luck in making good friends, but remember never judge someone by race." In the event, this was difficult advice to follow.

The persistence of racism, like the persistence of patriarchy, is a sobering historical and psychological reality. Patriarchy, as Gerda Lerner (1986) observes, has been another name for civilization. The race, class, and gender hierarchy, when reimposed generation after generation, guarantees the continuation of this equation. As women of color remind white women of their complicity and their privilege, so white women remind women of color that they have a common interest in breaking this cycle.

In joining a complex exploration of women's psychology with a study of girls' development we discovered once again the redemptive power of beginning with girls. In Toni Morrison's (1995) story "Recitatif," the narration of the Passion is carried by the voices of a black girl and a white girl—eight-year-olds Roberta and Twyla—who meet as roommates in the shelter where they were "dumped" by their mothers. Over the years, these two evangelists continue to run into each other intermittently and each time tell one another the story of their lives as young girls, as adolescents, as married women, as mothers picketing on opposite sides of a busing demonstration in a time of racial strife, and finally as two women who meet each other on Christmas Eve. At the center of their recitatif is the story of Maggie—the old, sandy-colored kitchen woman who worked at the shelter from early in the morning till two o'clock, who wore "this really stupid little hat, a kid's hat with ear flaps," who had legs like parentheses that rocked when she walked, who couldn't talk—"the kids said she had her tongue cut out, but I think she was just born that way: mute." Even for a mute, "it was dumb—dressing like a kid and never saying anything at all."

Roberta, in the middle of the racial strife over busing, tells Twyla that Maggie was black, and accuses Twyla of kicking Maggie, as the older girls at the shelter did when Maggie fell one day as she was crossing the field running to get her bus. In their final meeting some years later, on Christmas Eve, Roberta goes over the story of betrayal:

> Listen to me. I really did think she was black. I didn't make that up. I really thought so. But now I can't be sure. I just remember her as old, so old. And because she couldn't talk—well, you know, I thought she was crazy. She'd been brought up in an institution like my mother was and like I thought I would be too. And you were right. We didn't kick her. It was the [older] girls. Only them. But, well, I wanted to. I really wanted them to hurt her. I said we did it, too. You and me, but that's not true. And I don't want you to carry that around. It was just that I wanted to do it so bad that day— wanting to is doing it.

Twyla says, "We were kids, Roberta . . . Eight." But that's not the point. In the end, the passion lies in Roberta's weeping as she asks the previously unasked question: "Oh, shit, Twyla. Shit, shit, shit. What the hell happened to Maggie?"

In Morrison's radical and bold retelling of the Passion story as a story about mothers and daughters, girls and women, the passion is in the absences—in the parenthesis around race, in the muting of the interior world of women, in the breaking of relationship, in the ambiguity and silence of Maggie. And hope lies in the recitatif, in the telling of the story, the ongoing conversation of the two evangelists, the black girl and the white girl who begin talking with one another in the shelter where they have been dumped as children and then, when they have left the shelter and become women, run into one another in Howard Johnson's on the Turnpike, in the Gourmet Food Emporium, on the picket line, at the diner on Christmas Eve, and each time pick up and continue their conversation.

Notes

Prologue

1. Previously named the Harvard Center for the Study of Gender, Education, and Human Development, the research collaborative was renamed in 1988 to reflect a shift in the focus of the research.

2. The Women Teaching Girls, Girls Teaching Women retreats included the two principals, several teachers, and counselors from the Mary E. Curley Middle School and the Lewis Middle School. The women were Valeria Lowe-Barehmi (principal), Brenda Jones (principal), Mary Ahern, Emily Carrington, Janet Ferone, Maria Gonzalez-Baugh, Marie-Amy Moreno, Ciel Parteleno-Barehmi, Georgina Perry, Suzanne Ricco, Audrey Sturgis, and Patricia Woodruff.

3. The Laurel School is a private girls' school in Cleveland, Ohio, and the site of research of the Harvard Project on Women's Psychology and Girls' Development. Lyn Mikel Brown was the project director of the Laurel Study, Carol Gilligan the principal investigator (see Brown, 1989, 1991a, 1991b; Brown and Gilligan, 1992; Gilligan, 1990a).

4. See Amy M. Sullivan, "From Mentor to Muse: Recasting the Role of Women in Relationship with Urban Adolescent Girls," in *Urban Adolescent Girls: Resisting Stereotypes,* ed. B. Leadbeater and N. Way (New York: Teachers College Press, 1996).

1. Holding Difference, Sustaining Hope

1. We have changed girls' names and some identifying details for reasons of confidentiality.

2. "Social location" refers to who and where people are in relation to the systems they inhabit, a "standpoint" that frequently varies (widely) from that of the dominant culture. Feminist theorists have pointed to the importance of standpoint in how women define themselves. See, for example, Nancy Hartsock, *Money, Sex, and Power: Toward a Feminist Historical Materialism* (Boston: Northeastern University Press, 1983), particularly the final chapter, "The Feminist Standpoint: Developing the Ground for a Specifically Feminist Historical Materialism." See also

Patricia Hill Collins, *Black Feminist Thought* (Boston: Beacon Press, 1990), who speaks to the necessity of self-definition for black women; and Ruth Frankenberg, *White Women, Race Matters: The Social Construction of Whiteness* (Minneapolis: University of Minnesota Press, 1993), who discusses what she terms a "white anti-racist standpoint," referring to the self-conscious and self-critical engagement with a *dominant* position in the racial order (p. 265).

3. The authors are Diane Argyris, Jane Attanucci, Betty Bardige, Lyn Mikel Brown, Kay Johnston, Carol Gilligan, Barbara Miller, Richard Osborne, Mark Tappan, Janie Ward, and David Wilcox. Drawing on Kay Johnston's work on problem-solving using Aesop's fables as a means of determining that people know and can articulate the logic of both justice and care as strategies for solving moral conflicts, and Jane Attanucci's work on self in relationship to others, the Listening Guide is an interpretive method centered on voice and relationship with other people. The Guide has developed as the method has changed. The most recent description of how the Listening Guide is used is included in *Meeting at the Crossroads* (Brown and Gilligan, 1992).

4. Carol Gilligan was principal investigator for the Understanding Adolescence Study.

5. Michelle Fine is currently Professor of Psychology at the City University of New York Graduate Center and Senior Consultant to the Philadelphia Schools Collaborative, which is engaged in restructuring comprehensive high schools. Her work has included ethnographies of urban schools, where she has paid particular attention to the intersection of gender, race, social class, and educational equity.

6. We did not introduce similarly direct questions about class in the interviews. Although this country is clearly stratified across socioeconomic lines, this reality remains unspoken or denied. Research has repeatedly shown that most people in the United States, regardless of socioeconomic status, identify themselves as middle class (Rubin, 1994). Class as a direct subject of conversation in research with girls seems to us a priority for subsequent research.

It is also important to note that in asking girls about sexual decision-making, we did not directly ask about sexual orientation. We deliberately phrased questions to include the experience of both lesbian and heterosexual girls and to leave open the opportunity for girls to raise this issue, but in the absence of asking directly about sexual orientation, none of the girls brought up the issue.

7. Sarah Ingersoll and Mark Schernwetter completed their graduate programs, and so left the project. Janie Ward was a consultant throughout this project. Graduate student and high school teacher Beverly Smith, who is African American, analyzed the interviews of the African American girls in the study, as did Jamelle Gardine, an undergraduate and Caribbean American woman. Both wrote papers on their interpretations: Beverly Smith, "Raising a Resister," October 1991; Jamelle

Gardine, "Will We Succeed? Black Mothers and Daughters Negotiating a Doubling of Difference," October 1991.

8. Some students who met "at-risk" predictors, such as chronic tardiness or frequent absence combined with being a racial or ethnic minority and having come from a single-parent family (generally mother only), were not included in this study. Teachers explained reasons for tardiness or frequent absences—working before school or looking after other children while the mother worked, for example—and showed that these students were not "at risk."

9. We had initially identified both boys and girls, because we felt that boys in this group were also disenfranchised from mainstream culture, albeit in different ways. Fifteen boys were included in the original sample. However, because close to half of the boys chose not to participate in the third year of our study, and because we did not feel we could hear the complexity in these boys' voices without any men of color in our community (see the fuller discussion of interpretive community in this chapter), we decided to focus our analysis on the interviews with girls.

10. We use both "Hispanic" and "Latina" in this book. Although the latter is currently the term preferred by many, the girls in this study who are from Central America refer to themselves as "Hispanic" or "Spanish," and we retained their usage, one that was also prevalent at the time of our study.

11. The most recent statistics on status dropout rates for students aged 16 to 24 are: white students, 7.7 percent; black students, 13.7 percent; Hispanic students, 29.7 percent; 11 percent overall. The rates for students in low-income families are considerably higher: white students, 19 percent; black students, 24 percent; Hispanic students, 44.7 percent (NCES, 1993). John Ogbu (1991) argues that conventional explanations of variability between different minority groups in terms of school performance are lacking in three important ways. First, "the wider historical and societal forces that can encourage or discourage the minorities from striving for school success" have been ignored. Second, conventional explanations "do not consider a group's collective orientation toward school and striving for success as a factor in academic achievement. They assume that school success is a matter of family background and individual ability and effort." Third, according to Ogbu, "theories fail to consider the minorities' own notions of the meaning and the 'how-to' of schooling in the context of their own social reality" (p. 7). Required for a better understanding, Ogbu believes, is a "cultural model" that incorporates the perceptions and understanding that ethnic/racial minorities have of the social realities of their lives and schooling. (See also Suarez-Orozco and Suarez-Orozco, 1995.)

12. After the first year, the transcription became more detailed as we noted long pauses, overlaps, and interruptions that were important. Lyn Mikel Brown, Kathleen Curtis, Judith Dorney, Carol Gilligan, Sarah Ingersoll, Annie Rogers, Lori Stern,

Amy Sullivan, Jill McLean Taylor, Deborah Tolman, and Janie Ward were interviewers for the girls in the study.

13. School administrators requested that we ask no personal questions about sexuality in the eighth grade, but they agreed to the inclusion of a question about a real-life dilemma regarding a sexual decision because the students had participated in a six-week sexuality education class that year, and administrators were eager to learn if students included relevant information from it in their responses. The dilemma, which involved an adolescent girl's difficulty in responding to her boyfriend's pressure to become sexually active, had been introduced by a participant in an earlier study with adolescent mothers in an adolescent parenting program (Taylor, 1989). The school gave us permission to ask about sexual decisions in the girls' own relationships in the ninth and tenth grades. Although we asked no direct questions about physicial or emotional abuse, several of the girls introduced these subjects.

14. Some of these relational categories were drawn from the work of James Youniss and Jacqueline Smollar (1985) on adolescent relationships with family and friends.

15. See the "Appendix: Coding Sheet for Shifts in Voice of Psychological Distress and Psychological Resistance" in A. Rogers, L. Brown, and M. Tappan (1994), pp. 35–36.

16. In 1993, a New Zealand nursing student was asked to leave the training program for disagreeing with an elder on a Maori *marae,* or community meeting place. Her disagreement was with the elder's characterization of who the white settlers of New Zealand were, as this in no way reflected the history of her family. The phrase "subliminally gives girls a message of compliance" spoken by the young woman on television was instantly recognizable to a white woman of Jill's age and and middle-class background.

3. Cultural Stories

1. For a discussion of this point, see Abena Busia, "After/Words," in *Theorizing Black Feminisms: The Visionary Pragmatism of Black Women,* ed. Stanlie James and Abena Busia, 288–289 (New York: Routledge, 1993).

2. The literature related to these points is examined by Susan Miller-Havens, "Psychological Development of the Daughter in the Mother-Daughter Dyad," unpublished paper, Harvard University Graduate School of Education, 1985. See also Committee on Adolescence Group for the Advancement of Psychiatry, *Crises of Adolescence: Teenage Pregnancy: Impact on Adolescent Development* (New York: Brunner/Mazel, 1986).

3. All but one of the girls reported that they were living with their mothers during the three years of the study. One African American girl was living with her grand-

mother. Fourteen were living with both parents (eight Portuguese, two Latina, two black, two white), five with a mother and stepfather or a man in relationship with their mother (two black, three white), and six with their single mothers (two black, two Hispanic, two white).

4. Lyn Brown, in working with the text of one of the boys in the study who struggled with the question, alerted us to this by pointing out that she had not heard any of the girls in the Laurel School Study (Brown and Gilligan, 1992) *not* respond.

5. This concept comes from Dana Crowley Jack, *Silencing the Self: Women and Depression* (Cambridge: Harvard University Press, 1991). Jack describes two parts of the self as women talk about the sources of their sadness and feelings of loss. The "I" is the voice of personal experience and observation, the "authentic self." The other voice is an objective, moralistic, and judgmental tone that Jack hears as relentlessly condemning the authentic self. Like the superego, it has the feeling of something *over* the "I," hence the "Over-Eye." The Over-Eye includes a "cultural consensus about feminine goodness, truth, and value, [which] have the power to override the authentic self's viewpoint" (p. 94).

6. Hair has traditionally been a central identity and political issue among black women. See, for example, Okazawa-Rey, Robinson, and Ward (1987), and Russell, Wilson, and Hall (1992).

7. Teresa Bernardez has warned against generalizing the idea that all Latina women have trouble expressing anger (1988, 1991). The same is true of generalizing to white women, since many women, especially working-class women, openly express their anger, usually to the dismay of middle-class women (and men).

8. *Pakeha* is the Maori word for white New Zealanders. It is now widely used to distinguish between New Zealanders with Maori ancestry and those with European ancestry.

9. These and other questions in this section come either from the memorandum to all participants sent out by Lyn Brown, Janie Ward, and Joyce Grant before the retreat, or from the agenda for the retreat.

10. Because we were unable to come to an agreement about what exactly happened and why, and out of respect for the strong feelings and differences in interpretation among group members on this issue, we write here about the process of the argument and not the content.

4. Talking (and Not Talking) about Sexuality

1. The phrase "pleasure and danger" comes from the title of what may have been the most influential conference and book about female sexuality in the feminist community in the last ten years: *Pleasure and Danger: Exploring Female Sexuality,* ed. Carole S. Vance (Boston: Routledge and Kegan Paul, 1984).

2. There is continued concern around negative body image and eating disorders among preadolescents and adolescents, which differ across gender, race, and ethnicity. Findings from the Minnesota Adolescent Health Survey administered in 1986–87 to 36,000 seventh- through twelfth-grade students (94 percent white, 6 percent from racial or ethnic backgrounds) demonstrated that nearly one third (32 percent) of the girls reported a high degree of concern about their appearance compared to 13 percent of boys (Minnesota Women's Fund, 1990). According to an Arizona University Study (Parker et al., 1995) being thin is the goal for white junior high and high school girls, 90 percent of whom are dissatisfied with their bodies; 62 percent state that they have dieted within the last year. The same study reports that there is less emphasis on thinness for black girls, 70 percent of whom report that they *are* satisfied with their bodies. However, 51 percent of black girls in the study said they had dieted within the last year. According to figures from the Anorexia and Eating Disorders Association (1995) 1 percent of college-age girls suffer from anorexia and 5 percent from bulimia.

3. See the discussion of these values in Chapter 2.

4. Following the taped interview, Sandy and the interviewer discussed her family situation and her personal dilemma. Sandy agreed that the interviewer could speak about this to her school counselor, who was already aware of the situation and had taken steps to address it.

5. There is a wide range of literature on adolescent pregnancy from a public health perspective that looks at prevention and intervention (see Tolman, 1994, n16 for a comprehensive list). For work on adolescent mothers, see Butler and Burton (1990); Dore and Dumois (1990); Furstenburg, Brooks-Gunn, and Morgan (1987); Hayes and Hofferth (1987); Musick (1993); Taylor (1989); and Jacobs (1994).

5. Developing Ties

1. Many of the social networks of traditional extended families and racially or ethnically homogeneous communities may be disrupted or diminished, however, with increasing urbanization and concentration of urban poverty (Cross, 1990; Deng and Bonacich, 1991).

2. The question *Can you tell me about another person who is important to you?* was preceded by a series of questions about girls' relationships with their mothers; this sequence may have been influential in some girls' naming another adult woman as someone important to them. Surprisingly, however, the sequence of questions about mothers did not lead any of the girls to speak of their fathers as "another person who is important" to them. The majority of girls responded to this question by naming either one or more girlfriends or an adult woman other than their mother.

3. When Lilian's interviewer began the question about sexual interest and sexual decision-making, *As teenagers, boys and girls have to make decisions a lot of times when they are going out with someone . . .* , Lilian asked, "With a boy?" Her interviewer confirmed this: *Yes, with a boy. Can you describe when you had to make a decision in that relationship?* "Not really, no." *Do you go out with boys?* "No." *Not really?* "No." Lilian's interviewer again tries to ask about sexual decision-making, to which Lilian first responds, "I don't know, I don't know . . . I'm sort of lost," and then, "I understand what you're saying. I'm just sort of, I'm trying to think . . . I really don't go out with boys. I get along with boys as good friends, we're basically good friends." *I was thinking more, kind of, an intimate relationship with someone, with a boy . . . just a situation with a boy where you had to make . . . a sexual decision?* "I don't know, I'd rather not talk about it." *You'd rather not.* "If you don't mind." Then, perhaps in an effort to focus her interviewer's attention elsewhere, Lilian asks, "Would you like a piece of gum?" Although the interview protocol was designed so that questions about sexual interest and experience could apply to either sex, Lilian's interviewer in tenth grade unfortunately lapsed into the general cultural assumption of heterosexuality and asked specifically about boys, thus closing off any possibility of more discussion.

4. Ada Maria Isasi-Diaz's comments were part of a discussion in a multicultural/multiracial gathering of women, in which Katie Cannon also participated. Naming themselves the Mud Flower Collective, the group met to explore possibilities for theological education in the context of Christian feminism. (See Mud Flower Collective, 1985, p. 128.)

6. Disappearance, Disappointment, and Betrayal

1. This passage from Audre Lorde's writing was distributed and discussed at the Women and Race retreats: "Each of us is called upon to take a stand. So in the days ahead, as we examine ourselves and each other, our works, our fears, our sisterhood and survivals, I urge you to tackle what is most difficult for us all: self scrutiny of our complacencies, the idea that since each of us believes she is on the side of right, she need not examine her position. I urge you to examine your position."

7. The Risk of Development

1. Although Rochelle, who is African American, and Dahlia, who is Portuguese, have not been represented individually in this book, information from their interview narratives about relationships with their mothers and other women, experiences at school, and future plans has been included in summary discussions.

2. Organizations such as Girls Incorporated, Big Sisters, and One-to-One (a national mentoring program for girls and boys) provide important opportunities for adults in the community to build relationships with adolescent and younger girls.

References

AAUW. 1991. *Shortchanging girls, shortchanging America: A nationwide poll to assess self-esteem, educational experiences, interest in math and science, and career aspirations of girls and boys ages 9 to 15.* Report by Greenberg-Lake Analysis Group, Inc. Washington, D.C.: American Association of University Women.

———. 1992. *The AAUW report: How schools shortchange girls.* Report by Wellesley College Center for Research on Women. Washington, D.C.: American Association of University Women and National Education Association.

Amott, Teresa. 1990. Black women and AFDC: Making entitlement out of necessity. In *Women, the state, and welfare,* ed. Linda Gordon. Madison: University of Wisconsin Press.

Anthony, E. James, and Bertram Cohler, eds. 1987. *The invulnerable child.* New York: Guilford Press.

Anyon, Jean. 1982. Intersections of gender and class. In L. Weis, ed., *Issues in education: Schooling and reproduction of class and gender inequalities.* Buffalo: State University of New York.

Anzaldúa, Gloria. 1987. *Borderlands la frontera.* San Francisco: Aunt Lute Books.

Apter, Terri. 1990. *Altered loves: Mothers and daughters during adolescence.* New York: St. Martin's Press.

Barbieri, Maureen. 1995. *Sounds from the heart: Learning to listen to girls.* Portsmouth, N.H.: Heinemann.

Bassin, Donna, Margaret Honey, and Meryle Mahrer Kaplan, eds. 1994. *Representations of motherhood.* New Haven: Yale University Press.

Bassoff, Betty, and Elizabeth Ortiz. 1984. Teen women: Disparity between cognitive values and anticipated life events. *Child Welfare* 63: 125–138.

Belenky, Mary, Blythe Clinchy, Nancy Goldberger, and Jill Tarule. 1986. *Women's ways of knowing: The development of self, voice, and mind.* New York: Basic Books.

Belk, Sharyn, William Snell, Wayne Holtzman, Julita Hernandez-Sanchez, and Renan Garcia-Falconi. 1989. The impact of ethnicity, nationality, counseling orientation, and mental health standards on stereotypic beliefs about women: A pilot study. *Sex Roles* 21: 671–695.

Bell-Scott, Patricia, and Beverly Guy-Sheftall. 1992. Introduction to *Double stitch: Black women write about mothers and daughters,* ed. P. Bell-Scott, B. Guy-Sheftall, J. Royster, J. Sims-Wood, M. DeCosta-Willis, and L. Fultz. Boston: Beacon Press.

Bernal, Guillermo. 1982. Black families. In M. McGoldrick, J. Pearce, and J. Giordano, eds., *Ethnicity and family therapy,* 187–207. New York: Guilford Press.

Bernardez, Teresa. 1988. Women and anger: Cultural prohibitions and the feminine ideal. Working Paper, no. 31, Stone Center, Wellesley College, Wellesley, Mass.

———. 1991. Adolescent resistance and the maladies of women: Notes from the underground. In *Women, girls, and psychotherapy: Reframing resistance,* ed. Carol Gilligan, Annie Rogers, and Deborah Tolman. New York: Harrington Park Press.

Binion, Victoria. 1990. Psychological androgyny: A black female perspective. *Sex Roles* 22: 13–24.

Bowman, Phillip, and Cleopatra Howard. 1985. Race-related socialization, motivation and academic achievement: A study of black youths in three-generation families. *Journal of the American Academy of Child Psychiatry* 24: 134–141.

Boyd-Franklin, Nancy, and Nydia García–Preto. 1994. Family therapy: A closer look at African American and Hispanic Women. In L. Comas-Diaz and B. Greene, eds. *Women of Color,* 234–264. New York: Guilford Press.

Boyer, Debra, and David Fine. 1992. Sexual abuse as a factor in adolescent pregnancy and child maltreatment. *Family Planning Perspectives* 24, no. 4: 4–11.

Boykin, Wade, and Franklin Toms. 1985. Black child socialization: A conceptual framework. In H. McAdoo and J. McAdoo, eds., 33–52. *Black children: Social, educational, and parental environments.* Beverly Hills, Calif.: Sage Publications.

Brantlinger, Ellen. 1993. *The politics of social class in secondary school.* New York: Teachers College Press.

Brown, Lyn Mikel. 1989. Narratives of relationship: The development of a care voice in girls ages 7 to 16. Ph.D. diss., Harvard University Graduate School of Education.

———. 1991a. A problem of vision: The development of voice and relational voice in girls ages 7 to 16. *Women's Studies Quarterly* 19: 52–71.

———. 1991b. Telling a girl's life: Self-authorization as a form of resistance. *Women and Therapy* 11: 71–86.

Brown, Lyn, Dianne Argyris, Jane Attanucci, Betty Bardige, Carol Gilligan, Kay Johnston, Barbara Miller, Richard Osborne, Mark Tappan, Janie Ward, Grant

Wiggins, and David Wilcox. 1988. *A guide to reading narratives of conflict and choice for self and moral voice.* Project on Women's Psychology and Girls' Development, Monograph No. 1, Harvard University Graduate School of Education, Cambridge, Mass.

Brown, Lyn Mikel, and Carol Gilligan. 1990. Listening for self and relational voices: A responsive/resisting reader's guide. Paper presented at the annual meeting of the American Psychological Association, Boston, August.

————. 1992. *Meeting at the crossroads: Women's psychology and girls' development.* Cambridge: Harvard University Press.

Brown, Lyn Mikel, Mark Tappan, and Annie Rogers. 1993. Interpreting loss in ego development in girls: Regression or resistance. In *The narrative study of lives,* ed. R. Josselson and A. Lieblich. Vol. 2. Newbury Park, Calif.: Sage Publications.

Brown-Collins, Alice, and Deborah Sussewell. 1986. The African-American woman's emerging selves. *Journal of Black Psychology* 13: 1–11.

Burgos, Nielsa, and Yolanda Diaz Perez. 1986. An exploration of human sexuality in the Puerto Rican culture. *Journal of Social Work and Human Sexuality* (Special Issue on Ethnoculture) 4: 135–150.

Burlew, Ann. 1982. The experiences of Black females in traditional and non-traditional professions. *Psychology of Women Quarterly* 63: 312–326.

Burton, Linda. 1990. Teenage childbearing as an alternative life-course strategy in multigenerational black families. *Human Nature* 1: 123–143.

Butler, Janice, and Linda Burton. 1990. Rethinking teenage childbearing: Is sexual abuse a missing link? *Family Relations* 39: 73–80.

Campbell, Anne. 1987. Self definition by rejection: The case of gang girls. *Social Problems* 34: 451–466.

Canino, Gloria. 1982. Transactional family patterns: A preliminary exploration of Puerto Rican female adolescents. In *Work, family, and health: Latina women in transition,* ed. Z. E. Zambrana, 27–36. New York: Hispanic Research Center.

Cannon, Katie, and Carter Heyward. 1992. Alienation and anger: A black and white women's struggle for mutuality in an unjust world. Work in Progress, Paper no. 54. Stone Center, Wellesley College, Wellesley, Mass.

Cardoza, Desdemona. 1991. College attendance and persistence among Hispanic women. *Sex Roles* 24, no. 3–4: 133–147.

Carothers, Suzanne. 1990. Catching sense: Learning from our mothers to be black and female. In *Uncertain terms: Negotiating gender in American culture,* ed. Faye Ginsburg and Anna Lowenhaupt Tsing. Boston: Beacon Press.

Carrasquillo, Angela. 1991. *Hispanic children and youth in the United States: A resource guide.* New York: Garland Publishing.

Cary, Lorene. 1991. *Black ice.* New York: Knopf.

Cervantes, Lorna de. 1981. Poem for the young white man who asked me how I, an intelligent, well-read person, could believe in the war between races. *Emplumada*. Pittsburgh: University of Pittsburgh Press.

Children's Defense Fund. 1994. *Wasting America's future: The Children's Defense Fund report on the cost of child poverty,* by Arloc Sherman. Boston: Beacon Press.

Chodorow, Nancy. 1974. Family structure and feminine personality. In *Women, culture and society,* ed. M. Rosaldo and L. Lamphere. Stanford: Stanford University Press.

———. 1978. *The reproduction of mothering: Psychoanalysis and the sociology of gender.* Berkeley: University of California Press.

Chodorow, Nancy, and Susan Contratto. 1982. The fantasy of the perfect mother. In *Rethinking the family: Some feminist questions,* ed. Barrie Thorne with Marilyn Yalom. New York: Longman.

Collins, Patricia Hill. 1986. Learning from the outsider within. *Social Problems* 33: 14–32.

———. 1987. The meaning of motherhood in black culture and black mother-daughter relationships. *Sage* 4: 3–10.

———. 1989. Comparison of two works on black family life. *Signs* 14: 875–884.

———. 1990. *Black feminist thought.* Boston: Beacon Press.

———. 1994. Shifting the center. In *Representations of motherhood,* ed. D. Bassin, M. Honey, and M. Kaplan. New Haven: Yale University Press.

Comas-Diaz, Lilian. 1985a. Cognitive and behavioral group therapy with Puerto Rican women: A comparison of content themes. *Hispanic Journal of Behavioral Sciences* 7: 273–283.

———. 1985b. The cultural context: A factor in assertiveness training with mainland Puerto Rican women. *Psychology of Women Quarterly* 9: 463–476.

———. 1987. Feminist therapy with mainland Puerto Rican women. *Psychology of Women Quarterly* 11: 461–474.

———. 1989. Culturally relevant issues and treatment implications for Hispanics. In *Crossing cultures in mental health,* ed. D. R. Koslow and E. P. Salett, 31–48. Washington, D.C.: SITAR International.

———. 1994. An integrative approach. In *Women of color: Integrating ethnic and gender identities in psychotherapy,* ed. L. Comas-Diaz and B. Greene. New York: Guilford Press.

Comas-Diaz, Lilian, and Beverly Greene, eds. 1994. *Women of color: Integrating ethnic and gender identities in psychotherapy.* New York: Guilford Press.

Committee on Adolescence. 1986. *Crises of adolescence. Teenage pregnancy: Impact on adolescent development.* New York: Brunner/Mazel.

Coultas, Valerie. 1989. Black girls and self-esteem. *Gender and Education* 1: 283–294.

Cross, William. 1980. *Black identity: Rediscovering the distinction between personal identity and reference group orientation.* Ithaca, N.Y.: Cornell University, African Studies and Research Center.

————. 1990. Race and ethnicity: Effects on social networks. In *Extending families: The social networks of parents and children,* ed. M. Cochran, M. Larner, D. Riley, L. Gunnarsson, and C. Henderson, Jr. Cambridge: Cambridge University Press.

Darder, Antonia. 1994. How does the culture of the teacher shape the classroom experience of Latino students?: The unexamined question in critical pedagogy. In *Handbook of schooling in urban America,* ed. Stanley William Rothstein, 195–221. Westport, Conn.: Greenwood Press.

Davis, M. S. 1977. Sex-risk factors in the career development of 61 female high school students. Abstract in *Dissertation Abstracts International* 38: 1874B. Ann Arbor: University Microfilms, No. 77–21, 704.

Debold, Elizabeth. 1990. The flesh becomes word. Paper presented at the conference on "Diversity in Ways of Knowing" of the Association for Women in Psychology, Western Massachusetts and Vermont Region, November.

————. 1991. The body at play. *Women and Therapy* 11: 169–183.

Debold, Elizabeth, Marie Wilson, Idelisse Malave. 1993. *Mother daughter revolution.* Reading, Mass.: Addison-Wesley.

Delpit, Lisa D. 1993. The silenced dialogue: Power and pedagogy in educating other people's children. In *Beyond silenced voices: Class, race, and gender in United States schools,* ed. Lois Weis and Michelle Fine, 119–139. Albany: State University of New York Press.

————. 1995. *Other people's children.* New York: New Press.

Demb, Janet. 1990. Black, inner-city, female adolescents and condoms: What the girls say. *Family Systems Medicine* 8: 401–406.

Deng, Zhong, and Phillip Bonacich. 1991. Some effects of urbanism on black social networks. *Social Networks* 13: 35–50.

Dore, Martha, and Ana Dumois. 1990. Cultural differences in the meaning of adolescent pregnancy. *Families in Society* 71: 93–101.

Dornbusch, S. M., Anne Petersen, and Frances M. Hetherington. 1991. Projecting the future of research on adolescence. *Journal of Research on Adolescence* 1: 7–17.

Dorney, Judith. 1990. Women teaching girls: Relationships in the practice of teaching. Unpublished manuscript, Harvard Project on the Psychology of Women and the Development of Girls, Cambridge, Mass.

————. 1991. "Courage to act in a small way": Clues toward community and change among women teaching girls. Ph.D. diss., Harvard University Graduate School of Education.

Du Bois, W. E. B. 1989. *The souls of black folk.* New York: Penguin Books. First published in 1903.

Durant, Robert. 1989. Sexual behavior and contraceptive risk taking among sexually active adolescent females. *Journal of Adolescent Health Care* 10: 1–9.

Ehrenreich, Barbara, and Dierdre English. 1978. *For her own good: 150 years of the experts' advice to women.* New York: Anchor/Doubleday.

Enchi, Fumiko. 1971. *The waiting years.* Trans. John Bester. New York and Tokyo: Kodansha.

Espin, Oliva. 1984. Cultural and historical influences on sexuality in Hispanic/Latin women: Implications for psychotherapy. In *Pleasure and danger: Exploring female sexuality,* ed. C. Vance, 149–164. Boston: Routledge and Kegan Paul.

Ethier, Kathleen, and Kay Deaux. 1990. Hispanics in ivy: Assessing identity and perceived threat. *Sex Roles* 22: 427–440.

Falicov, Celia. 1982. Mexican families. In *Ethnicity and family therapy,* ed. M. McGoldrick, J. Pearce, and J. Giordano, 134–163. New York: Guilford Press.

Fernandez Kelly, Patricia. 1990. Delicate transactions: Gender, home, and employment among Hispanic women. In *Uncertain terms: Negotiating gender in American culture,* ed. Faye Ginsburg and Anna Lowenhaupt Tsing. Boston: Beacon Press.

Fine, Michelle. 1986. Why urban adolescents drop into and out of public high school. *Teachers College Record* 87: 393–409.

———.1987. Silencing in public schools. *Language Arts* 64: 157–174.

———. 1988. Sexuality, schooling and adolescent females: The missing discourse of desire. *Harvard Educational Review* 58: 29–53.

———. 1991. *Framing dropouts: Notes on the politics of an urban public high school.* New York: State University of New York Press.

Fine, Michelle, and Pearl Rosenberg. 1983. Dropping out of high school: The ideology of school and work. *Journal of Education* 165: 257–272.

Fine, Michelle, and Nancy Zane. 1989. On being wrapped tight: When low-income females drop out of high school. In *Dropouts in schools: Issues, dilemmas, and solutions,* ed. L. Weiss. Albany: State University of New York Press.

Fordham, Signithia. 1991. Racelessness in private schools: Should we deconstruct the racial and cultural identity of African-American adolescents? *Teachers College Record* 92: 470–484.

———. 1992. *Disruptive voices: The possibilities of feminist research.* Ann Arbor: University of Michigan Press.

———. 1993. "Those loud black girls": (Black) women, silence, and gender "passing" in the academy. *Anthropology and Education Quarterly* 24: 3–32.

Fordham, Signithia, and John Ogbu. 1986. Black students' school success: Coping with the "burden of 'acting white.'" *Urban Review* 18, no. 3: 176–206.

Fox, Greer, and Judith Inazu. 1980. Mother-daughter communication about sex. *Family Relations* 29: 352–374.

Freeman, Ellen. 1984. Urban black adolescents who obtain contraceptive services before or after their first pregnancy: Psychosocial factors and contraceptive use. *Journal of Adolescent Health Care* 5: 183–190.

Freire, Paolo. 1970. *The pedagogy of the oppressed.* New York: Seabury Press.

Fulani, Lenora. 1988. *The psychopathology of everyday racism and sexism.* New York: Harrington Park Press.

Fullilove, Mindy. 1990. Black women and AIDS prevention: A view towards understanding the gender rules. *Journal of Sex Research* (Special Issue: Feminist Perspectives on Sexuality) 27: 47–64.

Funiciello, Theresa. 1993. *Tyranny of kindness: Dismantling the welfare system to end poverty in America.* New York: Atlantic Monthly Press.

Furstenberg, Frank, Jeanne Brooks-Gunn, and S. Philip Morgan. 1987. *Adolescent mothers in later life.* Cambridge: Cambridge University Press.

Galbo, Joseph. 1984. Adolescents' perceptions of significant adults: A review of the literature. *Adolescence* 19, no. 76: 951–970.

———. 1989. The teacher as significant adult: A review of the literature. *Adolescence* 24, no. 95: 549–556.

Garbarino, James. 1992. *Children and families in the social environment.* 2d. ed. New York: Aldine de Gruyter.

García-Coll, Cynthia. 1992. Cultural diversity: Implications for theory and practice. Paper presented at Wellesley College, Wellesley, Mass., March.

García-Coll, Cynthia, and M. De Lourdes Mattei, eds. 1989. *The psychosocial development of Puerto Rican women.* New York: Praeger.

García-Preto, Nydia. 1982. Puerto Rican families. In *Ethnicity and family therapy,* ed. M. McGoldrick, J. Pearce, and J. Giordano, 164–186. New York: Guilford Press.

Gardner, Saundra. 1993. "What's a nice working-class girl like you doing in a place like this?" In *Working class women in the academy: Laborers in the knowledge factory,* ed. Michelle Tokarczyk and Elizabeth Fay, 49–59. Amherst: University of Massachusetts Press.

Garmezy, Norman, and Michael Rutter, eds. 1983. *Stress, coping, and development in children.* New York: McGraw-Hill.

Geronimus, Arline. 1986. The effects of race, residence and prenatal care on the relationship of maternal age to neonatal mortality. *American Journal of Public Health* 76: 1416–1421.

———. 1987. Teenage maternity and neonatal mortality: A new look at American patterns and their implications for developing countries. *Population and Development Review* 13: 245–279.

Geronimus, Arline, and John Bound. 1990. Black/White differences in women's reproductive-related health status: Evidence from vital statistics. *Demography* 27: 3457–3466.

Gibbs, Jewelle Taylor. 1985. City girls: Psychosocial adjustment of urban black adolescent females. *Sage* 2: 28–36.

———. 1986. Psychosocial correlates of sexual attitudes in urban adolescent females: Implications for intervention. *Journal of Social Work and Human Sexuality* 5: 81–97.

———. 1990. *Children of color: Psychological interventions with minority youth.* San Francisco: Jossey-Bass.

———. 1991. Black adolescents at-risk: Approaches to prevention. In *The encyclopedia of adolescence,* ed. R. Lerner, A. Petersen, and J. Brooks-Gunn, 73–78. New York: Garland Publishing.

Gibson, John, and Judith Kempf. 1990. Attitudinal predictors of sexual activity in Hispanic adolescent females. *Journal of Adolescent Research* 5: 414–430.

Gibson, Margaret, and John Ogbu, eds. 1991. *Minority status and schooling: A comparative study of immigrant and involuntary minorities.* New York: Garland Publishing.

Gibson, P. 1989. *Gay male and lesbian youth suicide.* Report of the Secretary's Task Force on Youth Suicide, 3-110-3-142. Pub. no. (ADM) 89-1623. Washington, D.C.: U.S. Dept. of Health and Human Services.

Giddings, Paula. 1984. *When and where I enter: The impact of Black women on race and sex in America.* New York: Bantam Books.

Gilligan, Carol. 1977. In a different voice: Women's conceptions of self and of morality. *Harvard Educational Review* 47: 481–517.

———. 1982. *In a different voice: Psychological theory and women's development.* Cambridge: Harvard University Press.

———. 1988. Remapping the moral domain: New images of self in relationship. In *Mapping the moral domain: A contribution of women's thinking to psychological theory and education,* ed. C. Gilligan, J. Ward, and J. Taylor, 3–19. Cambridge: Harvard University Press.

———. 1990a. Joining the resistance: Psychology, politics, girls and women. *Michigan Quarterly Review* 29: 501–536.

———. 1990b. Teaching Shakespeare's sister: Notes from the underground of female adolescence. In *Making connections: The relational worlds of adolescent girls at Emma Willard School,* ed. C. Gilligan, N. Lyons, and T. Hanmer, 6–29. Cambridge: Harvard University Press.

———. 1991. Women's psychological development: Implications for psychotherapy. *Women and Therapy* 11, no. 3–4: 5–31.

———. 1993. *In a different voice.* New Preface. Cambridge: Harvard University Press.

———. In press. The centrality of relationship in human development: A puzzle, some evidence, and a theory. In *Development and vulnerability in close relationships,* ed. Gil Noam and Kurt Fischer. New York: Lawrence Erlbaum.

Gilligan, Carol, Lyn Brown, and Annie Rogers. 1990. Psyche embedded: A place for body, relationships, and culture in personality theory. In *Studying persons and lives,* ed. A. Rabin, R. Zucker, R. Emmons, and S. Frank, 86–147. New York: Springer.

Gilligan, Carol, Nona Lyons, and Trudi Hanmer, eds. 1990. *Making connections: The relational worlds of adolescent girls at Emma Willard School.* Cambridge: Harvard University Press.

Gilligan, Carol, Annie Rogers, and Normi Noel. 1992. Cartography of a lost time: Women, girls, and relationships. Unpublished manuscript, Harvard University Graduate School of Education, Project on Women's Psychology and Girls' Development, Cambridge, Mass.

Gilligan, Carol, Annie Rogers, and Deborah Tolman, eds. 1991. *Women, girls, and psychotherapy: Reframing resistance.* New York: Haworth Press. (Published also as *Women in Therapy* 11, no. 3–4.)

Gilligan, Carol, Jill McLean Taylor, Deborah Tolman, Amy Sullivan, Pamela Pleasants, and Judith Dorney. 1992. The relation world of adolescent girls considered to be at risk. Final report to the Boston Foundation for Understanding Adolescents: A study of urban teens considered to be at risk and a project to strengthen connections between girls and women. July.

Gilligan, Carol, Janie Ward, and Jill Taylor, eds. 1988. *Mapping the moral domain: A contribution of women's thinking to psychological theory and education.* Cambridge: Harvard University Press.

Goertz, Margaret, Ruth Ekstrom, and Donald Rock. 1991. High school dropouts: Issues of race and sex. In *The encyclopedia of adolescence,* ed. R. Lerner, A. Petersen, and J. Brooks-Gunn, 250–253. New York: Garland Publishing.

Gordon, Linda, ed. 1990. *Women, the state, and welfare.* Madison: University of Wisconsin Press.

Grant, Linda. 1994. Helpers, enforcers, and go-betweens: Black females in elementary school classrooms. In *Women of color in U.S. society,* ed. Maxine Baca Zinn and Bonnie Thornton Dill. Philadelphia: Temple University Press.

Gray, Jacquelyn. 1985. A Black American princess: New game, new rules. *Washington Post,* March 17, E1-E5.

Greene, Beverly. 1990a. Sturdy bridges: The role of African-American mothers in the socialization of African-American children. *Women and Therapy* 10: 205–225.

———. 1990b. What has gone on before: The legacy of racism and sexism in the lives of Black mothers and daughters. *Women and Therapy* 9: 207–230.

Guinier, Lani. 1994. Different voices, common talk: Why we need a national conversation about race. Address to the National Press Club, Washington, D.C., November.

Hacker, Andrew. 1992. *Two nations: Black and white, separate, hostile and unequal.* New York: Charles Scribner and Sons.

Handler, Arden. 1990. The correlates of the initiation of sexual intercourse among young urban black females. *Journal of Youth and Adolescence* 19: 159–170.

Hardy-Fanta, Carol, and M. Montana. 1982. The Hispanic female adolescent: A group therapy model. *International Journal of Group Psychotherapy* 32: 351–366.

Harris, Maria. 1988. *Women and teaching.* New York: Paulist Press.

Hayes, Christina, and Sandra Hofferth. 1987. *Risking the future: Adolescent sexuality, pregnancy and childbearing.* Vol. 1. Washington, D.C.: National Academy Press.

Herman, Judith. 1981. *Father-daughter incest.* Cambridge: Harvard University Press.

———. 1992. *Trauma and recovery.* New York: Basic Books.

Higginbotham, Elizabeth, and Lynn Weber. 1992. Moving up with kin and community: Upward social mobility for black and white women. *Gender and Society* 6: 416–440.

Higginbotham, Evelyn Brooks. 1992. African-American women's history and the metalanguage of race. *Signs* 17: 251–274.

Higgins, Anne. 1986. *Dropout prevention planning survey: Seventh and eighth grades.* Cambridge: Harvard Graduate School of Education.

Hill, Robert B. 1971. *The strengths of Black families.* New York: Emerson Hall Publishing.

Hines, Paulette, and Nancy Boyd-Franklin. 1982. Black families. In *Ethnicity and family therapy,* ed. M. McGoldrick, J. Pearce, and J. Giordano, 84-106. New York: Guilford Press.

Hirsch, Marianne, and Evelyn Fox Keller. 1991. Conclusion: Practicing conflict in feminist theory. In *Conflicts in feminism,* ed. M. Hirsch, E. Fox Keller. New York: Routledge.

Hogan, Dennis, Nan Marie Astone, and Evelyn Kitagawa. 1985. Social and environmental factors influencing contraceptive use among black adolescents. *Family Planning Perspectives* 17: 165–169.

Hogan, Dennis, and Evelyn Kitagawa. 1985. The impact of social status, family structure, and neighborhood on the fertility of Black adolescents. *American Journal of Sociology* 90: 825–855.

hooks, bell. 1984. *From margin to center.* Boston: South End Press.

———. 1989. *Talking back: Thinking feminist, thinking black.* Boston: South End Press.

———. 1990. *Yearning: Race, gender, and cultural politics.* Boston: South End Press.

———. 1993a. Keeping close to home: Class and education. In *Working class women in the academy: Laborers in the knowledge factory,* ed. Michelle Tokarczyk and Elizabeth Fay, 99–111. Amherst: University of Massachusetts Press.

————. 1993b. *Sisters of the yam.* Boston: South End Press.

hooks, bell, and Mary Childers. 1990. A conversation about race and class. In *Conflicts in feminism,* ed. Marianne Hirsch and Evelyn Fox Keller, 60–81. New York: Routledge.

Hurrelmann, Klaus. 1989. Adolescents as productive processors of reality: Methodological perspectives. In *The social world of adolescents: International perspectives,* ed. K. Hurrelmann and U. Engel, 107–118. Walter de Gruyter: New York.

————. 1991. Parents, peers, teachers and other significant partners in adolescence. In *Unrelated adults in adolescents' lives: Perspectives from four countries,* ed. S. F. Hamilton, 31–39. Occasional Paper no. 29. Ithaca, N.Y.: Cornell University, Western Societies Program.

Jackson, Derrick Z. 1995. Affirmative action series. *Boston Globe,* March 15, 17, 22, 24, 29, 31.

Jacobs, Janet. 1994. Gender, race, class and the trend toward early motherhood. *Journal of Contemporary Ethnography* 22: 442–462.

Jones, Jacqueline. 1986. *Labor of love, labor of sorrow: Black women, work, and the family, from slavery to the present.* New York: Vintage.

Jordan, Judith, Alexandra Kaplan, Jean Baker Miller, Irene Stiver, and Janet Surrey. 1991. *Women's growth in connection: Writings from the Stone Center.* New York: Guilford Press.

Joseph, Gloria. 1984. Mothers and daughters: Traditional and new populations. *Sage* 1: 17–21.

Joseph, Gloria, and Jill Lewis. 1981. *Common differences: Conflict in black and white perspectives.* Garden City, N.Y.: Anchor.

Kincaid, Jamaica. 1983. *Annie John.* New York: New American Library.

Kinzer, N. 1973. Women in Latin America: Priests, machos, and babies, or Latin American women and the Manichean heresy. *Journal of Marriage and the Family* 35: 299–312.

Konopka, Gisela. 1966. *Young girls: A portrait of adolescence:* Englewood Cliffs, N.J.: Prentice-Hall.

Kozol, Jonathan. 1991. *Savage inequalities: Children in America's schools.* New York: Crown Publishers.

Ladner, Joyce. 1971. *Tomorrow's tomorrow: The Black woman.* New York: Doubleday.

Ladner, Joyce, and R. Gourdine. 1984. Intergenerational teenage motherhood: Some preliminary findings. *Sage* 1: 22–24.

Lerner, Gerda. 1986. *The creation of patriarchy.* New York: Oxford University Press.

Lerner, Michael, and Cornel West. 1995. *Jews and blacks: Let the healing begin.* New York: G. P. Putnam's Sons.

Lewis, Diane K. 1975. The black family: Socialization and sex roles. *Phylon* 36: 221–237.

Loevinger, Jane, and Ruth Wessler. 1970. *Measuring ego development.* San Francisco: Jossey-Bass.

Lopez, Tiffany, ed. 1993. Introduction to Sandra Cisneros's "Eleven." In *Growing up Chicana/o.* New York: Avon Books.

Lorde, Audre. 1984a. Age, race, class and sex: Women redefining difference. In *Sister outsider: Essays and speeches by Audre Lorde,* 114–123. Freedom, Calif.: The Crossing Press.

———. 1984b. The transformation of silence into language and action. *Sister outsider: Essays and speeches by Audre Lorde,* 40–44. Freedom, Calif.: The Crossing Press.

Luker, Kristin. 1984. *Abortion and the politics of motherhood.* Berkeley: University of California Press.

Luttrell, Wendy. 1993. "The teachers, they all had their pets": Concepts of gender, knowledge, and power. *Signs* 18: 505–547.

Lyons, Nona. 1983. Two perspectives on self, relationships and morality. *Harvard Educational Review* 53: 125–145.

Marin, Gerardo, and Barbara Marin. 1991. *Research with Hispanic Populations.* Applied Social Research Methods Series, vol. 23. Newbury Park, Calif.: Sage Publications.

Markstrom-Adams, Carol. 1989. Androgyny and its relation to adolescent psychosocial well-being: A literature review. *Sex Roles* 21: 325.

Martin, Jane Roland. 1994. Methodological essentialism, false differences, and other dangerous traps. *Signs* 19: 630–657.

Martín-Baró, Ignacio. 1994. *Writings for a liberation psychology,* ed. Adrianne Aron and Shawn Corne. Cambridge: Harvard University Press.

Mays, Vickie, and Susan Cochrane. 1988. Issues in the perception of AIDS risk and risk reduction activities by black and Hispanic/Latina women. *American Psychologist* 43: 949–957.

Mays, Vickie, and Lilian Comas-Diaz. 1989. Feminist therapy with ethnic minority populations: A closer look at Blacks and Hispanics. In *Feminist psychotherapies: Integration of therapeutic and feminist systems,* ed. M. Dutton-Douglas and L. Walker, 228–251. Norwood, N.J.: Ablex.

Mbiti, John. 1969. *African religions and philosophies.* New York: Anchor Books.

McAdoo, Harriet, ed. 1987. *Black families.* Beverly Hills, Calif.: Sage Publications.

McAdoo, Harriet, and John McAdoo, eds. 1985. *Black children: Social, educational, and parental environments.* Beverly Hills, Calif.: Sage Publications.

McCrate, Elaine. 1989. Discrimination returns to education and teenage childbearing. Working Paper, Bunting Institute, Radcliffe College, Cambridge, Mass.

McDermott, Raymond. 1989. Making dropouts. In *What do anthropologists have to say about dropouts? The first centennial conference on children at risk,* ed. H. T. Trueba, G. Spindler, and L. Spindler. New York: Falmer Press.

McGoldrick, Monica. 1982. Ethnicity and family therapy: An overview. In *Ethnicity and family therapy,* ed. M. McGoldrick, J. Pearce, and J. Giordano, 3–30. New York: Guilford Press.

McGowan, Owen T. P. 1976. Factors contributing to school leaving among immigrant children: The case of the Portuguese in Fall River, Massachusetts. Ph.D. diss., Catholic University of America.

Medina, Carmen 1987. Latino culture and sex education. *SIECUS Report* 15, no. 3: 1–2.

Medrano, Louisa. 1994. AIDS and Latino adolescents. In *Sexual cultures and the construction of adolescent identities.* Philadelphia: Temple University Press.

Mendelsohn, Janet. 1990. The view from step number 16. In *Making connections: The relational world of adolescent girls at Emma Willard School,* ed. C. Gilligan, N. Lyons, and T. Hanmer, 233–257. Cambridge: Harvard University Press.

Miles, Matthew, and A. Michael Huberman. 1984. *Qualitative data analysis.* London: Sage.

Miller, F. 1988. Network structure support: Its relationship to the psychosocial development of Black females. *Journal of Black Psychology* 15: 17–39.

Miller, Jean Baker. 1976. *Toward a new psychology of women.* Boston: Beacon Press.

———. 1982. Women and power. Work in Progress, Stone Center, Wellesley College, Wellesley, Mass.

———. 1986. *Toward a New Psychology of Women.* 2nd ed. Boston: Beacon Press.

———. 1988. Connections, disconnections and violations. Work in Progress, Stone Center, Wellesley College, Wellesley, Mass.

Minnesota Women's Fund. 1990. *Reflections of risk: Growing up female in Minnesota: A report on the health and well-being of adolescent girls in Minnesota.* Minneapolis: Minnesota Women's Fund.

Mirza, Heidi. 1992. *Young, female and black.* London: Routledge.

Mishler, Elliot. 1986. *Research interviewing: Context and narrative.* Cambridge: Harvard University Press.

———. 1992. Narrative accounts in clinical and research interviews. Paper presented at the conference on "Discourse and the Professions" of the Swedish Association for Applied Linguistics, Uppsala, Sweden.

Moitoza, Everett. 1982. Portuguese families. In *Ethnicity and family therapy,* ed. M. McGoldrick, J. Pearce, and J. Giordano, 412–437. New York: Guilford Press.

Molina, Papusa. 1990. Recognizing, accepting and celebrating our differences. In *Making face, making soul (haciendo caras): Creative and critical perspectives by feminists of color,* ed. Gloria Anzaldúa, 326–331. San Francisco: Aunt Lute Books.

Moore, Kristin, and Charles Betsey. 1986. *Choice and circumstance: Racial differences in adolescent sexuality and fertility.* New Brunswick, N.J.: Transaction Books.

Moraga, Cherrie, and Gloria Anzaldúa. 1981. *This bridge called my back: Writing by radical women of color.* New York: Kitchen Table-Women of Color Press.

Morrison, Toni. 1970. *The bluest eye.* New York: Washington Square Press.

———. 1995. Recitatif. In *Skin deep: Black women and white women write about race,* ed. Marita Golden and Susan Shreve, 87–110. New York: Doubleday.

Mud Flower Collective [Katie Cannon, Beverly Harrison, Carter Heyward, Ada Maria Isasi-Diaz, Bess Johnson, Mary Pellauer, Nancy Richardson]. 1985. *God's fierce whimsy: Christian feminism and theological education.* New York: Pilgrim Press.

Mullings, Leith. 1994. Images, ideology, and women of color. In *Women of color in U.S. society,* ed. M. Baca Zinn and B. Thornton Dill. Philadelphia: Temple University Press.

Mulroy, Elizabeth, ed. 1988. *Women as single parents: Confronting institutional barriers in the courts, the workplace, and the housing market.* Dover, Mass.: Auburn House.

Musick, Judith. 1993. *Young, poor, and pregnant: The psychology of teenage motherhood.* Chicago: University of Chicago Press.

Myers, Lena. 1989. Early gender role socialization for Black women: Affective or consequential. *Western Journal of Black Studies* 13: 173–178.

Nathanson, Constance. 1991. *Dangerous passage: The social control of sexuality in women's adolescence.* Philadelphia: Temple University Press.

National Center for Education Statistics (NCES). 1993. *Dropout rates in the United States: 1992.* NCES 93–464. Washington, D.C.: U.S. Department of Education, Office of Educational Research and Improvement.

Ogbu, John. 1987. Variability in minority responses to schooling: Nonimmigrants vs. immigrants. In *Interpretive ethnography of education at home and abroad,* ed. G. Spindler and L. Spindler, 255–278. Hillsdale, N.J.: Lawrence Erlbaum.

———. 1991. Immigrant and involuntary minorities in comparative perspective. In *Minority status and schooling,* ed. M. Gibson and J. Ogbu. New York: Garland Publishing.

Okazawa-Rey, Margot, Tracey Robinson, and Janie Ward. 1987. Black women and the politics of skin color and hair. In *Women, power and therapy: Issues for women,* ed. M. Braude, 89–102. New York: Haworth Press.

Orfield, Gary. 1994. Going to work: Weak preparation, little help. In Gary Orfield and Faith Paul. *High hopes, long odds.* Indianapolis: The Lilly Endowment.

Parker, Sheila, Mimi Nichter, Mark Nichter, Nancy Vukovic, Colette Sims, and Cheryl Ritenbaugh. 1995. Body image and weight concerns among African

American and white adolescent females: Differences that make a difference. *Human Organization* 54: 103ff.

Pearce, Diana. 1990. Welfare is not for women: Why the war on poverty cannot conquer the feminization of poverty. In *Women, the state, and welfare,* ed. Linda Gordon. Madison: University of Wisconsin Press.

Pennebaker, James. 1990. *Opening up: The healing power of confiding in others.* New York: Morrow.

Pepler, Debra, and Iara Lessa. 1993. The mental health of Portuguese children. *Canadian Journal of Psychiatry* 38: 46–50.

Petchesky, Rosalind. 1984. *Abortion and women's choice: The state, sexuality, and reproductive freedom.* New York: Longman.

Petersen, Anne. 1988. Adolescent development. *Annual Review of Psychology* 39: 583–607.

Phinney, Jean, and Steven Tarver. 1988. Ethnic identity search and commitment in Black and white eighth graders. *Journal of Early Adolescence* 8: 265–277.

Phinney, Virginia, Larry Jensen, Joseph Olsen, and Bert Cundick. 1990. The relationship between early development and psychosexual behaviors in adolescent females. *Adolescence* 25: 321–332.

Polakow, Valerie. 1993. *Lives on the edge: Single mothers and their children in the other America.* Chicago: University of Chicago Press.

Reid, Pamela. 1984. Feminism versus minority group identity: Not for black women only. *Sex Roles* 10: 247–255.

————. 1991. Socialization of Black female children. In *Encyclopedia of adolescence: A developmental perspective,* ed. P. Berman and E. Ramey, 85–87. New York: Garland Publishing.

————. 1993. Poor women in psychological research: Shut up and shut out. *Psychology of Women Quarterly* 17: 133–150.

Reid, Pamela, and Lilian Comas-Diaz. 1990. Gender and ethnicity: Perspectives on dual status. *Sex Roles* 22: 397–408.

Reissman, Catherine. 1993. *Narrative analysis.* Qualitative Research Methods Series 30. Newbury Park, Calif.: Sage Publications.

Ribeiro, Jose. 1981. Cultural, social and psychological factors related to academic success of Portuguese youth. Ph.D. diss., Boston College.

————. 1992. Personal Communication, Cambridge, Mass.

Rich, Adrienne. 1976. *Of woman born: Motherhood as experience and institution.* New York: Norton.

Robinson, Tracey, and Janie Ward. 1991. "A belief in self far greater than anyone's disbelief": Cultivating resistance among African American female adolescents. *Women and Therapy* 11: 87–103.

Rogers, Annie. 1989. Translating girls' voices. Paper presented at the Big Brothers/ Big Sisters of America National Conference, Norfolk, Va.

———. 1993. Voice, play, and a practice of ordinary courage in girls' and women's lives. *Harvard Educational Review* 63: 265-295.

Rogers, Annie, Lyn Brown, and Mark Tappan. 1991. Interpreting loss in ego development in girls: Regression or resistance? Symposium paper delivered at the Annual Meeting of the American Psychological Association, San Francisco, August.

———. 1994. Interpreting loss in ego development in girls: Regression or resistance? In *The narrative study of lives,* ed. Amia Lieblich and Ruthellen Josselson. Vol 2. Newbury Park, Calif.: Sage Publications.

Root, Maria. 1990. Disordered eating in women of color. *Sex Roles* 22: 7–8.

Rose, Mike. 1989. *Lives on the boundaries: The struggles and achievements of America's underprepared.* New York: Free Press.

Rotheram, Mary Jane, and Jean S. Phinney. 1987. Definitions and perspectives in the study of children's ethnic socialization. In *Children's ethnic socialization,* ed. J. S. Phinney and M. J. Rotheram, 10–28. Newbury Park, Calif.: Sage Publications.

Rothstein, Stanley, ed. 1993. *Handbook of schooling in urban America.* Westport, Conn.: Greenwood Press.

Rubin, Lilian. 1992. *Worlds of pain: Life in the working-class family.* New York: Basic Books. First published in 1976.

———. 1994. *Families on the fault line: America's working class speaks about the family, the economy, race, and ethnicity.* New York: HarperPerennial.

Russell, Kathy, Midge Wilson, and Ronald Hall. 1992. *The color complex: The politics of skin color among African Americans.* New York: Anchor Doubleday.

Rutter, Michael. 1980. *Changing youth in a changing society: Patterns of adolescent development and disorder.* Cambridge: Harvard University Press.

Sadker, Myra, and David Sadker. 1994. *Failing at fairness: How America's schools cheat girls.* New York: Charles Scribner's Sons.

Sander, Joelle. 1991. *Before their time: Four generations of teenage mothers.* New York: Harcourt Brace Jovanovich.

Santiago, Esmeralda. 1993. *When I was Puerto Rican.* Reading, Mass.: Addison-Wesley Publishing.

Schulz, Amy. 1994. "I don't want a life like that": Constructing a life between cultures. In *Women creating lives,* ed. C. Franz and A. Stewart. Boulder, Colo.: Westview Press.

Scott, Clarissa, Lydia Shifman, Lavdena Orr, Roger Owen, and N. Fawcett. 1988. Hispanic and Black American adolescents' beliefs relating to sex and contraception. *Adolescence* 23: 667–688.

Scott, Kesho Yvonne. 1991. *The habit of surviving: Black women's strategies for life.* New Brunswick, N.J.: Rutgers University Press.

Scott-Jones, Diane, and Maxine Clark. 1986. The school experiences of Black girls: The interaction of gender, race, and socioeconomic status. *Phi Delta Kappan* 67: 520–526.

Scott-Jones, Diane, and Sharon Nelson-LeGall. 1986. Defining Black families, past and present. In *Redefining social problems,* ed. Edward Seidman and Julian Rappaport. New York: Plenum.

Scott-Jones, Diane, and Sherry Turner. 1988. Sex education, contraceptive and reproductive knowledge, and contraceptive use among black adolescent females. *Journal of Adolescent Research* 3: 171–187.

Shorris, Earl. 1992. *Latinos.* New York: Norton.

Sidel, Ruth. 1990. *On her own.* New York: Penguin Books.

Silko, Leslie Marmon. 1994. Language and literature from a Pueblo Indian perspective. In *Signs of life in the USA,* ed. Sonia Maasik and Jack Solomon. Boston: Bedford Books of St. Martin's Press.

Smith, Althea. 1986. Positive marginality: The experience of Black women leaders. In *Redefining social problems,* ed. L. Seidman and J. Rappaport, 101–120. New York: Plenum Press.

Smith, Elsie. 1982. The Black female adolescent: A review of the literature. *Psychology of Women Quarterly* 6: 261–288.

Smith, Estellie. 1980. The Portuguese female immigrant: The marginal man. *International Migration Review* 14: 77–92.

Sohlberg, V. Scott, Karen O'Brien, Pete Villareal, Richard Kennel, and Betsy Advise. 1993. Self-efficacy and Hispanic college students: Validation of the college self-efficacy instrument. *Hispanic Journal of Behavioral Sciences* 15: 80–95.

Solomon, Patrick. 1992. *Black resistance in high school: Forging a separatist culture.* New York: State University of New York Press.

Soto, Elaine. 1979. Biculturality and conflict in Puerto Rican women living in the United States. Ph.D. diss., New York University.

Spelman, Elizabeth. 1988. *Inessential women: Problems of exclusion in feminist thought.* Boston: Beacon Press.

Spencer, Margaret Beale. 1985. Racial variations in achievement prediction: The school as a conduit for macrostructural cultural tension. In *Black children: Social, educational, and parental environments,* ed. H. McAdoo and J. McAdoo, 85–112. Beverly Hills, Calif.: Sage Publications.

Spencer, Margaret, and Spencer Dornbusch. 1990. Challenges in studying minority youth. In *At the threshold: The developing adolescent,* ed. S. S. Feldman and G. R. Elliott. Cambridge: Harvard University Press.

Spencer, Margaret, and Carol Markstrom-Adams. 1990. Identity processes among racial and ethnic minority children in America. *Child Development* 61: 290–310.

Spindler, George, and Louise Spindler, eds. 1987. *Interpretive ethnography of education: At home and abroad.* Hillsdale, N.J.: Lawrence Erlbaum.

Stack, Carol. 1974. *All our kin: Strategies for survival in a Black community.* New York: Harper and Row.

Steiner-Adair, Catherine. 1990. The body politic: Normal female adolescent development and the development of eating disorders. In *Making connections: The relational worlds of adolescent girls at Emma Willard School,* ed. C. Gilligan, N. Lyons, and T. Hanmer, 162–182. Cambridge: Harvard University Press.

Steinhauer, Jennifer. 1995. Study cites adult males for most teen-age births. *New York Times,* August 2, p. A10.

Steinitz, Victoria A., and Ellen R. Solomon. 1986. *Starting out: Class and community in the lives of working-class youth.* Philadelphia: Temple University Press.

Stern, Lori. 1990. Conceptions of separation and connection in female adolescents. In *Making connections: The relational worlds of adolescent girls at Emma Willard School,* ed. C. Gilligan, N. Lyons, and T. Hanmer, 73–87. Cambridge: Harvard University Press.

———. 1991. Disavowing the self in female adolescence. *Women and Therapy* 11: 105–117.

Stevens, Evelyn. 1973. Machismo and Marianismo. *Society* 10, no. 6: 57–63.

Stevenson, Robert B., and Jeanne Ellsworth. 1993. Dropouts and the silencing of critical voices. In *Beyond silenced voices: Class, race, and gender in United States schools,* ed. Lois Weis and Michelle Fine, 259–271. Albany: State University of New York Press.

Stiffman, Arline. 1990. Racial differences in support for adolescent mothers who use health clinics. Paper presented at the Third Biennial Conference of the Society for Research on Adolescence, Atlanta, March.

Stiffman, Arline, F. Earls, L. Robins, K. Jung, and P. Kulbok. 1987. Adolescent sexual activity and pregnancy: Socioenvironmental problems, physical health, and mental health. *Journal of Youth and Adolescence* 16: 497–509.

Suarez-Orozco, Carola, and Marcelo Suarez-Orozco. 1995. *Transformation: Immigration, family life, and achievement motivation among Latino youth.* Stanford: Stanford University Press.

Sullivan, Amy M. 1993. Connections of promise: Women in the lives of adolescent girls considered to be at risk. Qualifying Paper, Harvard University Graduate School of Education.

———. 1996. From mentor to muse: Recasting the role of women in relationship with urban adolescent girls. In *Urban adolescent girls: Resisting stereotypes,* ed. B. Leadbeater and N. Way. New York: Teachers College Press.

Takesheni, Ruby, ed. 1992. *Adolescence in the 1990's: Risk and opportunity*. New York: Teachers College Press.

Tappan, Mark, and Lyn Mikel Brown. 1992. *Ethics and interpretation: The role of values in psychology and human development*, ed. W. Kurtines, M. Azmitia, and J. Gewirtz, 105–130. New York: John Wiley and Sons.

Tatum, Beverly. 1992. Talking about race, learning about racism: The application of racial identity development in the classroom. *Harvard Educational Review* 62: 1–24.

Taylor, Jill McLean. 1989. Development of self, moral voice, and the meaning of adolescent motherhood. Ph.D. diss., Harvard University Graduate School of Education.

———. 1991. Breaking the silence: Questions about race. Symposium paper presented at the Annual Meeting of the American Psychological Association, San Francisco, August.

———. 1994. Adolescent development: Whose perspective? In *Sexual cultures: Adolescence, community, and construction of identity*, ed. J. Irvine. Philadelphia: Temple University Press.

Taylor, Jill, and Janie Ward. 1991. Culture, sexuality, and school: Perspectives from focus groups in six cultural communities. *Women's Studies Quarterly* 19: 11–137.

Thomas, A. Dorothy. 1995. United States feminism and international women's human rights. Paper presented at the Bunting Institute Colloquium Series, Radclifte College, April 12.

Thomas, Veronica. 1983. Perceived traditionality and nontraditionality of career aspects of Black college women. *Perceptual and Motor Skills* 57: 979–982.

———. 1986. Career aspirations, parental support, and work values among black female adolescents. *Journal of Multicultural Counseling and Development* 14: 177–185.

Thomas, Veronica, and Leslie Shields. 1987. Gender influences on work values of Black adolescents. *Adolescence* 22, no. 85: 37-43.

Tolman, Deborah. 1990. Discourses of adolescent girls' sexual desire in developmental psychology and feminist scholarship. Qualifying Paper, Harvard University Graduate School of Education.

———. 1991. Adolescent girls, women and sexuality: Discerning dilemmas of desire. *Women and Therapy* 11: 55–69.

———. 1992. Voicing the body: A psychological study of adolescent girls' sexual desire. Ph.D. diss., Harvard University Graduate School of Education.

———. 1994. Daring to desire: Culture and the bodies of adolescent girls. In *Sexual cultures and the construction of adolescent identities*, ed. J. Irvine. Philadelphia: Temple University Press.

Tolman, Deborah, and Elizabeth Debold. 1994. Conflicts of body and image: Female adolescents, desire, and the no-body body. In *Feminist perspectives of eating disorders,* ed. M. Katzman, P. Fallon, and S. Wooley, 301–317. New York: Guilford Press.

Tomatis, Alfred A. 1991. *The conscious ear: My life of transformation through listening.* Barrytown, N.Y.: Station Hill Press.

Torres-Matrullo, C. 1976. Acculturation and psychotherapy among Puerto Rican women in mainland United States. *International Journal of Group Tensions* 13: 100–105.

Treuba, Henry, George Spindler, and Louise Spindler, eds. 1989. *What do anthropologists have to say about dropouts? A first centennial conference on children at risk.* New York: Falmer Press.

Tucker, Sandra 1989. Adolescent patterns of communication about sexually related topics. *Adolescence* 24: 269–278.

U.S. Bureau of the Census. 1994. *Statistical abstract of the United States.* Washington, D.C.: U.S. Department of Commerce.

Valdivieso, Rafael, and Siobhan Nicolau. 1994. "Look me in the eye": A Hispanic cultural perspective on school reform. In *Schools and students at risk,* ed. R. Rossi. New York: Teachers College Press.

Vasquez, M. 1982. Confronting barriers to the participation of Mexican-American women in higher education. *Hispanic Journal of Behavioral Sciences* 4: 147–165.

Vasquez-Nuttall, Ena, Z. Avila-Vavas, and G. Morales-Barreto. 1984. Working with Latin American families. In *Family therapy with school-related problems,* ed. J. Hansen and B. Okun, 74–90. Rockville, Md.: Aspen Systems Corporation.

Vasquez-Nuttall, Ena, and Ivonne Romero-Garcia. 1989. From home to school: Puerto Rican girls learn to be students in the United States. In *The psychosocial development of Puerto Rican women,* ed. Cynthia García-Coll and Maria De Lourdes Mattei. New York: Praeger.

Vasquez-Nuttall, Ena, Ivonne Romero-Garcia, and B. De Leon. 1987. Sex roles and perceptions of femininity and masculinity of Hispanic women: A review of the literature. *Psychology of Women Quarterly* 11: 409–425.

Villarosa, Linda, ed. 1994. *Body and soul: The black woman's guide to physical health and emotional well-being.* New York: HarperCollins.

Wade-Gayles, Gloria. 1984. The truths of our mothers' lives: Mother-daughter relationships in Black women's fiction. *Sage* 1: 8–12.

———. 1993. *Pushed back to strength: A black woman's journey home.* Boston: Beacon Press.

Wallace, Michele. 1990. *Invisibility blues: From pop to theory.* New York: Verso.

Ward, Janie Victoria. 1988. Urban adolescents' conceptions of violence. In *Mapping the moral domain: A contribution of women's thinking to psychological theory and education,* ed. C. Gilligan, J. Ward, and J. Taylor, 175–200. Cambridge: Harvard University Press.

———. 1990. Racial identity formation and transformation. In *Making connections: The relational worlds of adolescent girls at Emma Willard School,* ed. C. Gilligan, N. Lyons, and T. Hanmer, 215–232. Cambridge: Harvard University Press.

———. 1991. Eyes in the back of your head: Moral themes in African American narratives of racial conflict. *Journal of Moral Education* 20: 267–281.

Ward, Janie, and Jill Taylor. 1991. Sex education for immigrant and minority students: Developing a culturally appropriate curriculum. In *Sexuality and the curriculum,* ed. J. Sears. New York: Teachers College Press.

Washington, Mary Helen. 1975. *Black-eyed Susans.* New York: Anchor/Doubleday.

Way, Niobe. 1995. "Can't you see the courage, the strength that I have?": Listening to urban adolescent girls speak about their relationships. *Psychology of Women Quarterly* 19: 107–128.

Webb, Nancy. 1995. The textbook business: Education's big dirty secret. *Harvard Education Letter.* July/August.

Webber, Kikanza. 1980. Reflections on Black American women: The images of the eighties. *Western Journal of Black Studies* 4: 242–250.

Weis, Lois. 1990. *Working class without work: High school students in a deindustrializing economy.* New York: Routledge.

Weis, Lois, E. Farrar, and H. Petrie. 1989. *Dropouts from school: Issues, dilemmas and solutions.* Albany: State University of New York Press.

Welwood, John. 1990. *Journey of the heart: Intimate relationship and the path of love.* New York: Harper Perennial.

Werner, Emmy. 1989. High-risk children in young adulthood: A longitudinal study from birth to 32 years. *American Journal of Orthopsychiatry* 59: 72–81.

West, Cornel. 1993. *Race matters.* New York: Vintage Books.

Wheelock, Anne. 1992. *Crossing the tracks: How "untracking" can save America's schools.* New York: New Press.

Williams, Constance. 1991. *Black teenage mothers: Pregnancy and childrearing from their perspective.* Lexington, Mass.: Lexington Books.

Willie, Charles. 1985. *Black and white families: A study in complementarity.* Dix Hills, N.Y.: General Hall.

Wilson, Pamela. 1986. Homosexuality, ethnoculture, and social work. *Journal of Social Work and Human Sexuality. Special Issue* 4, no. 3: 29–46.

Winters, A., and J. Frankel. 1984. Women's work role as perceived by lower status white and black female adolescents. *Adolescence* 19: 403–415.

Wolfman, Brunetta R. 1984. Women and their many roles. Work in Progress, Stone Center, Wellesley College, Wellesley, Mass.

Wolforth, Sandra. 1978. *The Portuguese in America.* San Francisco: Reed and Eterovich.

Women's Action Coalition. 1993. *WAC Stats: The facts about women.* 2d ed. New York: New Press.

Woolf, Virginia. 1938. *Three guineas.* New York: Harcourt Brace Jovanovich.

Wyatt, Gail. 1989. Reexamining factors predicting African-American and white American women's age at first coitus. *Archives of Sexual Behavior* 18: 271–289.

Wyatt, Gail, and Sandra Lyons-Rowe. 1990. African American women's sexual satisfaction as a dimension of their sex roles. *Sex Roles* 22: 509–524.

Youniss, James, and Jacqueline Smoller. 1985. *Adolescent relations with mothers, fathers, and friends.* Chicago: University of Chicago Press.

Zabin, L., M. Hirsch, E. Smith, R. Streett, and J. Hardy. 1986. Evaluation of a pregnancy prevention program. *Family Planning Perspectives* 18, no. 3: 119–126.

Zane, Nancy. 1988. *In their own voices: Young women talk about dropping out.* Washington, D.C.: NOW Legal Defense and Education Fund.

Zayas, Luis. 1987. Toward an understanding of suicide risks in young Hispanic females. *Journal of Adolescent Research* 2: 1–11.

Zimmerman, James. 1991. Crossing the desert alone: An etiological model of female adolescent suicidality. *Women and Therapy* 11: 223–240.

Zinn, Maxine Baca, and Barrie Thornton Dill, eds. 1994. *Women of color in U.S. society.* Philadelphia: Temple University.

Index